THE AMERICAN REPUBLIC

The Fourth Form Government

C. Michael Barry

iUniverse, Inc.
Bloomington

The American Republic
The Fourth Form Government

iUniverse books may be ordered through booksellers or by contacting:

iUniverse
1663 Liberty Drive
Bloomington, IN 47403
www.iuniverse.com
1-800-Authors (1-800-288-4677)

ISBN: 978-1-4620-0416-4 (sc)
ISBN: 978-1-4620-0417-1 (hc)
ISBN: 978-1-4620-0418-8 (e)

Library of Congress Control Number: 2011910769

Printed in the United States of America

iUniverse rev. date: 9/30/2011

Contents

Preface

"I pledge allegiance to the Flag, of the United States of America, and to the Republic for which it stands, one Nation, under God, indivisible, with liberty and justice for all."

I would like to offer my inspiration to make a pledge to our Constitution, which is:

> *I pledge allegiance to the Constitution of the United States of America and to the Republic for which it stands, formed from republican principles under God's providential care, indivisible, with liberty and justice for all.*

Our republic *stands* upon principles that unite our land. Our Republic *stands* upon those principles that form our Constitution and our Union. Therefore, I believe that an accurate understanding of our Framers' new government is a key to understanding our present issues. To provide this understanding, I strive to find from original sources the Framers' thoughts and reasons for their calling our American form of government *a new type of republic.*

We are the republic of the United States of America. The Framers formed our Union out of the dust of revolution and from hearts of heroes who held celestial thoughts, who set their minds and wills to fight all forms of tyranny, to keep their and our souls free, and to keep their and our minds open to the God of creation by faith based on reason. Their conscience was the mind-set that broke the chains of monarchial government and evaluated the accounts of history to establish a *more perfect union.* They rose from their prayers to raise a nation founded upon principles that guide the law of the land for the common good of its citizens. Though God creates, man corrupts. Therefore, our struggle for the people's sovereignty continues to be a struggle of right over wrong; Truth over partial facts. That struggle weighs God's words against those of men who desire to strike God's words from history and to elevate their own over humanity; who diligently strive to strike from time this form of government the Framers of our Constitution nominated the best form of government.

We are the republic of the United States of America knit together by the principles of our republican form of government that unite *we the people who hold these truths to be self-evident, which holds that we are endowed by our creator with certain unalienable rights to pursue life, liberty, and happiness.*

Our united voice hails from the multitude of our free society and albeit the hands that vote make the majority, the Constitution never denies the minority their rights, and it protects the whole from the few who would usurp the sovereignty of the people. Thus, our united voices by principle guide our ship of state upon these pacific waters by the Framers' compass of republican principles of government. Our banner is our stars and stripes that stir our hearts and minds to remember our heritage. The wind that unfurls our flag is the breath of God and his Spirit writes our pledge of allegiance to our Constitution that embraces the whole of his humanity.

Our character is the fabric of his Spirit of free will and his word of righteousness that guides our path in society as individuals. We are a collective of thanksgivings for these natural rights, so our understanding of them as natural law honors our sovereign union and pledges our united obligation to one another to protect these principles. We develop our strength of character when we possess the moral courage to govern ourselves. We do this by ensuring that we elevate by education these republican principles, which through virtue guide our hearts and minds in order to develop our consciences. We live united to honor God by instilling in our prosperity the truth upon which our culture thrives. Truth breathes life into those of us who are free and may in those who hope to be free. Our Framers established our Constitution to create our form of government. It, as practical law, institutes our civil law. Our practice of it disciplines us to remember our pledge, but if not, divided we shall fall.

One reason I write is to correct the assumption that democracy is a legitimate movement in America. It is precisely because it is contrary in the most part to our Constitutional principles that I write. As such, it erodes our rights, our laws, and our understanding of the principles of our republican form of government. We should note that as a republic, we possess laws not of man, but of God. The former law, of man, is positive; the latter law of God is natural law. James Wilson notes that man's law is arbitrary; God's law is absolute. As an empire, our natural law applies to the whole or extent of our country and its people. Jefferson points out man's long struggle to obtain what our Framers established in America, our republican form of government unequaled then as now.

"During the throes and convulsions of the ancient world, during the agonizing spasms of infuriated man, seeking through blood and slaughter his long-lost liberty, it was not wonderful that the agitation of the billows should reach even this distant and peaceful shore; that this should be more felt and feared by some and less by others, and should divide opinions as to measures of safety. However, every difference of opinion is not a difference of principle. We have called by different names brethren of the same principle. We are all Republicans, we are all Federalists. If there be any among us who would wish to dissolve this Union or to change its republican form, let them stand undisturbed as monuments of the safety with which error of opinion may be tolerated where reason is left free to combat it. I know, indeed, that some honest men fear that a republican government can not be strong, that this Government is not strong enough; but would the honest patriot, in the full tide of successful experiment, abandon a government which has so far kept us free and firm on the theoretic and visionary fear that this Government, the world's best hope, may by possibility want energy to preserve itself? I trust not. I believe this, on the contrary, the strongest Government on earth. I believe it the only one where every man, at the call of the law, would fly to the standard of the law, and would meet invasions of the public order as his own personal concern. Sometimes it is said that man can not be trusted with the government of himself. Can he, then, be trusted with the government of others? Or have we found angels in the forms of kings to govern him? Let history answer this question.

"Let us, then, with courage and confidence pursue our own Federal and Republican principles, our attachment to union and representative government."

Thomas Jefferson
First Inaugural Address, March 4, 1801

Introduction

My thesis is that the American Republic is a mix of the three ancient forms of government, which includes unique innovations by our Framers. It is the fourth form of government. Secondly, I want to show that the form and structure of our government combats the evils and weaknesses of the three ancient forms. Thirdly, I shall prove that our Framers' intent as ratified in our Constitution is the only orthodox method of understanding it and the principles of our law. Given the history of our government's progress, we know that we possess solid basis for knowing its principles, interpreting its meaning, and either legislating law or adjudicating law. Fourthly, I provide an answer to those who follow Dr. Rakove's conclusion about modern American polity. Jack Rakove, Coe Professor of History and American Studies at Colgate University quotes Dr. Judith Shklar from her lecture on "*Democracy and the Past: Jefferson and His Heirs*," which she delivered at Stanford University, April 1988. The Los Angeles Times printed her quote on May 14, 1995. The LA Times provides no specific reference for her quote in its article. Dr. Rakove references John Quincy Adams as Dr. Shklar's source for her quote. Dr. Rakove states that she takes her quote from the 1833 memoirs of Adams. The quote is as follows,

> "Democracy has no forefathers, it looks to no posterity, it is swallowed up in the present and thinks of nothing but itself."

The Los Angeles Times is the only return from my web search for this quote. Such issues influence our beliefs. Therefore, I fully cover why America is a republic of compound principles that eliminate democracy in its most vile and evil nature and principles. First, I use the word Democracy, as capitalized, to refer to the Democratic Party present in the United States (U. S.). As a form of government, I present the word in lower case. I also use the word as defined by James Madison, to mean a pure democracy. The modern usage focuses upon democracy in a sense unfamiliar and least descriptive of a democracy, which does not suit the nature and principles of democracy, as we know it diachronically. Our challenge is that proposed by Madison, which is to be careful of mixing concepts. I purpose to unravel that mix in this book and to establish the uniqueness of our American form of republican government. I use republican to mean our form of government and not the resident party, unless specifically indicated by context or otherwise.

Each chapter concerns itself with a particular subject that explains the differences between a republic and a democracy as understood in three eras of history, ancient, 16th through 19th centuries, and modern America. I do not delve into postmodern thought directly, although I may touch upon some of its tenets when I address interpretation, but I do not attempt herein to explore the rules, maxims, or vocabulary of interpretation in this volume. Each era influences our mixed views of our republic and the manner in which we draw conclusions. I rely upon terms and definitions to convey meaning and intent. Throughout the book, I review and cite the Framers' research to substantiate my thesis that America is not a democracy. I sort their collective reasoning from their papers, and their arguments in the 1787 Debates, which contribute to this book's content. I apply these findings to the platforms from which our political parties take their respective positions on current issues. I do not concentrate on the undercurrents in platform rhetoric because I believe that republican principles speak directly to both thought and action, which we can use to evaluate personal speech and personal or party platform planks. Therefore, I view our republican principles as capable of evaluating each issue for relevance to our common good in harmony with our structure of government. Each chapter deals with a specific aspect of government that is relevant to our modern understanding of how past meets present and why and when we have a collision of ideas. Each chapter ends with a conclusion that highlights the core of the chapter and that segues to the next chapter.

An insertion here seems appropriate after our newly appointed Supreme Court Justice Kagan advises us that we should not desire any opinion outside the bounds of the Constitution. Our question is, whether the final acceptance of the Constitution must include those principles enumerated by the Framers that formed our Constitution and the people ratified? As she responds to a question regarding the Declaration of Independence and its mention of nature's law, she invites us as a Union to answer whether the roots of our government grow from the soil of our fight for independence. Her assumption seems to be that natural rights lay outside the purview of our Constitution. We do need to understand that the principles in the Declaration of Independence are fountainheads for our republican birth. Yet, we need to ask, is it not true that our Constitution includes a Bill of Rights? Is it not of historical import that the intent of the Bill of Rights was to limit legislative *and* Executive acts against encroachments upon our *natural rights*? We must answer both questions in the affirmative.[1] Therefore, we must be concerned that ideas contrary to natural rights that hope to strip the people of their natural rights granted by our Creator specifically addresses our interests in religion from which originates virtue upon which character and conscience exhibits itself righteously or not. From this, I add my previous concerns that our Judiciary finds precedent to exclude natural rights, which, in turn, raises questions about the Judiciary's interpretational process. I will add an observation regarding the Establishment Clause, which reads from Black's Law Dictionary as follows,

> (1959) The First Amendment [1791] provision that prohibits the federal and state governments from establishing an official religion, or from favoring or disfavoring an official religion over another.[2]

I find this interesting because the actual Amendment I of 1791 reads as follows,

> "Congress shall make no law respecting an establishment of religion, or prohibiting the free exercise thereof;...."[3]

I see the first item as an innovation of the second, because *prohibiting the free exercise thereof* seems to mean something entirely different from *or from favoring or disfavoring an official religion over another.* Again, I see the first as pertaining to worship, but the second provides the cover for neutrality, in my opinion. Our question is, is this the intended meaning of Amendment I?

The liberal movement as represented in some of its publications works to accomplish globalization for the benefit of humanity. I see this effort as a worthy goal, however, we must question how "free" is its implementation? Do developing countries want Western help in the way liberals wave the flag of humanitarianism? Is the struggle to raise self and country more productive than third party ideologies? While I am aware of these ideologies and their resultant programs, my purpose is to ask North Americans whether they are willing to give up our independence, our fight for freedom, and our rule of law to immerse ourselves in the affairs of other states. The United States is a great resource to other countries and peoples today as in the past. If we believe in the market place of ideologies, then why do liberals feel such zeal to order the world?

*New Politics, Vol XIII No 3, Summer 2011; Democracy A Journal of Ideas No. 21, Summer 2011; Political Science Quarterly, The Journal of Public and International Affairs; The New Republic, August 18, 2011.

I am a highly interested retiree of middle class heritage. I possess college degrees that provide me with a foundation in diverse subjects to which my self-study adds depth. I focus on the Framers' republican principles as our beacon that guides life's scope that plays a meaningful role in our civil and personal lives.

Chapter 1:

Montesquieu: On the Nature and Principles of the Three Governments[4]

Montesquieu provides a survey of insights that the Framers referenced. He described the three forms of government and he set out their nature and principles that express its character. In studying the papers of the Framers, we discover how much they read and relied upon Montesquieu's writings, but they did use many other writers. While, his three forms are not consistent with other writers who use some different terms in their list of forms, his extended discussion of democracy covers essential differences between a republican form and a democracy. The Framers use monarchy, aristocracy, and democracy as the ancient forms. The commonality between Montesquieu and the Framers is the term republican. Our focus in Montesquieu is his description of a democratic republic, an economic democratic republic, and a republic. In the Framers, our focus is on the three primary forms that lead to evils and their modifications that introduce the fourth form of government.

Section 1: Montesquieu's Three Forms of Government

Montesquieu names three forms of government, which are Republican, Monarchical, and Despotic. He defines republican government as one in which the people either as a body or some portion of the people possess sovereign power. Under the Republican head, Montesquieu lists democracy, so we find that he includes a democratic republic. Key to our understanding is that both a republic and a democracy vest power in the people. Our various authors herein cited, define the essential idea of democracy by a variety of definitions, which we deal with as they arise. My treatment of democracy revolves around the Framers definition, which Madison provides and we discuss later.

Each form of government has a nature and a principle and these emit fundamental laws.[5] The Framers refer to these three forms consistently, but their evaluation of democracy coincides with that of Montesquieu's. I narrowed my focus to Montesquieu's pictures of government to the democratic and republican forms because I juxtapose democracy and a republic. In America, Jackson's *Era of Democracy* produced a split, which introduced the Democratic Party. The word *democratic* became associated with the Democratic political party in 1829 in America, three years after Jefferson's death.[6] Actually, the Democratic Party was pro-slavery and some states promoted it. Some say that Jefferson founded the Republican Party in 1792 to defend "*agrarian interests and states' rights*". Some also say that in 1854, the Republican Party was reformed and Jefferson's party became an anti-slavery coalition.[7] However, we might view this as an early testimony to the confusion of the nature and principles of our form of government as early as 1829. As we shall demonstrate, Jefferson represents a constitutional republic, which is the form the Framers developed and considered worthy to emulate.

Section 2: Nature and Principle of Government

Montesquieu recognizes that the nature of government makes it what it is by its structure. Its principle makes it act. This principle is the human passions. My intention is to demonstrate that the American Republic is not a democracy, so I reference the Framers' prolific writings for their collective conclusions from which I draw my thesis. I look to James Madison for his definitions of democracy and republics that he presents in his various papers to demonstrate the character and principles that the Constitutional Convention delegates relied upon. John Adams' study of ancient and modern constitutions provides us with an understanding of their nature and their principles, which identifies their form of government. In addition, I consult many diverse papers from not a few Framers. I use direct quotes with references for you to examine more fully at your leisure. The Glossary provides 18th century terms and definitions juxtaposed with modern terms and definitions to flavor the feast of ideas we investigate.

Section 3: Pure Democracy

Since the states leaned towards democracy, the Framers spent considerable energy to define its meaning and to present their case against it for the Federal system.

Madison states this:

> "A pure democracy, by which I mean a society consisting of a small number of citizens, who assemble and administer the government in person, can admit of no cure for the mischiefs of faction. A common passion or interest will, in almost every case, be felt by a majority of the whole; a communication and concert result from the form of government itself; and there is nothing to check the inducements to sacrifice the weaker party or an obnoxious individual. Hence it is that such democracies have ever been spectacles of turbulence and contention; have ever been found incompatible with personal security or the rights of property; and have in general been as short in their lives as they have been violent in their deaths. Theoretic politicians, who have patronized this species of government, have erroneously supposed that by reducing mankind to a perfect equality in their political rights, they would, at the same time, be perfectly equalized and assimilated in their possessions, their opinions, and their passions."[8]

> "Hence, it clearly appears, that the same advantage, which a republic has over a democracy, in controlling the effects of faction, is enjoyed by a large over a small republic, is enjoyed by the Union over the States composing it."[9]

Democracy unmixed is a dangerous form of government for the people. Madison distinguishes between a republic and a democracy, which informs us that democracy was a direct representational form of government, while our republic is an indirect representational form, but both forms give the government to the people through different structures and principles. The Framers concluded that although the ancients knew about representation, they attempted it only with the executive, but even this was rare. Great Britain tried indirect representation first, which the Framers modified. We find three ideas that are sprinkled throughout the Framers' discourses. First, they attempt to separate the mixing of concepts of a republic with a democracy. Secondly, we have the structural distinction between a republic and a democracy. Thirdly, we have innovative ideas that apply to the United States only. In the quote below, Madison clarifies the first two of these ideas.

> "The error which limits republican government to a narrow district has been unfolded and refuted in preceding papers. I

remark here only that it seems to owe its rise and prevalence chiefly to the confounding of a republic with a democracy, applying to the former reasonings drawn from the nature of the latter. The true distinction between these forms was also adverted to on a former occasion. It is, that in a democracy, the people meet and exercise the government in person; in a republic, they assemble and administer it by their representatives and agents. A democracy, consequently, will be confined to a small spot. A republic may be extended over a large region.[10]

A. On Democracy:

"As for democracy, I believe it can suit only with the convenience of a small town, accompanied with such circumstances as are seldom found. But this no way obliges men to run into the other extreme, in as much as the variety of forms, between mere democracy and absolute monarchy, is almost infinite. And if I should undertake to say, there never was a good government in the world, that did not consist of the three simple species of monarchy, aristocracy, and democracy, I think I may make it good. This at the least is certain, that the government of the Hebrews, instituted by God, had a judge, the great Sanhedrim, and general assemblies of the people. Sparta had two kings, a Senate of twenty-eight chosen men, and the like assemblies. All the Dorian cities had a chief magistrate, a Senate, and occasional assemblies ...

"It is conferred, that a pure democracy can never be good, unless for a small town, &c."[11]

B. Popular Government:

"As to popular government in the strictest sense, that is, pure democracy, where the people in themselves, and by themselves, perform all that belongs to government, I know of no such thing; and, if it be in the world, have nothing to say for it."[12]

"If it be said, that those governments, in which the democratical part governs most, do more frequently err in the choice of men, or the means of preserving that purity of manners which is required for the well-being of a people, than those wherein aristocracy prevails, I confess it, and that in Rome and Athens, the best and wisest men did for the most part incline to aristocracy. Xenophon, Plato, Aristotle, Thucydides, Livy, Tacitus, Cicero, and others, were of this sort. But if our author there seek patrons for his absolute monarchy, he will find none but Phalaris, Agathocles,

> Dionysius, Catiline, Cechegus, Lentulus, with the corrupted crew of mercenary rascals who did, or endeavoured to set them up: these are they, quibus ex honesto nulla est spes: they abhor *the dominion of the law*, because it curbs their vices, and make themselves subservient to the lusts *of a man* who may nourish them."[13]

> "Being no way concerned in the defence of democracy, &c. I may leave our knight, like Don Quixote, fighting against the phantasms of his own brain, and saying what he pleases against such governments as never were, unless in such a place as St. Marino, near Siniglaglia in Italy, where a hundred clowns govern a barbarous rock that no man invades, and relates nothing to our question. The republic of St. Marino, next to that of Millingen in Switzerland, is the smallest republic in Europe. The limits of it extend no farther than the base of the mountain on which it is seated. Its insignificance is its security. No neighbouring prince ever thought it worth his while to destroy the independency of such a Beehive. See Blainville's Travels, vol. ii. p. 227. Addison's Remarks on several parts of Italy."[14]

Mr. Adams cautions against using the label democracy for mixed governments:

> "However, more ignorance cannot be expressed, than by giving the name of democracy to those governments that are composed of the three simple species, as we have proved that all the good ones have ever been: for, in a strict sense, it can only suit with those, where the people retain to themselves the administration of the supreme power; and more largely, when the popular part, as in Athens, greatly overbalances the other two, and the denomination is taken from the prevailing part."[15]

How Democracy arises, Mr. Adams says,

> "Democracy is next to be considered, in what manner it arises, and what kind of man it produces when arisen. The change from oligarchy to democracy is produced through the insatiable desire of becoming as rich as possible. As those who are governors in it govern on account of their possessing great riches, they will be unwilling to restrain by law such of the youth as are dissolute, from having the liberty of squandering and wasting their substance; that so, by purchasing the substance of such persons, and lending them on usury, they may still become richer, and be held in greater honour. While they neglect education, and suffer the youth to grow licentious, they sometimes lay under a necessity of becoming poor, such as are of no ungenerous

disposition: these sit in the city, some of them in debt, others in contempt, hating and conspiring against those who possess their substance, and with others very desirous of a change. But the money-catchers, still brooding over it, and drawing to themselves exorbitant usury, fill the city with drones and poor. They neglect every thing but making of money, and make no more account of virtue than the poor do. When these governors and their subjects meet on the road, at public shows, in military marches, as fellow soldiers or sailors, or in common dangers, the poor are by no means contemned by the rich. A robust fellow, poor and sunburnt, beside a rich man, bred up in the shade, swoln with flesh, and panting for breath, and in agony in battle, thinks it is through his own and his fellows fault that such men grow rich, and says, Our rich men are good for nothing. The city soon grows into sedition between the oligarchic and democratic parties; and the poor prevailing over the rich, kill some and banish others, and share the places in the republic, and the magistracies, equally among the remainder, and for the most part the magistracies are disposed in it by lot. In what manner do these live, and what sort of republic is this? A democracy. The city is full of all freedom of action and speech, and liberty to do in it what any one inclines: every one will regulate his own method of life in whatever way he pleases. In such a republic will arise men of all kinds. This is the finest of all republics, variegated like a robe with all kinds of flowers, and diversified with all sorts of manners. The multitude, it is likely, judge this republic the best, like children and women gazing at variegated things. In truth it contains all kinds of republics, and it appears necessary for any one, who wants to constitute a city, as we do at present, to come to a democratic city, as to a general fair of republics, and choose the form that he fancies: he will not be in want of models. Is not this a sweet and divine manner of life for the present? To be under no necessity to govern, although you were able to govern; nor to be subject, unless you incline; nor to be engaged in war when others are; nor to live in peace when others do so, unless you be desirous of peace; and though there be a law restraining you from governing or administering justice, to govern nevertheless, and administer justice if you incline? Have you not observed, in such a republic, men condemned to death or banishment continuing still, or returning like heroes, and walking up and down openly, as if no one observed them? Is not this indulgence of the city very generous, in magnificently despising all care of education and discipline, and in not regarding from what sort of pursuits one comes to act in public affairs, but honouring him, if he only say he is well affected towards the multitude? These things, and such as

> these; are to be found in a democracy; and it would be a pleasant sort of republic, anarchical and variegated, distributing a certain equality to all alike, without distinction."[16]

Adams finds no comfort in the ability of democracies to safeguard the people. Their final vote against democracy came with the ratification of our Constitution, which is a settled opinion by majority will of those who signed our Constitution. The majority will of the people came with ratification.

C. Democracy in the Debates:

Mr. Hamilton:

Alexander Hamilton does not use the word democracy in any of his *Federalist* Articles. On the other hand, he uses "republic" (or a derivative) approximately, 16 times, Republican 13 times, Republicanism 3 times, Republican government 27 times, and Republican principles 3 times. See below his misgivings regarding both the "*vices of democracy*" and the "*weakness of a republican government*" on the floor of the Convention. He was an advocate for a government modeled after Great Britain with the Executive reflecting a monarchy.[17]

Mr. Gerry

> "The evils we experience flow from the excess of democracy. The people do not want virtue, but they are the dupes of pretended patriots."[18]

His context is Massachusetts campaigns in which the people were "daily misled into the most baneful measures and opinions by the false reports ... which no one on the spot can refute." When we attach this sentiment to Montesquieu's study[19] that virtue gone awry is ambition, then we see continuity in history about human nature. He goes on to discuss government employee salaries as too little. This, however, is not my focus. Whatever the subject, do we the people really want to hear the arguments in order to determine the truth in order to discover the virtue or ambition in the speakers? Either virtue or self-interested design is the backbone of government. Should we look again at the Framers' motives, sincerity, and effort to discover a "*more perfect union*" that exemplifies good government?

Section 4: Nature of Democracy in a Republic

In a democratic republic, democracy has a specific nature. Montesquieu's observation is that democracy produces factions, each with a spirit that represses the others. He sees that a popular government divides people into classes upon which democracy depends and thrives. History is our witness that only virtue sustains government.[20] He says,

> "Desires change their objects: that which one used to love, one loves no longer."[21]
>
> "Ambition is pernicious in a republic."[22]

In the first quote, Montesquieu addresses how our passions are whimsical and change from virtuous love to ambition for some need or desire. In the second quote, how love changed to ambition undermines virtue and destroys a republic. He also points out that in classical times education did not contradict itself. A society that opposes its ties with religion with those of the world nullifies its virtue. When children receive one instruction from their parents, another from their schoolmasters, and still another from the world the latter upsets the first two, then the government fails in its principle.[23].

He relates this love in a democracy as love that is everything and education must inspire it. Education begins at home. Montesquieu says that a democratic republic dedicates itself to the love of democracy, which is the love of equality, which limits ambition to happiness with service to homeland rather than to other citizens. Democracy's love is of frugality. The democratic emphasis, Montesquieu writes, focuses love on equality and on frugality where all possess the same happiness, the same advantages, the same expectation, rather than each their own conscience. In a democracy, all possess a common frugality that limits the desire to possess. With such a principle, a democratic republic must have a quantity of middling, sober, and happy people. Further, such a republic must establish its love of equality and its frugality by its laws.[24] A democratic republic must pass laws that regulate dowries, gifts, inheritances, testaments, and all other types of contracts. A democratic republic must regulate wills in order to control the stability of the fundamental laws of equality. Montesquieu points this out by stating that inheritance law, especially one that forbids passing to one-person two inheritances, was "*a good law for democracy*".[25] Historically we see that governments that attempted democracy must also attempt to make laws that made fortunes equal, because equality is the élan vital of democracy. Therefore, the government places burdens on the rich to reduce fortunes, upon the citizens to reduce differences, upon the land to provide only for one's daily bread. In a democracy, the people prosper at the expense of the successful and it establishes equality by placing burdens on the rich to relieve burdens on the poor.[26] In conclusion, we note that a republic places the government in the people that parallel democracy's *demos*. Later, we see how the Framers further separated our Republic from a democracy.

Section 5: Commercial Democracy

Montesquieu does warn us about a commercial democracy,

> "The ill comes when an excess of wealth destroys the spirit of commerce; one sees the sudden rise of the disorders of inequality which had not made themselves felt before.
>
> "In order for the spirit of commerce to be maintained, the principal citizens must engage in commerce themselves; this spirit must reign alone and not be crossed by another; all the laws must favor it; these same laws, whose provisions divide fortunes in proportion as commerce increases them, must make each poor citizen comfortable enough to be able to work as the others do and must bring each rich citizen to a middle level such that he needs to work in order to preserve or to acquire."[27]

He points out that a free enterprise system is in conflict with a democratic spirit of commerce. Does a social welfare system take from the rich and from the worker? Our personal schemes rest upon the passions of human nature. Shall we ever learn this lesson? Mr. Morris' concern that reason fails to challenge passion and that the schemes of the rich manipulate our passions, finds proof in modern science. I address passion later.

> "We should remember that the people never act from reason alone. The Rich will take advantage of their passions & make these the instruments for oppressing them. The Result of the Contest will be a violent aristocracy, or a more violent despotism. The schemes of the Rich will be favored by the extent of the Country. The people in such distant parts can not communicate & act in concert. They will be the dupes of those who have more knowledge & intercourse. The only security against encroachments will be a select & sagacious body of men, instituted to watch against them on all sides. He meant only to hint these observations, without grounding any motion on them."[28]

This last sentence is the root of a bicameral legislature with the Senate as those who answer passion with *"cool headed deliberation"*.

Mr. Gerry reflects upon democratical tendencies in the states.

> "In Massachusetts, particularly he saw the danger of this calamitous event-In that State there are two parties, one devoted to *democracy, the worst he thought of all political evils*, the other as violent in the opposite extreme. From the collision of these in opposing and resisting the Constitution, confusion was greatly to be feared. He had thought it necessary, for this & other reasons

> that the plan should have been proposed in a more mediating shape, in order to abate the heat and opposition of parties."[29]

Mr. Gerry identifies the conflict democracy has with other parties. He considers it "the worst *of all political evils*". One may stamp out a fire, but a smoldering ember can burn down a forest.

Section 6: Modern Democracy

The theory of *demos* concerns the whole of society that is the people, which differentiates between a class, a section, or any interest in society. An expressed issue is with how to know who *the people* are. A question that our Constitution asks is, what "acts of government" belong to the people? The answer our American Constitution mandates is the people act to elect the governing, to amend our Constitution to seal its weaknesses, and to ensure our government operates only within its enumerated jurisdictions. Our Constitution prescribes republican principles, which we shall discuss throughout this book, to guide our actions.[30] We shall contrast our republican form with democracy more closely, next.

A. Democratic Representation:
   Modern democracy prescribes two forms:

   a. Direct representation occurs when all citizens participate in decision-making

   b. Indirect representation (Representative) occurs when citizens choose representatives who are directly involved and usually perform without further consultation, but they are responsible to the citizenry.

These two ideas are the *sheet anchors* of modern democracy that constitute an agreement among modern pundits as to what democracy is, but pundits admit little agreement as to what a democratic regime actually is. We shall review ancient democratic representation in Chapter 2. We shall see how our Constitution deals with representation in Chapter 6.

Modern pundits present two conflicting criteria that occur when an assessment of any particular decision-making instance surfaces, which are:

1. Who made the assessment?

   This presents a problem that addresses *collective choice*.[31]

2. What interested party does it serve?

> This question surfaces the problems of *social welfare* and *social choice*[32].

I shall not address these questions or their ancillary problems for they are not germane to our major concern, which is, why the United States is not a democracy. *Black's Law Dictionary* defines neither of these phrases.

B. Western Theory of Democracy

The West uses the above two criteria to establish whether a state is a democracy, which are as follows:

a. European: "a state is democratic if there is some way of attributing every major political decision to the people, either because they take part in making it, or because it ultimately depends upon their consent."

b. Soviet: "...decisions are democratic if they furthered (or perhaps only if were intended to further) the interests of the people, even though taken by a ruling party which forbad popular membership of its ranks."

1. Western Democratic Parties:

> The usual reason for a party is to develop polices for the people to choose and to seek free and periodic elections for the power to implement them. This forms the democratic framework for any modern western democracy.

2. U.S. Democratic Party:

We will discuss this aspect of democracy in the United States in Chapter 2, Section 5. I place this in this context for its involvement with the constitutionality of the New Deal (President Roosevelt 1933-1945) that addresses whether this Progressive form of democracy is constitutional, which was argued before the USSC (West Coast Hotel v. Parish (1937)) overruled (Adkins v. Children's Hospital, 261 U.S. 525 (1923)).

Section 7: Social Democracy

The reason for our Framers' fear of democracy is what we see in its modern version. The first term that makes the meaning of the Framers' fear clear is ... democratic socialism:

> "Socialism pursued by democratic means—e.g., through persuasion of the electorate in a state ruled by representative institutions. ("The parliamentary road to socialism.") Normally

> contrasted with socialism and communism imposed by force, following a revolution or *coup d'état.*
>
> "Many Western parties profess Democratic socialism, e.g., the UK Labor Party, prior to its emergence as New Labor, but very few such parties profess it today."[33]

Under the guise of democracy, its modern version works persistently to change government from the inside. Scruton is not saying it does not exist. He is saying that it is subtly boiling. It permeates our society. In this sense, "*we are all democrats*", as Ron Paul titles his paper. I see the next term describes our frog in the pot. Its insidious heating is its silent weapon of destruction. The new word, the new concept, and the new method is ...Democratization.

> "Quantitative or statistical research, by contrast, does a very good job in showing that relationships exist (for example, capitalist development relates to democratization) but does not generally do a good job at telling us what is the nature or underlying dynamic of this relationship.[34]
>
> "The introduction of collective choice into institutions and associations that are not themselves parts of government: e.g. places of work, schools and universities, churches and local communities. Democratization is a major political movement in Western countries that often see it as an essential feature of gradualist social reform in accordance with a respect for existing institutions."[35]

I shiver at the realization that our republican government exists in quicksand ideology that subtly forms through the sieve of educational ignorance and subterfuge. It does reflect Dr. Westin's differentiation between the passionate and the dispassionate, see Chapter 4, Section 3.

Section 8: Constitutional and Procedural Democracy

Gutmann and Thompson say that "*Constitutional and procedural democracy both protect individual rights against majority rule, but constitutional democrats do not.*" These two groups have different agendas that attempt to function on behalf of minority rights against *majoritarianism*. Their "*democratic process,*" splits along their names, Constitutional democrats and Procedural democrats, to deal with deliberative disagreements.[36]

Section 9: Conclusion

Montesquieu's great ideas on republics founded on democracy reveal some explicit collisions of ideas with a republic founded on the three ancient forms plus the unique American experience. The Framers attempt to nullify these differences between our federated extended republic and a republic founded on a democracy, or an aristocracy, or a monarchy. All three ancient forms have something to offer, but overall none alone are either sufficient or efficient to secure the people from its ultimate dominion. It seems that the result of a democratic republic is a mishmash of laws. We have some democratical ideas vying against republican, that is, American Constitutional government, ideas with all sounding as confirming the common good of our federal and national systems. Democratical strategies must ensure that the mores of the people remain fixed upon democratical principles, because a state gradually descends into oblivion and only rises with effort. A democratic republic rests upon virtue and that produces censors who must exist because both crime and negligence destroy virtue.[37] Montesquieu's observation extrapolated informs us that democracy is at variance with our mixed form of government. We can look to our educational system to see how democratical principles operate. Our question is, does it fit the republican principles that undergird our Constitution?

Montesquieu is the primary modern source on government of interest to the Framers with John Locke and Rousseau, who made predictions that we find realized today. The latter's concept of morals might be of interest to us.[38] Other writers rise whose thoughts clarify the thoughts of our constitutional Framers. The Framers did plumb the depths of the available original materials of the ancients and of modern governments. While these resources provide fathomable insights, they also looked to American history and their present lessons learned for the development of our unique American government's nature, principles, and structure. I find this provocative in reviewing history in our contemporary environment.

When I check *Black's Law Dictionary, Ninth Edition*, for the modern definition of democracy, it defines democracy as a government *by the people*. We note that this definition's use of *elected representatives* is inconsistent with the ancient idea of a pure democracy as Madison defines it and the democracy that Cicero notes as popular rule. Our Framers give Great Britain credit for introducing indirect representation, but they modified its structure in our form of government. We must grasp the modern version of democracy to comprehend its influence upon our thinking today and to evaluate its relevance to our mixed republican Constitution, which we address in Chapter 2.

I offer a quote from an Anti-Federalist, Brutus, who is identified as Judge Robert Yates of New York, who says in his Article 10,

> "In a pure democracy the people are the sovereign, and their will is declared by themselves; for this purpose they must all come together to deliberate, and decide. This kind of government cannot be exercised, therefore, over a country of any considerable extent; it must be confined to a single city, or at least limited to such bounds as that the people can conveniently assemble, be able to debate, understand the subject submitted to them, and declare their opinion concerning it."[39]

While the definitions of a democracy vary among the authors we discuss, the one constant is that democracy does not work over the long haul, except in small populations, if that. We now have history and the present as testimonies that the Framers were correct. Our question is, should we allow America to be lumped with European democracy when our framers understood it and worked to limit its negatives? Maybe more relevant is our question, does the modern democratic movement emulate the communist style of democracy?

The modern call to democratic ideas seems to be a focus on the people as factions of rights within our society. What they hope to accomplish is to favor certain defined rights over majority rule. In this, they are antirepublican in the sense that majority rule is a fundamental principle of our republican form of government.

Chapter 2:

Modern Influences on Republicanism

Section 1: On Representative Democracy

History gives us variant definitions of democracy. Dr. Adrienne Koch begins her introduction with the innovative idea that our Constitution sets up principles of our *democratic Republic of the United States*[40]. An idea our Framers' would find alien, as we see that John Adams makes it clear. However, the literature is replete with confusion over this issue. My point is that the Framers did not see ancient democracy as a workable representation either as direct or indirect for the United States. I discuss this further in Chapter 8, Section 1. The confusion is between what our Framers took as democracy and the modernization of democracy in its terms as defined above and in Chapter 2. We must look at Madison's definition in Chapter 3, Section 2 combined with Montesquieu's analysis to understand their view. A modern democracy is said to be one in which the people elect representatives. We derive this thought from Great Britain's form of government. However, the Commons, which represented the common people, was a minority in the party until changes drew it closer to the American form of representation, reports James Wilson. The Framers write about Great Britain's progressive approach to the American form of government. When the people form a popular government, Cicero calls it a democracy. Madison's definition of democracy is the one we treat herein, as above noted with the quote of Brutus serving as explanation. Since the Framers saw the weaknesses of democracy, monarchy, and aristocracy, Madison could not apply the concept "*representative democracy*" to our form of government. In fact, as we will see, he advises us not to mix the ideas of democracy with our American Republic's form. If Dr. Koch like others represents the Framers' conception in modern terms, she does an injustice to the Framers. We elect our representatives through *indirect representation.* This form is the republican form of government that James Madison describes.[41] President Jackson's *"era of Democracy"* confuses the Framer's distinction by introducing the concept of *popular will,*[42] which is not the same as Madison's *majority rule.* We might equate the former with mob rule and the latter with organized debate. Popular will often escalates to ochlocracy. The states reflect democratic ideas, but our Framers chose a republican form of government for our Republic, which the people of the States ratified. Our Constitution guarantees to the states that the federal will be a republican form of government.

Section 2: The Seventeenth Amendment

Article I, Section 3.

> "The Senate of the United States shall be composed of two Senators from each State, chosen by the Legislature thereof, for six Years; and each Senator shall have one vote."

Amendment XVII [1913]

> "[1] The Senate of the United States shall be composed of two Senators from each State, elected by the people thereof, for six years; and each Senator shall have one vote. The electors in each State shall have the qualifications requisite for electors of the most numerous branch of the State legislatures."

The Seventeenth Amendment introduces the *democratical* idea of "*direct popular election*" of the Senate. We know this from the history of the Progressive movement dating to this time. In 1912, Progressives argued for popular direct election. Their argument was that "*the democratic principle required the Senate to be elected by the people*".[43] Their argument was fallacious because our Constitution does not provide such a principle and majority will protects us against popular will. We point out later that the Senate is in fact the aristocratical element in our government. The House of Representatives is its democratical portion. The people thinking democratical ideas favorable to themselves voted the change. What they did might be innocuous, but it led the people astray in thinking a democratic principle is better than the mixed republican principle. We do need to understand the difference, which is a vote by the *people at large* (democratical) and our majority vote (electoral), which may not be a popular vote. The Framers saw that passions often drive the public and by adding this layer of indirect representation, it would cool down passions. Does Madison, WI prove their point? The Framers thought State legislators being mature citizens would select from among themselves two fit Senators. We learn in time that Congressional representatives are not intimidated from using their office and power to advantage their personal, rather than our state or national, interests. Our Framers thought virtue would help keep representatives in order. They did not foresee professional politicians who would accumulate power through unlimited tenure, a change in moral values, or uncontrolled lobbying. The Framers' attempt to balance power in Congress becomes canceled (See Article 1, Section 3.). They designed it to give the people better representation and to balance the House, the popular, against the Senate, the aristocratical. I believe we have lost this focus. If modern democracy is about the Communist version, then the change is fundamental. The Framers hoped each state legislature would elect talented and virtuous persons because they knew their character. Our lesson learned may be that we the people do tend towards democracy.[44] In that case, we the people may decide to understand an amendment's effect upon our form of government and our power to control those we elect before we rush to amend the Constitution. Madison and Mason did advocate suffrage for the Senate as for the Presidency, but the majority did not.[45] I believe the current movement for popular voting found its first step toward its wish fulfillment in the XVII Amendment. If we eliminate the Electoral College as a non-popular entity, then we lose the proportionate voting power of each state based on representation, which our census determines.

Section 3: Dr. Adrienne Koch[46] on Representative Democracy

> "Both terms, 'democracy' and 'Republic,' prove to be double-barreled if one takes a closer look. As Madison never tired of repeating, there is a direct Democracy, feasible only for small communities like the ancient city-states, for example, where simple majority rule holds sway and where all who are citizens cast their vote ...
>
> "On the other hand, *representative* Democracy was in fact what Madison was prepared to endorse. Because of the need for adjectival qualification, he preferred to use the term "Republic"—especially since a strong tradition of political thought which was opposed to monarchy and centered in the doctrine of human equality had appealed to Americans since the rise of the Revolutionary sentiment. The maxim 'he who wears the shoe, knows best where it pinches' was the ancient and honorable cardinal principle of Republicanism. Thus the consent

> of the governed is the only legitimate basis of government, for it alone abolishes the prescriptive subordination of men in society into super and subordinate classes. Madison himself in innumerable contexts defined what he meant by a *democratic* Republic, or a *representative* democracy. European theory had made Republicanism, understood as the theory of representative democracy, familiar. Only America, Madison pointed out, could claim to have taken the concept of popular government, through elected representatives of "we the people," out of the realm of pure theory and into the realm of experimental practice; and only America had this experiment in nonmonarchial, representative government made for a large country, an 'extensive republic'." [47]

Dr. Koch thinks there is a need for an "*adjectival qualification*", which is Republic. Her reason is fallacious, because the word *republic* describes America's new type of government and because monarchy was a split between two federalist camps. Madison and his majority delegates wanted the executive to be dependent on Congress' oversight, so the split was not about our form of government, but about its structure. Our new republic as constitutionally defined is our form of government structured by its Articles. She does not reveal from what source she translates Jefferson's intent for our government to be a representative democracy, I believe, because he agreed with the delegates that democracy is unworkable. He did promote, as did Washington, Madison, Mason, and Wilson, to name the obvious, the people's suffrage to dominate representation. All of these were adverse to democracy as a form of government in general and in America especially. I have provided all references to a democracy from Madison's papers that I could find, and I found no such intention on his part that democracy is the sole or most important header in our form of government. Analysis indicates that the *adjectival qualification* is "*mixed*". However, the United States' history is replete with acceptance that it is a democracy, even Hollywood adds its voice, contra the Framers' voice. However, Madison's definition of a democracy leaves no doubt that he fails to grasp the idea of *representation* in ancient democracy as anything but limited and that to the executive. The only ancient part that is democracy is the idea that the people are sovereign because they are the decision-makers, but they thought the better term to define sovereignty was *republic*. "*We the people*" is a republican phrase that means the people elect their representatives by majority will and we retain absolute sovereignty over both our representation and our national, each state republic, and general, state and federal, governments through elected representatives. The states are all republics, and this is republicanism, not democracy. So, we have an indirect representation, which is the innovation wrapped in the republican idea of suffrage by majority will. Dr. Koch does not reveal her source that leads her to conclude that Madison means a representative democracy. John Adams informs us that such a concept is a contradiction (See Chapter 1, Section3: A.). I do not recollect from the writings of Madison or in the majority of Framers represented in the Debates that he or any Framer ever refers to the United States as a "*direct or representative democracy*". They missed their opportunity if they meant it by leaving it out of the Constitutional Debates, and Madison and Hamilton out of their Federalist articles. It is true that a direct democracy was an evil in Madison's and in the other Framers' opinion. In fact, Madison bends over backward to guard against using democratical terms as though republican to avoid such an interpretation as Dr. Koch states. The Massachusetts' Constitution provided protection against "*democratical pirates*". The move reflects the commercial coast that was a conservative reaction to revolutionary radicalism. It goes on to report the move for a "*bicameral legislature*", which our Constitution "*substantially embodied*". Does this legislative precaution also reflect France's Ambassador to the United States Edmond-Charles Genêt's influence toward radicalism existent in democracies and France's practice and its influence on our population? American crowds loudly applauded him, but our government coolly received him. John Adams was the chief architect of the Massachusetts document. We should remember that he moved to the republican view of a strong Executive from his monarchial-aristocratic position.[48]

Mr. Adams, Mr. Madison, and other Framers use the adjectival qualification *pure* to denote democracy and that a pure type restricts its meaning to the executive and to a small territory. All the Framers' references to a democratic form of government show that it turns into an evil form and is short lived. The majority of Framers in the convention or otherwise did not condone democracy as a viable form of government. Madison does draw a distinction in the mode of representing the people in ancient democracies and that of the United States as above cited. However, his use of the phrase "*The difference relied on...*" makes it clear that he sees a significant difference between the ancient mode and America's. We hone in on this thought later. Our question is, can the modernized version offer a modified version of democracy worthy to compete with our present constitutional establishment? Since "*pundits admit little agreement as to what a democratic regime actually is*", the question is rhetorical.

Ralph Ketcham, editor of *The Anti-Federalist Papers and the Constitutional Convention Debates* reports that the "...founders would not have been opposed to the modern connotations of the word 'democracy'...." I believe he is incorrect and the Framers' wisdom shines through by their rejection of these modern views of democracy. How can democracy evolve to a modern form if its nature and principles remain the same? Does not the news testify each day that democracy modernized is democracy anciently realized?[49] I appreciate his thoughts, however, my survey of the Framers' words suggest that they would not allow themselves to trust the redefining of democracy as enough to change the result of a democracy. In fact, those who cry for democracy rely upon the public's willingness to govern by mob rule. In tyranny, one finds some justification for rebellion, but in America our law justly interpreted and justly applied is sufficient for majority will to operate for the good of society. We might remember this quote when we tend to ignore our Framers' experience, which is:

> "Every exception not watched tends to assume the place of the principle."[50]

In this vein, Ketcham explains that the tension between "*unalienable rights*" and "*consent*" is what the Framers' intended in order to balance power through our Constitution. He draws the conclusion that,

> "all the members of the Federal Convention, and both sides in the ratification struggle, sought to fulfill the purposes of the Declaration of Independence to both protect rights and insure government consent."

I believe this is true and it is the reason we need to understand our history in order to ensure that our natural rights, our civil rights, and our consensual rights are protected from encroachment by any of our three branches of government.[51] I am glad he, unlike Justice Kagan, sees the relationship between our Declaration of Independence and the Framer's mode of government to protect it and our rights declared by it.

If Madison used "*extended republic*" to clarify his meaning that America is a large country, then any other usage readmits the confusion the Framers hoped to avoid between it and a democracy. Democracy limited to a small town might work, but it would not in an extended territory such as America. In fact, Madison never equates the two terms, extended republic and representative democracy. I distinguish between aspects of democracy as a democratical feature, which is substantively different from the object *democracy* in its entirety. This is peculiarly true of the ancient type and definitively true of the modern type. Madison's distinction from the American and the modernized seventeenth and eighteenth century European usage is that only in America is a republic so "*unmixed and extended*". In this context, I understand *unmixed* to eliminate democracy's influence upon our form of representation because our form is indirect representation. I am not sure of this, but as Samuel Johnson defines *unmixed*, I believe I am correct. As such, it is an American credit and carries America's stamp of uniqueness, which makes it a new term for a new world government that is pure, new, and uncorrupted.[52] Therefore, I depart from Ketcham's opinion that the Framers would not be "opposed to the modern connotations of the word 'democracy' to differentiate the difference". I explain in Chapter 5, Section 1 how the Framers understood a republic.[53]

One might make a case that Dr. Koch and Mr. Ketcham use historicism, which Leo Strauss identifies as a conflict between conventionalism, classical philosophy's rise from the natural to the eternal, and modern ideas that reject natural rights based on the belief that all human thought is historical. Madison makes this statement:

> "A government deriving its energy from the will of the society, and operating by the reason of its measures on the understanding and interest of the society. Such is the government for which philosophy has been searching, and humanity been sighing, from the most remote ages. Such are the republican governments, which it is the glory of America to have invented, and her unrivalled happiness to possess. May her glory be completed by every improvement on the theory which experience may teach; and her happiness be perpetuated by a system of administration corresponding with the purity of the theory."[54]

Madison does not recognize the modern idea, so his emphasis is upon the elevation of human reason by nature's God as enlightenment to guide humankind's self-governance.[55] If society has ceased its search by attaining its new form of government, then how can one believe he intends to name our form a democracy? Does this challenge our State Department's pride in exporting democracy? Madison sees that our form of government departs from all previous governments, as this excerpt from his above quote clarifies,

> "Such are the republican governments, which it is the glory of America to have invented, and her unrivalled happiness to possess."[56]

His claim remains to this day. He also suggests improvements to it. Maybe we the people should consider how to *improve* our government to better embrace republicanism in its application. In attempting to make our Republic a democracy, some overlook this plain fact, democracy serves only small communities, not an extended territory, in which the people must make all the decisions. Its passion is its Achilles' heel. Its sphere is small; its passion large, which may boil over and become mob rule. I think Madison's warning is applicable here as we see that our republican principles can fall victim to the Jacksonian fallacy that *what is part is the whole*. Madison calls our Republic a new form of government. A part may represent a whole as in a *synecdoche*, but this is not the case here. American representation is unique. The American Republic is unique. One element of a thing within another thing is not sufficient for the whole of the latter to take on the character of the former. We clarify more specifically later on.

Section 4. Other Sources of this Confusion are as follows

1. *Democracy in America,* renewed 1972, Alexis De Tocqueville;
2. *The American Commonwealth, Volume II,* pg. 923–4, 1995, James Bryce.

   Bryce recognizes three forms of government taken by free countries, which are:

   a. Greek republics with primary assemblies;

   b. Representative bodies, parliaments, and chambers;

   c. A compromise of a. and b. *either as an attempt to apply the principle of primary assemblies to large countries or as a modification of the representative system in the direction of direct popular sovereignty.*

   This latter is not what the Framers' intended, but what the Jacksonian Democratic Era accomplished. We see that Bryce notices this and promulgates it rather than the Framers' original idea.

3. Churchill notes the Jacksonian presidency gave rise to Western democratic urges and entered politics through his *economic policy.* I draw the same conclusion. However, we have seen that its earliest introduction was its import from France by Genêt. In any case, it certainly does not follow our republican Constitution.[57]

   "Democracy is the worst form of government, except for all those other forms that have been tried from time to time."

   (House of Commons speech on Nov. 11, 1947) Winston Churchill

Do we accept this to be inclusive of our form of republican government based on our Framers' conception of democracy? In their understanding, Jackson extended the Jeffersonian vision of the centrality of the people and he took Jefferson's view of the role of president further still. To Jackson, the idea of sovereignty of the many was compatible with a powerful Executive, which is the monarchial aspect the Framers made every attempt to quell. He saw that liberty required security, that freedom required order, and that the well-being of the parts of the Union required that the whole remain intact.

> "If he felt a temporary resort to autocracy was necessary to preserve democracy, Jackson would not hesitate to take the role.... In this, he set an example on which other presidents would draw in times of national struggle."[58]

His autocratic notion is the specific move toward despotism the Framers used the bicameral legislature to prevent. While his action may seem justifiable, our Constitution protects we the people by blocking such a move, up to then. If we need flexibility in the roles of leadership, then we the people must make the change through a Constitutional Convention. We should reward leaders who make the change by usurpation or innovation with impeachment. All of the above sources fail to grasp the major differences between the classical democracy, which modern democracy provides no protections against, and our American mixed Republican form that incorporates only a few democratical ideas and these with structural restraints built in to protect we the people from the inherent democratical vices. Actually, Jackson falls from the Framers' belief regarding *balance of power*, which, in part, was to restrict the Executive from evolving into Monarchianism or despotism. Our republican form grants total sovereignty to the people by natural law, by representation, and through their indirect representation through the House of Representatives, then by state representation through the Senate. I believe President Lincoln reflects the republican principle of union by the Constitutional Convention that the states voted to observe, but he also saw in crisis a need for autocracy. It was and is unconstitutional for any state to declare secession on its own or as a member of a group of states.[59] Was Lincoln a despot, or did he become autocratic due to the unusual forces of democratic tendencies in the South? If so, he reverses the Jacksonian tendency to popular will and the democratical ideas that embraced state rights to own slaves. Our question is whether we the people should meet any movement toward an imbalance of power with alarm and swift action to nullify it?

Section 5: Jacksonian Democracy and a Looming Question

Does the Jackson Democracy correlate with the *intent* of the Framers or the *spirit* of our Constitution? Jackson's idea of democracy, while an attempt to help the people, is contrary to that of the Convention's intent to establish a representative republic. Jackson's democracy is not in the spirit of our Constitution, because it matches a democratic idea of popular will with our republican principle of majority will. The former may become mob rule, while the latter occurs through organized suffrage. Popular will, in fact, introduces evils the Framers testify that the Constitution remedies. A key character of democracy is the creation of factions. If democracy is an evil, then what is our constitutional republican form? Madison answers,

> "In a confederacy founded on republican principles, and composed of republican members, the superintending

> government ought clearly to possess authority to defend the system against aristocratic or monarchical innovations."[60]

Besides this republican character, see Appendix B: Table of Government Powers for more detail. When we add the Soviet form of democracy in this mix, what form of democracy is the European Union or our internal Democratic Party? I see the Framers' intent is to intertwine the states' national and the federal governments by common interests, not factions as opposing our form of government, but as groups using its structure to protect their interest. We can only ensure stability in our government if our compact remains *substantially* or materially the same.[61] So, the people are the protectors of our republican constitutional Union's form or its direst enemy. We the people by right must protect it when our political institutions fail to do so. I think it safe to expand the extent of innovations to mean from whatever source threatens our republican principles. How could we the people stray so far from understanding these limits of constitutional republican government? Our question is whether we proudly accept our new form as the best of all possible governments, or do we join in the European movement and democratize America?

Section 6: Conclusion

Our form of government was intricately woven with cognizance of past (ancient), present (Framers), and the future (us). Our past must inform our present in order to preserve our future from here to eternity. Whatever we believe is the worth of freedom, it motivates us to evaluate carefully the influence of contemporary thinkers upon the Framers' intent for their intent is the best understanding of our form of government. As their intent is inherent within the republican principles that they embodied in our Constitution so too is the true grit of our law that the Constitution keeps positive elements in harmony with those natural laws that are unalienable. When I wrote *Unfurl the Flag*, I pondered how government alienated the people from their unalienable rights. Herein, I believe, is the greater answer. Our question is, shall we the people forfeit to government the ultimate interpretation of our Constitutional compact?

CHAPTER 3:

Differences between Jefferson and Jackson

If some see similarities in Jefferson's presidential actions and Jackson's, I see major distinctions between them. First, Jefferson had the opportunity to remove a foreign nation from continental America by buying the property. No one in or out of government objected. It was a no-brainer. The Louisiana Purchase gave the United States broader borders and greater security. Jackson made political decisions that were all about politics and power, and possibly, were personal. Secondly, John Meacham, author of *American Lion*, makes the following quote from the Republican newspaper, a well-established paper of the day, which demonstrates a blend of meanings that Madison separated.

> "We will not for an instant believe that he will descend from his high estate to take an active part in the ensuing election or consent to lend an improper and unrepublican influence in the appointment of his successor."[62]

The *Republican's* usage of *unrepublican* suggests a distinction between republican and democratic principles. Whether the distinction is conscious is questionable. Meacham admits that Jackson is a Jeffersonian Old Republican, *as opposed to a Federalist*, which means Jackson's focus is on those democratical ideas of Jefferson, which Jefferson shared with the majority Framers. This blend does inform us how Jefferson became associated with democracy, but it is entirely incorrect as our revelations so far testify. Meacham points out another fallacy, which is that Hamilton's Federalist arguments represent all Federalists. Madison and Hamilton disagreed over Monarchianism and aristocratism, but both were Federalist, until this designation changed to Federalist-Monarchists, that adopted democracy. The Convention settled the dispute by arguing against democracy, ensuring the federal system was republican, and voting to present our republican Constitution to the States for ratification. The people did ratify it. Jackson's distorted view of Jefferson remains embedded in the feelings of the United States and the Democratic Party. Jefferson and Madison's correspondence proves their alliance in constructing our compound republic. So, Jackson's perceived democratic influence from Jefferson is his failure to comprehend the Federalist arguments and the debates in the Convention. I find in Jackson a *party spirit* rather than the principles of republican government. In any case, Jackson creates the Democratic Party as denoted by the following quote from Meacham, as follows:

> "One of the results of Jackson's coalition victory in 1828 was a rising sense of party identity. Soon to be known as *the Democracy,* and eventually as the *Democratic Party."*[63]

Is the above quote the origin of the split between our Framers' structure of government and our current two-party system? If so, Jackson breaks the republican lineage that began with the Constitutional Convention of 1787 and ended with the Presidency of John Quincy Adams. The above might explain, if indeed it existed, Adams' fear for the future rather than anger over his loss to Jackson. In spite of differences over politics, Jefferson and Hamilton worked together on the Constitution. When the two views of the Federalists divided, they formed the monarchist federalists and the republican federalists. Hamilton was the chief architect of the former. As the people slowly began to understand the split, they began to elect republicans, which formed the majority in the Constitutional Convention. A search for democratic republicans always defaults to republican topics, in which I find no sentiment that attaches republican to democratic, except Hamilton and Adam's Federalist Monarchist scheme that incorporates democracy. It seems that those who favor democracy must invent its tie to any of our Framers, as did Jackson, which lessens the republican idea of majority rule to the democratical idea of popular rule. The latter idea came from the French revolution brought to America by Genêt. We note that Hamilton was killed in 1804 and Adams fled to the Federalist Republicans. The Federalist Monarchists became representatives of democracy. If we examine the sources in Chapter 2, Section 4, we find that these authors do not correspond with Madison's analyses regarding our "*extensive republic*" of the United States. James Bryce, a Scotsman, born in 1846, studied Roman history and law at Oxford and Oriel College, is close to our true form as he looks into the composition of the branches of the United States' general government, which differentiates our republican form from all previous types.[64] I conclude that the Democracies of Europe cannot conceive that their form of government is greatly flawed. Yet, America stands as a beacon of warning that democracy deteriorates over time. As history notes, Europe is internally at odds with the various aspects of factions that democracy engenders and it is falling apart. Such internal strife does yield fundamental changes, which are instability and insecurity.

Section 1: Error of Mixing Terms

One hears the voices of the past begin to murmur when we realize how far apart we are from their original intent as the following quotes, which comprise the totality of Madison's references throughout all of his Federalist articles, fail to identify either a pure or impure democracy as synonymous with either a republic or a representative republic.

> "To this accidental source of the error may be added the artifice of some celebrated authors, whose writings have had a great share in forming the modern standard of political opinions. Being subjects either of an absolute or limited monarchy, they have endeavored to heighten the advantages, or palliate the evils of those forms, by placing in comparison the vices and defects of the republican, and by citing as specimens of the latter the turbulent democracies of ancient Greece and modern Italy. Under the confusion of names, it has been an easy task to transfer to a republic observations applicable to a democracy only; and among others, the observation that it can never be established but among a small number of people, living within a small compass of territory.[65]
>
> "In a democracy, where a multitude of people exercise in person the legislative functions, and are continually exposed, by their incapacity for regular deliberation and concerted measures, to the ambitious intrigues of their Executive magistrates, tyranny may well be apprehended, on some favorable emergency, to start up in the same quarter.
>
> "But in a representative republic, where the Executive magistracy is carefully limited; both in the extent and the duration of its power; and where the legislative power is exercised by an assembly, which is inspired, by a supposed influence over the people, with an intrepid confidence in its own strength; which is sufficiently numerous to feel all the passions which actuate a multitude, yet not so numerous as to be incapable of pursuing the objects of its passions, by means which reason prescribes; it is against the enterprising ambition of this department that the people ought to indulge all their jealousy and exhaust all their precautions.[66]

> "As the natural limit of a democracy is that distance from the central point which will just permit the most remote citizens to assemble as often as their public functions demand, and will include no greater number than can join in those functions; so the natural limit of a republic is that distance from the centre which will barely allow the representatives to meet as often as may be necessary for the administration of public affairs."[67]

Madison makes ten references, all negative, to democracy in all of his *Federalist* articles and none agrees that it is synonymous with Koch's view of a republic. In fact, I find no indication that the Framers discovered an *indirect* democracy of the ancients that compares to our form of government. We should note in the last sentence of the above quote that *demos* does not mean all the people, but it can only "*include no greater number than can join in those functions*".

Section 2: Ancient Forms of Government

Cicero reports that ...:

> "In a democracy, where the right of making laws resides in the people at large, public virtue, or goodness of intention, is more likely to be found, than either of the other qualities of government. Popular assemblies are frequently foolish in their contrivance, and weak in their execution; but generally mean to do the thing that is right and just, and have always a degree of patriotism or public spirit.
>
> "In aristocracies there is more wisdom to be found, than in the other frames of government; being composed, or intended to be composed, of the most experienced citizens: but there is less honesty than in a republic, and less strength than in a monarchy.
>
> "A monarchy is indeed the most powerful of any; for by the entire conjunction of the legislative and Executive powers all the sinews of government are knit together, and united in the hand of the prince: but then there is eminent danger of his employing that strength to improvident or oppressive purposes.
>
> "Thus these three species of government have, all of them, their several perfections and imperfections. Democracies are usually the best calculated to direct the end of a law; aristocracies to invent the means by which that end shall be obtained; and monarchies to carry those means into execution. And the ancients, as was observed, had in general no idea of any other permanent form of government but these three: for though

> Cicero declares himself of opinion ... yet Tacitus treats this notion of a mixed government, formed out of them all, and partaking of the advantages of each, as a visionary whim, and one that, if effected, could never be lasting or secure.[68]

> "If, finally, all power is vested in the people, the state is a democracy."[69]

Cicero's definition points out that the people as a whole meet to manage government. They are their own representatives. While there is some confusion in terms, the Framers' idea gives us the context for the form of government they chose. We should understand Cicero's democracy as a popular government. The Framer's idea of representation is new. They did incorporate the democratical idea embedded in our House of Representatives, which instituted structural barriers against democracy's more pernicious characteristics, which also applies to a monarchy and an aristocracy. In all, our form of government is not a democracy. It is a mixed republic. I take, for example, two cases where Cicero points out the shortcomings of democracy.

1. "And finally, at Athens the Athenians themselves—to seek no other [authority—admit] that the absolute power of the people degenerated into the irresponsible madness of a mob...."[70]
2. "Now the equal rights of which democracies are so fond cannot be maintained. Indeed, no matter how free and untrammeled popular governments may be, they are still exceptionally prone to confer many favors on many men, and show decided preferences in the matter of individuals and in the matter of high rank."[71]

Section 3: Conclusion

Whatever term for democracy we employ, its weaknesses offset its advantages. If we limit its meaning to a government of the people, for the people and by the people, we miss represent our American heritage. Our government is a national/federal contract between the people and our elected and appointed representatives, those we elect from the national system, Senators and House of Representatives, those who form the federal system as appointees, such as Justices, diplomats, or bureaucrats, and the Executive we elect from the national population. The Framers thought it best to restrain the absolute freedom inherent in democracy. Again, when our society mixes principles, we find upheaval and disorder. We cannot yield to the popular belief that democracy means for the people, by the people, or of the people, as does our form of government. This tripartite phrase defines the Republic of the United States of America, our national treasure, and it is not a democracy. Yet, we may need to use our experience to adjust our structure of government to deal with modern problems or understand how its principles encompass them. Our form of mixed-government remains the best protection against corruption from our Federal and our National Systems, but as importantly, from ourselves once we know the history of governments. Is not our Framers' warning sufficient to deter us from advocating democracy unfettered to the world?

CHAPTER 4:

On Democracy

Section 1: Voices from Our Past, on Democracy

Adams on democracy and governments from his *A Defense of the United States Constitutions of the Americas*:

Mr. Adams' research shows us how dedicated he was to understanding how to form a *more perfect union.*

> "According to a story in Herodotus, the nature of monarchy, aristocracy, and democracy, and the advantages and inconveniences of each, were as well understood at the time ... as they are at this hour.
>
> "A variety of mixtures of these simple species were conceived and attempted, with different success, by the Greeks and Romans."[72]

If our Framers understood the three ancient forms then and vetoed all three, then how can democracy serve us today? We notice a different opinion about mixture of governments by the ancients. We also note that the Framers possessed mixed views about the definition of democracy. As I am working with the ideas by which the Constitutional Convention operated, I use Madison's definition. Here, Adams divides some attempts that I loosely list as follows, which are:

> -representations, instead of collections, of the people;
>
> -a total separation of the Executive from the legislative power, and of the judicial from both;

> -a balance in the legislature, by three independent, equal branches.

Adams prefers representation as opposed to assembles of the people. He also lists two other features that make America's form of government unique. He continues and distinguishes another problem that comes to fruition during the Convention Debates of 1787. Two options remained after the monarchies fell, which neither proved successful in government.

> "While it would be rash to say, that nothing further can be done to bring a free government, in all its parts, still nearer to perfection—the representations of the people are most obviously susceptible of improvement. The end to be aimed at, in the formation of a representative assembly, seems to be the sense of the people, the public voice: the perfection of the portrait consists in its likeness.
>
> "When the kings were abolished, the aristocracies tyrannized; and then no balance was attempted but between aristocracy and democracy. This, in the nature of things, could be no balance at all, and therefore the pendulum was for ever on the swing. It is impossible to read in Thucydides, lib. iii. his account of the factions and confusions throughout all Greece, which were introduced by this want of an equilibrium, without horror. During the few days that Eurymedon, with his troops, continued at Corcyra, the people of that city extended the massacre to all whom they judged their enemies."[73]

He also notes an idea proven by experience to be unworkable. Mr. Adams says,

> "Democracy, simple democracy, never had a patron among men of letters. Democratical mixtures in government have lost almost all the advocates they ever had out of England and America.[74]
>
> "Men of letters must have a great deal of praise, and some of the necessaries, conveniences, and ornaments of life. Monarchies and aristocracies pay well and applaud liberally. The people have almost always expected to be served gratis, and to be paid for the honour of serving them; and their applauses and adorations are bestowed too often on artifices and tricks, on hypocrisy and superstition, on flattery, bribes, and largesses. It is no wonder then that democracies and democratical mixtures are annihilated all over Europe, except on a barren rock, a paltry fen, an inaccessible mountain, or an impenetrable forest. The people of England, to their immortal honour, are hitherto an exception; but,

> to the humiliation of human nature, they shew very often that they are like other men.
>
> "The people in America have now the best opportunity, and the greatest trust, in their hands, that Providence ever committed to so small a number, since the transgression of the first pair: if they betray their trust, their guilt will merit even greater punishment than other nations have suffered, and the indignation of heaven. If there is one certain truth to be collected from the history of all ages, it is this: That the people's rights and liberties, and the democratical mixture in a constitution, can never be preserved without a strong Executive, or, in other words, without separating the Executive power from the legislative. If the Executive power, or any considerable part of it, is left in the hands either of an aristocratical or a democratical assembly, it will corrupt the legislature as necessarily as rust corrupts iron, or as arsenic poisons the human body; and when the legislature is corrupted the people are undone."[75]

Mr. Adams notes that the popular or democratical aspects of government are subject to corruption and he relates these peculiarities to a democracy. Since a dependent Executive fashioned after a monarch is an American addition, then it nullifies democracy as its form. The house demonstrates how our form incorporates the democratical idea of the people with the addition of suffrage, while the Senate represents the more mature aristocratical contribution to government. These embedded and structured units in our Republic strive to prevent their inherent vices from corrupting our representatives.

> "The rich, the well-born, and the able, acquire an influence among the people, that will soon be too much for simple honesty and plain sense, in a house of representatives. The most illustrious of them must therefore be separated from the mass, and placed by themselves in a Senate: this is, to all honest and useful intents, an ostracism.
>
> "A simple and perfect democracy never yet existed among men. If a village of half a mile square, and one hundred families, is capable of exercising all the legislative, Executive, and judicial powers, in public assemblies of the whole, by unanimous votes, or by majorities, it is more than has ever yet been proved in theory or experience. In such a democracy, the moderator would be king, the town-clerk legislator and judge, and the constable sheriff, for the most part; and, upon more important occasions, committees would be only the counsellors of both the former, and commanders of the latter. "[76]

Adams knows human nature and advises that the popular arm of Congress be guarded against by "...the most illustrious of them", which means those elected to the Senate. So, the Seventeenth Amendment stayed this safety net. Adams finds no ancient history that provides the practical use of a simple democracy and democracy, by all men of letters, failed the test of a good government. It appears that Europe does not remember its democratic past any better than we do ours. Mr. Adams continues,

> "It might be easier to determine the question concerning the practibility or impracticability, the utility or inutility, of a simple democracy, if we could find a number of examples of it. From the frightful pictures of a democratical city, drawn by the masterly pencils of ancient philosophers and historians, it may be conjectured that such governments existed in Greece and Italy, at least for short spaces of time: but no particular history of any one of them is come down to us; nor are we able to procure any more satisfaction to our curiosity from modern history. If such a phenomenon is at this time to be seen in the world, it is probably in some of those states which have the name of democracies, or at least in such as have preserved some share in the government to the people. Let us travel to some of those countries, and examine their laws.
>
> "The republic of St. Marino, in Italy, is sometimes quoted as an instance; and therefore it is of some importance to examine, 1. Whether in fact this is a simple democracy; and, 2. Whether, if it were such, it is not owing to particular circumstances, which do not belong to any other people, and prove it to be improper for any other, especially the United States of America, to attempt to imitate it."[77]
>
> "Yet enough appears to shew incontestibly, that St. Marino is by no means a perfect democracy. It is a mixture of monarchy, aristocracy, and democracy, as really as Sparta or Rome were; and as the Massachusetts, New-York, and Maryland now are, in which the powers of the governor, Senate, and assembly, are more exactly ascertained and nicely balanced, but they are not more distinct than those of the *capitaneos*, council of forty, and the *arengo* are in St. Marino."[78]

Adams points out that no democracy is pure and most governments mix the three ancient forms. I see Montesquieu's distinctions of great importance in understanding why America, even though expressed by the Framers as a federated republic, is so easily confused.[79]

Sovereignty resides in the people as unalienable and indivisible, but it does not reside as a democracy.

A. Sovereignty: Unalienable and Indivisible:

> "Should it be argued that a government like this, where the sovereignty resides in the whole body of the people, is a democracy, it may be answered, that the right of sovereignty in all nations is unalienable and indivisible, and does and can reside no where else; but not to recur to a principle so general, the exercise, as well as right of sovereignty, in Rome, resided in the people, but the government was not a democracy.

B. People are Sovereign:

> "In America, the right of sovereignty resides indisputably in the body of the people, and they have the whole property of land. There are no nobles or patricians—all are equal by law and by birth. The governors and senates, as well as representative assemblies, to whom the exercise of sovereignty is committed, are annually chosen. "Governments more democratical never existed; they are vastly more so than St. Marino. Yet the annual administration is divided into Executive, legislative, and judicial powers; and the legislature itself is divided into monarchical, aristocratical, and democratical branches; and an equilibrium has been anxiously sought for in all their deliberations and actions, with infinitely more art, judgment, and skill, than appears in this little Italian commonwealth."[80]
>
> "Although the government is called a democracy, we cannot here find all authority collected into one center; there are, on the contrary, as many distinct governments as there are cities and merindades. The general government has two orders at least; the lord or governor, and the biennial parliament."[81]
>
> "These officers, it is true, are elected by the citizens, but they must by law be elected, as well as the deputies to the biennial parliament or junta general, out of a few noble families, unstained, both by the side of father and mother, by any mixture with Moors, Jews, new converts, penitentiaries of the inquisition, &c. They must be natives and residents, worth a thousand ducats, and must have no concern in commerce, manufactures, or trades; and, by a fundamental agreement among all the merindades, all their deputies to the junta general, and all their regidores, sindics, secretaries, and treasurers, must be nobles, at least knights, and such as never exercised any mechanical trades

> themselves or their fathers. Thus we see the people themselves have established by law a contracted aristocracy, under the appearance of a liberal democracy. Americans, beware!"[82]

In the above, Mr. Adams finds even the appearance of democracy a cause for alarm. We should hear his voice for some are leading America to the edge of the democratic pit.

C. Democracy in a Small Area

> "Although we see here in the general government, and in that of every city and merindad, the three branches of power, of the one, the few, and the many; yet, if it were as democratical as it has been thought by some, we could by no means infer, from this instance of a little flock upon a few impracticable mountains, in a round form of ten leagues diameter, the utility or practicability of such a government in any other country.[83]

D. Democracy's Disposition to Division

> "The disposition to division, so apparent in all democratical governments, however tempered with aristocratical and monarchical powers, has shewn itself, in breaking off from it Guipuscoa and Allaba; and the only preservative of it from other divisions, has been the fear of their neighbours. They always knew, that as soon as they should fall into factions, or attempt innovations, the court of Spain would interpose, and prescribe them a government not so much to their taste."[84]

> "This is surely no simple democracy. Indeed a simple democracy by representation is a contradiction in terms."[85]

Section 2. Fourth Form of Government

A. Mixed Government Defined:

Adams points out that a mixed form of government did exist, but it was immature. The Framers matured it by structure for the American experiment.

> "Instead of a simple democracy, it is a mixed government, in which the monarchical power in the land amman, stadthalder or pro-consul, the aristocratical order in the Senate, and the democratical in the general assembly, are distinctly marked. It is, however, but imperfectly balanced; so much of the Executive power in an aristocratical assembly would be dangerous in the

> highest degree in a large state, and among a rich people. If this canton could extend its dominion, or greatly multiply its numbers, it would soon find the necessity of giving the Executive power to the land amman, in order to defend the people against the Senate; for the Senate, although it is always the reservoir of wisdom, is eternally the very focus of ambition."[86]

Our Framers knew a new form of government would be difficult for some to accept. Mr. Adams continues.

> "It is scarcely possible to believe that Mr. Turgot, by collecting all authority into one center, could have intended an aristocratical assembly. He must have meant, however, a simple form of government of some kind or other; and there are but three kinds of simple forms, democracy, aristocracy, and monarchy."[87]

B. Machiavelli: Longevity of the Three Forms

> "According to some authors, there are but three sorts of governments, viz. monarchy or principality, aristocracy, and democracy; and that those who intend to erect a new state, must have recourse to some one of these which he likes best. Others, and with more judgment, as many think, say there are six sorts; three of which are very bad, and the other three good in themselves, but liable to be so corrupted that they may become the worst. The three good sorts have been just now mentioned: the other three proceed from these; and every one of them bears such a resemblance to that on which it respectively depends, that the transition from one to the other is short and easy; for monarchy often degenerates into tyranny, aristocracy into oligarchy, and democracy into licentious anarchy and confusion: so that whoever sets up any one of the former three sorts of government, may assure himself it will not be of any long duration; for no precaution will be sufficient to prevent its falling into the other that is analogous to it, on account of the affinity which there seems to be in this case betwixt virtue and vice, perfection and imperfection."[88]

C. Mixed Government Best:

> "The best governments of the world have been composed of monarchy, aristocracy, and democracy."[89]

Madison views the vestiges of democratic principle in representation, which as Adams notes is not definitive of a democracy, but a general principle founded in unalienable rights.

Mr. Mason,

Democratic Arm of Our Republic: House of Representatives

> "...argued strongly for an election of the larger branch by the people. It was to be the grand depository of the *democratic* principle of the Govt. It was, so to speak, to be our House of Commons—It ought to know & sympathise with every part of the community; and ought therefore to be taken not only from different parts of the whole republic, but also from different districts of the larger members of it, which had in several instances particularly in Virga., different interests and views arising from difference of produce, of habits &c &c. He admitted that we had been too *democratic* but was afraid we sd. incautiously run into the opposite extreme. We ought to attend to the rights of every class of the people. He had often wondered at the indifference of the superior classes of society to this dictate of humanity & policy; considering that however affluent their circumstances, or elevated their situations, might be, the course of a few years, not only might but certainly would, distribute their posterity throughout the lowest classes of Society. Every selfish motive therefore, every family attachment, ought to recommend such a system of policy as would provide no less carefully for the rights and happiness of the lowest than of the highest orders of Citizens."[90]

I understand Mason to be addressing the hallmark of America's addition to government, that is, representation by a divided legislature. James Wilson, signer of the Declaration of Independence and the Constitution and nominated by President Washington with Senate confirmation as Associate Justice of the Supreme Court of the United States, makes this clear.

> "...the PEOPLE, as the fountain of government...can delegate it (power) in such proportions, to such bodies, on such terms, and under such limitations, as they think proper. I agree with the members in the opposition, that there cannot be two sovereign powers on the same subject."[91]

D. Article II, Sec. 4: On Impeachment...:

Article II provides an example of Wilson's meaning of *limitations*, which states,

> "Sect. 4. The president, vice-president and all civil officers of the United States, shall be removed from office on impeachment for, and conviction of treason, bribery, or other high crimes and misdemeanors."[92]

Wilson informs us with these words what the effect of digression from constitutional authority results in. What exactly do these words mean in terms of behavior? What is good behavior? Is it not strict compliance with the meaning, intent, and spirit of our Constitution? If so, then Madison's insight that its principles are our guide to understanding and evaluating the behavior of our representatives also provides us the cause of our action to ensure the effect comes in response to their improper behavior. Today, immediacy becomes our concern as an unrepublican government can so swiftly injure our government and have a negative impact upon the people and our allies. What is the answer to this dilemma?

E. Inconveniencies of Democracy:

Mr. Madison answers Col. Mason's concerns regarding the protection our form of government is to provide against democracy, popular rule, factions, and all other evils.

> "Interferences with these were evils which had more perhaps than anything else, produced this convention. Was it to be supposed that *republican liberty* could long exist under the abuses of it practised in some of the States ...
>
> "Had they not prevailed in the largest as well as the smallest tho' less than in the smallest; and were we not thence admonished to enlarge the sphere as far as the nature of the Govt. would admit. This was the only defence agst. the inconveniencies of d*emocracy* consistent with the democratic form of Govt. All civilized Societies would be divided into different Sects, Factions, & interests, as they happened to consist of rich & poor, debtors & creditors, the landed, the manufacturing, the commercial interests, the inhabitants of this district or that district, the followers of this political leader or that political leader, the disciples of this religious Sect or that religious Sect. In all cases where a majority are united by a common interest or passion, the rights of the minority are in danger ...
>
> "It was incumbent on us then to try this remedy, and with that view to frame a *republican* system on such a scale & in such a form as will control all the evils which have been experienced."[93]

Mr. Madison here clarifies for the convention that the new government is not democratic, but our system is a division and separation of majorities that protects against the experienced evils or "*inconveniencies of democracy*". Mr. Madison, Wednesday June 6, 1787; notes that a *free Govt* is not synonymous with a democratic govt. "*... to enlarge the sphere as far as the nature of the Govt. would admit.* This was the only "*defence agst. The inconveniencies of democracy consistent with the democratic form of Govt.*"

Mr. Hamilton on a strong Executive

> "Giving powers to Congs. must eventuate in a bad Govt. or in no Govt. ...
>
> "The Senate he feared from a similar cause, would be filled by certain undertakers who wish for particular offices under the Govt. This view of the subject almost led to him despair that a *Republican* Govt. could be established over so great an extent. He was sensible at the same time that it would be unwise to propose one of any other form. In his private opinion he had no scruple in declaring, supported as he was by the opinions of so many of the wise & good, that the British Govt. was the best in the world: and that he doubted much whether any thing short of it would do in America."[94]

While we see that when our separated powers do not act as devised that Mr. Hamilton is correct that it "*would be unwise to propose one of any other form*". Our form of government is the best for the people possess sovereign power. Hamilton thinks otherwise. He continues,

> "The members most tenacious of *republicanism*, he observed, were as loud as any in declaiming agst. the vices of *democracy*. This progress of the public mind led him to anticipate the time, when others as well as himself would join in the praise bestowed by Mr. Neckar on the British Constitution, namely, that it is the only Govt. in the world *which unites public strength with individual security*."[95]

Mr. Madison takes up the gauntlet and disproves the view of Hamilton. I see why the Framers were cautious and wisely wove the national system into the federal to incorporate more into the American federal system than ever existed in all the previous systems to protect the people from government. The question remains, will the people govern themselves? Or, will the people default to the angels who flock to Washington?

Mr. Madison continues on Hamilton's assault on the Executive.

> "As to the Executive, it seemed to be admitted that no good one could be established on *Republican* principles. Was not this giving up the merits of the question: for can there be a good Govt. without a good Executive. The English model was the only good one on this subject."[96]

So, I see why the Framers call our Republic compounded. Mr. Madison sees our American government as the most likely to protect the people from all the weaknesses of past governments. The Framers formed our republican government of the people as the best of all forms of governments. Hamilton continues his address on republican weaknesses.

F. On Foreign Interests:

Mr. Hamilton believes that,

> "One of the weak sides of Republics was their being liable to foreign influence & corruption. Men of little character, acquiring great power become easily the tools of intermeddling Neighbors."[97]

The Framers' answer was to counter balance the Executive with the powers of Congress with the bicameral members' particular interests balancing that body.

G. Congress to Check the Executive:

Governor Morris points out that the 2nd Branch, which is the Senate, is to check the 1st Branch, the House of Representatives.

> "The mode of appointing the 2nd branch tended he was sure to defeat the object of it. What is this object? to check the precipitation, changeableness, and excesses of the first branch."[98]

Governor Morris points out why the Framers combat democratic influences. The states' experiences with those of the ancients verify the need for division and separation in the federal system.

> "Every man of observation had seen in the democratic branches of the State Legislatures, precipitation-in Congress changeableness, in every department excesses against personal liberty private property & personal safety. What qualities are necessary to constitute a check in this case? Abilities and virtue, are equally necessary in both branches. Something more then is now wanted.
>
> "1. The checking branch must have a personal interest in checking the other branch, one interest must be opposed to another interest. Vices as they exist must be turned against each other.
>
> "2. It must have great personal property, it must have the aristocratic spirit; it must love to lord it thro' pride, pride is indeed the great principle that actuates both the poor & the rich. It is this principle which in the former resists, in the latter abuses authority.
>
> 3. "It should be independent. In Religion the Creature is apt to forget its *Creator.* That it is otherwise in political affairs, the late debates here are an unhappy proof. The aristocratic body, should be as independent & as firm as the democratic."[99]

We find again the cry for virtue for only with it can justice prevail in a republic, especially our Republic. This tendency to democratic principles seems to mean that human nature is adept at promoting its self-interests that create factions, sects, and divisions of other sorts, especially of representatives against the common interests. We find this same behavior in the New Testament as Paul combats denominationalism.[100] Our democratical unit is our House of Representatives balanced by the Senate and guarded by the Judiciary against constitutional corruption. Madison states his concern,

> "If the members of it *(the Senate)* are to revert to a dependence on the democratic choice, the democratic scale will preponderate. All the guards contrived by America have not restrained the Senatorial branches of the Legislatures from a servile complaisance to the democratic."[101]

I sense that the fear is that the balance of power is always at stake and the Executive is the most feared to become despotic. Even so, our contemporary degeneracy to a democratic form frustrates the Framers' resolve to avoid its negatives. It does give strength to the enemies of our Republic to manipulate the weaknesses of democracy outside the structure of our republican form of government. In the following passage, note the emphasis on separation of powers and the deterioration of government if we do not guard against democratic principles. He attacks longevity of Senators that gives them room for mischief. He advises us that the rich rule over the common in a commercial country through an oligarchy. But if, commerce ceases, then democracy prevails and its evils in a large territory as America covers will destroy the Union.

> "If the 2d. branch is to be dependent we are better without it. To make it independent, it should be for life. It will then do wrong, it will be said. He believed so: He hoped so. The Rich will strive to establish their dominion & enslave the rest. They always did. They always will. The proper security agst them is to form them into a separate interest. The two forces will then controul each other. Let the rich mix with the poor and in a Commercial Country, they will establish an oligarchy. Take away commerce, and the *democracy* will triumph."[102]

I find this quote a clear denial of the modern accusation that the Framers were elitists. They understood human nature and attempted to counterbalance it with opposing self-interests. It also warns us in the bravest words to watch the creep of corruption by the people by ensuring that the powers of our federal government are "*substantially maintained*", which I treat in Chapter 9, Section 2.

Section 3: On Passion

Our American variety of constitutional government does involve reason that our Framers hoped would override passion. One author who points out the advantages of passion advises candidates to exploit our feelings in order to win the election. Dr. Drew Westin, author of *The Political Brain, The Role of Emotion in Deciding the Fate of the Nation*, says that "*what a voter needs to know most in deciding whether to vote for one candidate or another is four things....*" The voter should ask, are the candidate's,

1. values relevant to the voters' values;
2. promises backed by values the candidate stick to in office (trust);
3. values of a character to honor my values and interests
4. stand on issues ones that matter to the voter and would the candidate decide issues as the voter would?[103]

He says that two visions encompass morality, which includes virtue, faith, and character, in contemporary American politics. He says, "*as progressives, we sell...the American people short when we fail to recognize...ultimately it is our emotions that provide the fuel—and the hope for those achievements.*"[104]

In his view, we have two visions of mind and brain:

1. dispassionate, which leads voters to rationally examine candidate issues and positions
2. passionate, which leads candidates to emotionally emit favorable responses to them.[105]

Therefore, voters ask, which I summarize below,

a. What are my feelings toward the candidate's party and principles?
b. How does the candidate make me feel?
c. How do I feel about the candidate's character?
d. How do I feel about the candidate's stand on issues?

He sums up by stating that progressives need to capitalize on this modern information by using narratives that tell what they stand for and stand against.[106]

I have to agree that this is a great collision of principles and it seems to reverse the high moral road that progressives or liberals left of Republicans elevated to sacred status. Yet, this sacrifice is necessary due to human nature and its positive response to emotive power. Our question is, whether American politics and its emotive trend secures to we the people our liberties, heals our divisions, and heads us toward reasonable debate. Which vision is most favorable to our Constitutional principles and which most facilitates our rule of law? I have to add that a republic of, for, and by the people must be mature in its governance or its wall of law will fall from the howling of wolves at our gates. Our question is, can we be passionate about truth, virtue, justice, peace, etc. because of their nature, principle, and positive effect and affect?

Section 4: Conclusion

The Framers' words challenge our present conventional wisdom and perception of government. They did rely upon reason and principles to effect voter reliability to elect and to monitor representatives. If reason gives way to passions, then democracy is not the government of choice. If our state governments tend to be democratic, then we must look to our Judiciary to ensure each state a republican form of Federal government. We must keep, by all cost, separate democratical ideas from intermingling with our federal system. Our question is, is this the reason our Constitution guarantees a federal republican form of government to the states? I wonder if the states as republics also have a call to be republican in nature and principle.

The democratic states of Europe are in turmoil because they have none of our protections. Yet our leaders tell us, and recently so, that our form of government is a democracy. Whom shall we believe? Shall we believe our Framers or those interpreters who describe us in European terms? Our Republic is not a democracy, but it does contain a few democratical ideas, but many more that are not representative of a democracy in extent or particulars, especially that of commerce.

The ancient idea of a democracy as a form of government is what our Framers call democracy. What is certain today is that the nature and principle of democracy has not changed since our Framers' review of it two hundred years ago, in spite of its modern revision and new definition. A face-lift does not change character. Our republican form of government is more expansive and protective of the people than any democracy. Can we promote our republican strength of mixed government to the world when we are confounded as to its prevalence among all other forms of government? What is a republic?

CHAPTER 5:
On Republics

Section 1: Definition of a Republic

What is a Republic? It is a public thing, which is a state and its institutions. Montesquieu reports that a republican government establishes that the people or a family possess sovereign power. In this state, integrity maintains the force of law through virtue, which depends upon the lawmaker viewing himself as subject to the law. He writes, when leaders fail to enforce the laws of the land, then the republic is already lost.[107] One distinguishes a republic when consent replaces submission.

> *"In a republic the foundation of public order is the ever lessening of submission inherited from ancestors who, being truly governed, submitted because they had to."*[108]

A republic centers on consent. Therefore, we use the term *republic* to denote a state in which citizens are directly or indirectly involved in public life, in which there is a rotation of office-holders, and in which there is an ethos of public service and duty—such is the meaning of the term in Harrington, Machiavelli, Montesquieu, and Rousseau.[109] When we add the adjective *mixed*, a republic includes a governmental structure that protects the public from corruptions through the weaknesses of the other three forms of government.

1. Republican government:

Mr. Madison's Republic:

> "A republic, by which I mean a government in which the scheme

of representation takes place, opens a different prospect, and promises the cure for which we are seeking. Let us examine the points in which it varies from pure democracy, and we shall comprehend both the nature of the cure and the efficacy, which it must derive from the Union."[110]

A pure democracy is without mixture of any other form of government. The Framers know of no other type. They turn to a republic as the basis for America's government. The Framers mix it with the best of the ancient three forms of government, then enhance the republics structure with new ideas.

2. Difference between a Democracy and a Republic:

> "There are two great points of difference between a democracy and a republic:
>
> "first, the delegation of the government, in the latter, to a small number of citizens elected by the rest;
>
> "secondly, the greater number of citizens, and greater sphere of country, over which the latter may be extended."[111]

Samuel Johnson states that a republic is a *commonwealth*, which is a state where more than one person holds power. He defines a *republican* as a person who believes that a commonwealth without monarchy is the best form of government. His definition explains the feud between Madison and Jefferson as Federalist-republicans and Hamilton and Adams' view of federalism as Federalist Monarchists.

Black's defines a *republic* as a system of government where the people possess sovereign power. It goes on to connect a republic with a pure democracy. Madison does not use that definition. *Black's* lists no definition for a representative democracy, but it does list a *democracy* as a government by the people who elect representatives. Madison warns against confusing the two terms. Madison distinguishes between a democracy and a republic. Madison further amplifies his thought in his 1833 paper on *Majority Government*, in which he says this,

> "Those who framed and ratified the Constitution believed that as power was less likely to be abused by majorities in representative Govts than in democracies, where the people assembled in mass, and less likely in the larger than in the smaller communities, under a representative Govt. inferred also, that by dividing the powers of Govt. and thereby enlarging the practicable sphere of government, unjust majorities would be formed with still more difficulty ..."

So, Madison draws a clear distinction in his advocacy of indirect representative republican government and an assemblage democracy. In the latter, his experience finds unjust majorities rising against minorities whereas the separation of powers curtails this inclination of human nature. I imagine he does this because the ancient democracies knew of *representatives*, but used them in a limited manner.

Section 2: Madison Defines a Republic

> "If we resort for a criterion, to the different principles on which different forms of government are established, we may define a republic to be, or at least may bestow that name on, a government which derives all its powers directly or indirectly from the great body of the people; and is administered by persons holding their offices during pleasure, for a limited period, or during good behavior."[112]

A. Powers of Government:

1. Federal vs. National
   - FEDERAL form regards the Union of sovereign states, which are the individuals making up each state as a *confederacy*.
   - NATIONAL government regards the people as a nation, which is a *consolidation* of the population of all the States.

> "...first, to ascertain the real character of the government in question;
>
> "... the Constitution is to be founded on the assent and ratification of the people of America, given by deputies elected for the special purpose; but, on the other, that this assent and ratification is to be given by the people, not as individuals composing one entire nation, but as composing the distinct and independent States to which they respectively belong. It is to be the assent and ratification of the several States, derived from the supreme authority in each State, the authority of the people themselves. The act, therefore, establishing the Constitution, will not be a NATIONAL, but a FEDERAL act.
>
> "...secondly, to inquire how far the convention were authorized to propose such a government; and
>
> "...thirdly, how far the duty they owed to their country could supply any defect of regular authority."[113]

Let us carefully analyze Madison's perspective. In the first place, *"the*

supreme authority in each State" is ***"the authority of the people themselves."*** The *people* are those who make up each respective independent state, and each State is sovereign. In this character, their assent and ratification is federal. The people will vote state by state for ratification or not. From their act of voting, they form the supreme authority that establishes the Constitution and by it they establish the federal branches of government. I understand this as meaning that the people are the authority that breathes the breath of life into the delegated government. The people become neither national nor federal when they amend the Constitution, because a proportion of states is necessary rather than a majority of citizens in each state. Ratification requires less than unanimity of states, therefore the action adopts a national character. (See Appendix D: Table of Constitutional Principles) Our republican principles clearly identify we the people in our respective capacities, unlike modern democracy.

2. Popular and Majority vs. Unanimous Vote

> "That it will be a federal and not a national act...the act of the people, as forming so many independent States, not as forming one aggregate nation, is obvious from this single consideration, that it is to result neither from the decision of a MAJORITY of the people of the Union, nor from that of a MAJORITY of the States. It must result from the UNANIMOUS assent of the several States that are parties to it, differing no otherwise from their ordinary assent than in its being expressed, not by the legislative authority, but by that of the people themselves. Were the people regarded in this transaction as forming one nation, the will of the majority of the whole people of the United States would bind the minority, in the same manner as the majority in each State must bind the minority; and the will of the majority must be determined either by a comparison of the individual votes, or by considering the will of the majority of the States as evidence of the will of a majority of the people of the United States. Neither of these rules have been adopted. Each State, in ratifying the Constitution, is considered as a sovereign body, independent of all others, and only to be bound by its own voluntary act. In this relation, then, the new Constitution will, if established, be a FEDERAL, and not a NATIONAL constitution.[114]

The people must vote unanimously by direct vote, which makes their act federal, because each state stands as sovereign in its ratification of the compact. In making this point, Madison also explains the difference between the national and the federal governments. The people form a national Union when they vote as one aggregate nation, whether as a majority of the people of the Union or as a majority of the aggregate States. This is the meaning of *we the people.*

3. Origin of Powers

   a. House of Representatives from the National Government (the people individually) is *for the people*

"The next relation is, to the sources from which the ordinary powers of government are to be derived. The House of Representatives will derive its powers from the people of America; and the people will be represented in the same proportion, and on the same principle, as they are in the legislature of a particular State. So far the government is NATIONAL, not FEDERAL.[115]

   b. Senate Derives Federal Power from the States

"The Senate, on the other hand, will derive its powers from the States, as political and coequal societies; and these will be represented on the principle of equality in the Senate, as they now are in the existing Congress. So far the government is FEDERAL, not NATIONAL.[116]

   c. Executive Power from a Mix of National and Federal

The Executive power will be derived from a very compound source. The immediate election of the President is to be made by the States in their political characters. The votes allotted to them are in a compound ratio, which considers them partly as distinct and coequal societies, partly as unequal members of the same society. The eventual election, again, is to be made by that branch of the legislature which consists of the national representatives; but in this particular act they are to be thrown into the form of individual delegations, from so many distinct and coequal bodies politic. From this aspect of the government it appears to be of a mixed character, presenting at least as many FEDERAL as NATIONAL features.[117]

B. Operation of Government:

   a. Federal Operation:

"The difference between a federal and national government, as it relates to the OPERATION OF THE GOVERNMENT, is supposed to consist in this, that in the former the powers operate on the political bodies composing the Confederacy, in their political capacities;...[118]

b. National Operation

"...in the latter, on the individual citizens composing the nation, in their individual capacities. On trying the Constitution by this criterion, it falls under the NATIONAL, not the FEDERAL character; though perhaps not so completely as has been understood. [119]

c. Mix of National (as Individuals) and Federal (as collective and political capacities)

"...In several cases, and particularly in the trial of controversies to which States may be parties, they must be viewed and proceeded against in their collective and political capacities only. So far the national countenance of the government on this side seems to be disfigured by a few federal features. But this blemish is perhaps unavoidable in any plan; and the operation of the government on the people, in their individual capacities, in its ordinary and most essential proceedings, may, on the whole, designate it, in this relation, a NATIONAL government.[120]

d. Extent of Government Powers is National

"But if the government be national with regard to the OPERATION of its powers, it changes its aspect again when we contemplate it in relation to the EXTENT of its powers. The idea of a national government involves in it, not only an authority over the individual citizens, but an indefinite supremacy over all persons and things, so far as they are objects of lawful government. Among a people consolidated into one nation, this supremacy is completely vested in the national legislature. Among communities united for particular purposes, it is vested partly in the general and partly in the municipal legislatures. In the former case, all local authorities are subordinate to the supreme; and may be controlled, directed, or abolished by it at pleasure. In the latter, the local or municipal authorities form distinct and independent portions of the supremacy, no more subject, within their respective spheres, to the general authority, than the general authority is subject to them, within its own sphere. In this relation, then, the proposed government cannot be deemed a NATIONAL one; since its jurisdiction extends to certain enumerated objects only, and leaves to the several States a residuary and inviolable sovereignty over all other objects. It is true that in controversies relating to the boundary between the two jurisdictions, the tribunal which is ultimately to decide, is to be established under the general government. But this does not change the principle of the case. The decision is to be impartially made, according to the rules of the Constitution; and all the usual and most effectual precautions are taken to secure this impartiality. Some such tribunal is clearly essential to prevent an appeal to the sword and a dissolution of the compact; and that it ought to be established under the general rather than under the local governments, or, to speak more properly, that it could be safely established under the first alone, is a position not likely to be combated.[121]

"If we try the Constitution by its last relation to the authority by which amendments are to be made, we find it neither wholly *national* nor wholly *federal.* Were it wholly national, the supreme and ultimate authority would reside in the MAJORITY of the people of the Union; and this authority would be competent at all times, like that of a majority of every national society, to alter or abolish its established government. Were it wholly federal, on the other hand, the concurrence of each State in the Union would be essential to every alteration that would be binding on all. The mode provided by the plan of the convention is not founded on either of these principles. In requiring more than a majority, and particularly, in computing the proportion by *states,* not by citizens, it departs from the *national,* and advances towards the *federal* character. In rendering the concurrence of less than the whole number of states sufficient, it loses again the *federal* and partakes of the national character.

"The proposed Constitution, therefore, is, in strictness, neither a national nor a federal Constitution, but a composition of both. In its foundation it is federal, not national; in the sources from which the ordinary powers of the government are drawn, it is partly federal and partly national; in the operation of these powers, it is national, not federal; in the extent of them, again, it is federal, not national; and, finally, in the authoritative mode of introducing amendments, it is neither wholly federal nor wholly national."[122]

Madison aligns the national with the people by stating that,

"When the people have formed a constitution, they retain those rights which they have not expressly delegated. It is a question whether what is thus retained can be legislated upon."[123]

In the same source, Madison states that,

"If we advert to the nature of republican government, we

shall find that the censorial power is in the people over the government, and not in the government over the people."[124]

e. Essential: Derived from the great body of the society:

"It is *essential* to such a government, that it be derived from the great body of the society, not from an inconsiderable proportion, or a favoured class of it; otherwise a handful of tyrannical nobles, exercising their oppressions by a delegation of their powers, might aspire to the rank of republicans, and claim for their government the honourable title of republic."[125]

f. Sufficient: Appointments directly or indirectly by the people:

"It is sufficient for such a government, that the persons administering it be appointed, either directly or indirectly, by the people; and that they hold their appointments by either of the tenures just specified; otherwise every government in the United States, as well as ever other popular government that has been, or can be well organized or well executed, would be degraded from the republican character. According to the constitution of every state in the union, some or other of the officers of government are appointed indirectly only by the people. According to most of them, the chief magistrate himself is so appointed. And according to one, this mode of appointment is extended to one of the co-ordinate branches of the legislature."[126]

From these quotes, we do derive the place of democratical ideas in our republic, but our Framers differentiate all the elements to comprise our republican form of government. They do not count America as a type of democracy, but they explicitly designate our form of government as a compounded republic. We continue this differentiation.

g. Tenure is Definite or Period of Years:

"According to all the constitutions also, the tenure of the highest offices is extended to a definite period, and in many instances, both within the legislative and Executive departments, to a period of years. According to the provisions of most of the constitutions, again, as well as according to the most respectable and received opinions on the subject, the members of the Judiciary department are to retain their offices by the firm tenure of good behavior.

"On comparing the constitution planned by the convention, with the standard here fixed, we perceive at once, that it is, in the most rigid sense, conformable to it ...

"The duration of the appointments is equally conformable to the republican standard, and to the model of the state constitutions.

"Could any further proof be required of the republican complexion of this system, the most decisive one might be found in its absolute prohibition of titles of nobility, both under the federal and the State governments; and in its express guaranty of the republican form to each of the latter."[127]

I note *in loco* Madison's explanation of the answer to this question:

"...by what authority this bold and radical innovation was undertaken."[128]

C. Empire of Laws the Best of Republics:
John Adams writes,

"The only valuable part of the British constitution is so; because the very definition of a republic is 'an empire of laws, and not of men.' That, as a republic is the best of governments, so that particular arrangement of the powers of society, or, in other words, that form of government, which is best contrived to secure an impartial and exact execution of the laws, is the best of republics."[129]

Is Adams saying that there is a difference between manmade law and the laws of an empire? Yes. However, he uses the meaning of his era, for which Samuel Johnson lists three meanings in his dictionary. First, we have imperial power, supreme dominion, and sovereign command. Secondly, he says an empire is a region over which dominion extends. Thirdly, he tells us that an empire occurs when command over it exists.[130]

This perfectly coincides with Madison's definition. America is a vast land over which the people possess command and, therefore, are sovereign over it. In *Black's Law Dictionary*, I find a simple definition that does not match our discovery here. Black reports that an empire is the region that an emperor controls. Black's does define emperor as the tile the Romans took after the fall of the republic. Johnson tells us that an emperor is superior to a king. In this case, Johnson is able to reveal our Framers' conception of the American empire. It is sovereign dominion of the people over the entire land. In *Black's* definition, the focus is upon the reigning person as emperor rather than the sovereign people in an empire.[131]

Section 3: Nature of a Republic

In a republic of whatever type, Montesquieu views the full power of education as necessary to sustain love for the laws and the homeland, which inculcates a public interest over self-interest, and this produces individual virtues.[132]

A. Democratic Republic:

Montesquieu notes that a people may establish democracy upon commerce where equality gives way to some who amass fortunes and virtue sustains mores. In it, commerce encourages frugality, economy, moderation, work, wisdom, tranquility, order, and rule. The democratic republic finds threat from commerce when an excess of wealth destroys the spirit of commerce due to inequalities. To counterbalance this, legislators must ensure that the spirit of commerce has no competition, and the laws must support it as above noted. The republic must equalize its citizens. Give to the poor wealth enough to be happy and take from the rich to bring them to a middle level of property in order that each must work in order to survive or to accumulate and to preserve. See Chapter 1, Section 5. All of this is democracy, Montesquieu writes. He says,

> "In a good democracy where spending should be only for necessities, each person should have them, for from whom would he receive them?"[133]

B. Capitalist Republic:

According to Montesquieu, we find in a capitalist republic, competition and self-interest are aspects of achievement and these the republic controls by virtue and by opposing self-interests. Through all of this, a government establishes frugality. Using self-interests as minorities to balance power is a prominent theme among the Framers.

Montesquieu believes that free republics, which are governments of the many, provide an environment of acquisition as opposed to preservation. In this state, traders feel safe, which encourages them to risk to gain more "*for they expect much of their fortune*". Commerce leads from one variety to another, from small to great, which mix by necessity with public business. A consequence of big business is that it becomes daring and that leads from a desire to gain little to a desire to gain a "*great deal*". This consequence begins from a desire to gain little or less, but its compensation is from gaining continually. I find a difference between large corporations and the small business. A large corporation seeks large profits, while the small business seeks continuous, but smaller, profits. The large corporation must meet consumption demands of investors, while the small business must meet subsistence demands of business and personal origin. The large corporation enlarges its scope of interest to politics, deals, law, tax structure, and other means to capture larger share and more control over resources. The small business must operate more frugally because it has less money and influence over resources and politics. Economic commerce seems to occur when two nations or more possess differing climates that make one nation need or desire the commodities of the other. While Montesquieu has much to say, I will end with his thought, "***that only goodness of government brings prosperity***". Montesquieu does point out how the discovery of gold caused Spain to suffer bankruptcy, because as its volume doubled, its value declined. I draw a general conclusion from his insights, which is that the fewer laws that pertain to commerce, the more traders engage profitably in commerce.[134] Does this not also emphasize why government should not liberally print money? Our government prints money and thereby devalues it. Our question is, does the emphasis on profit actually lead to greed? This seems to be the case from modern experience as transnational corporations operate in third world countries and abandon national allegiance. Our next question concerns virtue in commerce, which is, does the principle of virtue decrease greed or is the world of finance and commerce unrestrained to the point that it implodes itself without conscience or concern for our destiny?

We have mixed Montesquieu's commercial republic with all sorts of socialized and democratized solutions to appease various groups. We note that we call this democratic, but it is actually socialist or socialism. Johnson offers no word for either. I do find a definition for socialist in American English that occurs in 1827. Socialism comes along in 1837. *Barnhart* relates its appearance to Robert Owen who strove for social reform. He sees an earlier possible connection with Saint-Simon who founded French socialism about 1831.[135] Unfortunately, some of our representatives cater to self-interest groups that are political self-appeasers. A government without established principles is a tyranny upon the people. A people with principle or principles in collision will become societally chaotic, which may lead to mob violence, revolution, and that to despotism. Any solution to government that goes beyond our constitutional limits provides legislators and the Judiciary fuel for law making laws. I think another worrisome aspect is capitalism without virtue, which is like law or medicine without conscience.

I have a library of books on economics and every form of it by whatever name. Since there is no theory that demonstrates dominance, we have a cacophony of theories that one can only hope works. Our diversity in application of theories seems to make it impossible to determine what works and what does not. What I observe is that the theory intends good things, but it is unpredictable how humans practice it. We come again to the nature of humans. The motive to achieve, to succeed, to possess, to accumulate, and to escape even the middle class standard of living drives minds and behavior to a dopamine high that disregards the rules of law and virtue.

Free market is a term for an assortment of exchanges between persons as individuals, groups, or corporations for the purpose of exchanging commodities for mutual benefit. We find in this arrangement a resolution to the exploiter/exploited dynamic prevalent in the mercantile era. Today, we use the terms *zero-sum* or *negative-sum* to indicate a win-win exchange, which depends upon the parties agreeing by bargaining on a value for the commodity. Yet, do all exchanges meet this criterion of *free*? Consumers rarely get to bargain over prices. We either pay it or not. Our conditioning is to pay without a say. Item returns are getting more difficult, warranties are too troublesome to attempt, and rebates are not cash for cash, but for more product that the consumer may not need or want, whereas cash enables free choice. Justice is not in favor of the common people. Law must possess fact; principle must possess commitment to truth; good faith must include parity.

Section 4: Conclusion

Capitalism is the choice of our Framers. Capitalism is by experience the best form of commerce. Many pundits advocate *laissez faire* from all quarters to permit entrepreneurs and employers total control over business. Maybe that is the answer, if only human nature would permit it. Does our experience prove that "*the love of money is the root of all evil"* is true in the commercial world?[136]

I see why capitalism in its modern form must be reevaluated. A commercial republic's nature and principles are distinct from those of a commercial democracy. The latter taints the former. The mix of various ideas corrupts the whole system. With the loss of virtue in our society, so follows the loss of fair play. The old quip *buyer beware* is the more to be practiced, but it works best when virtue is more popular than profit. Certainly, the customer should beware of fraud, but the buyer cannot know all the deceptive ploys of the sociopath or the profit driven entity that constructs business instruments that operate behind legal guises. Today, we have poor-quality materials that an untrained person cannot detect until used. The buyer bleeds from the thousand forays into his wallet by all aspects of society's necessary services, personal desires, future security, and corrupt behavior. Truth in business comes from character, not regulation. Our question is, if we live in a one-world government, as a democracy, are we agreeable to its outcome?

Chapter 6:

Property in Our Republic

Section 1: John Adams on Ownership

Our government seems to be off track with our republican economy. Montesquieu gave us his take on a commercial democracy. John Adams wrote his view on ownership. He realized that *"a great majority of every nation is wholly destitute of property ..."*. In his opinion, he considers ownership a right. If it is a right, then it falls under the egis of republican principles.[137] Property right is as real as our right to life, liberty, and our pursuit of happiness. Is ownership a natural right? My research suggests that it was so considered by our Framers.

Section 2: Madison on Property

James Madison said more on this idea of property.[138] His idea defines property in two ways. First, he sees it as,

> *"that dominion which one man claims and exercises over the external things of the world, in exclusion of every other individual."*

In this sense, he sees that *"a man's land, or merchandise, or money is called his property."* Secondly, property,

> *"...embraces everything to which a man may attach a value and have a right; and which leaves to everyone else the like advantage."*

In this version, property exists as *"opinions and the free communication of them*". Madison sees one's religious opinions as property that brings with it the right of profession and practice as conscience dictates. Is it a right for corporations to own natural resources like water? Is this a collision between natural rights and positive law? Madison believes that...

> *"government is instituted to protect property of every sort ... This being the end of government, that alone is a just government, which impartially secures to every man, whatever is his."*

Does this quote emphasize corporate ownership or our commonwealth citizens' rights? If citizens are the subject of our Constitution, then how does the Bench justify any interest beyond its constitutional limits? If our Bill of Rights protects the citizen from the Federal System, as the five or six lawyers I interviewed stated, they are the only interest the Federal System has in constitutional civil rights adjudication. In my personal working in the world experience, I know that corporations are no more angelic in their management of power than are our representatives in Washington or in our States. I have some issues that I feel fall between the separation of State and Federal legal divide, but our interest is on limited federal government. All rights retained by the states must be the legal category for my complaints regarding civil rights.

On Two Forms of Property Rights

James Madison reports that there are "Two Forms of Property Rights: Right of Property and Rights in Property."

> "A just security to property is not afforded by that government, under which unequal taxes oppress one species of property and reward another species: where arbitrary taxes invade the domestic sanctuaries of the rich, and excessive taxes grind the faces of the poor; where the keenness and competitions of want are deemed an insufficient spur to labor, and taxes are again applied, by an unfeeling policy, as another spur; in violation of that sacred property, which Heaven, in decreeing men to earn his bread by the sweat of his brow, kindly reserved to him, in the small repose that could be spared from their supply of his necessities.
>
> "If there be a government then which prides itself in maintaining the inviolability of property; which provides that none shall be taken *directly* even for public use without indemnification to the owner, and yet *directly* violates the property which individuals have in their opinions, their religion, their persons, and their faculties; nay more, which *indirectly* violates their property, in their actual possessions, in the labor that acquires their daily subsistence, and in the hallowed remnant of time which ought to

so relieve their fatigues and soothe their cares, the influence will have been anticipated, that such a government is not a pattern for the United States.

"If the United States mean to obtain or deserve the full praise due to wise and just governments, they will equally respect the rights of property, and the property in rights: they will rival the government that most sacredly guards the former; and by repelling its example in violating the latter, will make themselves a pattern to that and all other governments."[139]

Madison penned these words after the Convention of 1787. How can the Bench rule that a corporation can declare improvement of a property to be justification to remove persons from their homes even with just compensation? Among our republican principles the primary right is life. What is greater, higher, more important than life? Constitutionally, there is no thing greater than life. The Benches' ruling that it "*is an incident of federal sovereignty and an 'offspring of political necessity*'" is not sound republican reasoning by the principles of republicanism.[140] First, this quote suggests the bench believes it has sovereign property rights to understand constitutional principles. Secondly, if property is a right, how does Madison understand *right*? Is it a natural right as is one's right to worship God? Thirdly, our Constitution provides for eminent domain in the Fifth Amendment as due process of law.[141] Is that positive law? Fourthly, the Bench, in my opinion, incorrectly advances itself to be superior to the States in this matter, especially since our Constitution does not grant this superiority except in pursuance to those clauses that limit its jurisdiction. Fifthly, we again see the Bench's bias toward corporations as it subordinates our human or natural rights and promotes to an equal status an artificial entity. Is this not a tyranny over the many by Judiciary fiat? Likewise, how can taxation be just when it displaces people from their homes in favor of property values in their community that favor the well to do to rid themselves of the not so well to do? I smell an innovation. Tax laws should respect the wage earner's position, not the government's laws above the citizen. Arbitrary federal laws that outlaw the citizen is against liberty, which is the second highest republican principle. A tax clause that excuses tax collection from individuals below the average local income seems more republican, especially in light of all the tax monies transferred to underwrite all types of big money special interests to government. It seems to me that Madison voices the opinion of the majority. In the Convention of 1787, Madison makes these comments:

"Why was America so justly apprehensive of Parliamentary injustice? Because Great Britain had a separate interest real or

> supposed, & if her authority had been admitted, could have pursued that interest at our expense. We have seen the mere distinction of color made in the most enlightened period of time, a ground of the most oppressive dominion ever exercised by man over man. What has been the source of those unjust laws complained of among ourselves? Has it not been the real or supposed interest of the major number? Debtors have defrauded their creditors. The landed interest has borne hard on the mercantile interest. The Holders of one species of property have thrown a disproportion of taxes on the holders of another species. The lesson we are to draw from the whole is that where a majority are united by a common sentiment, and have an opportunity, the rights of the minor party become insecure. In a Republican Govt. the Majority if united have always an opportunity. The only remedy is to enlarge the sphere, & thereby divide the community into so great a number of interests & parties, that in the 1st. place a majority will not be likely at the same moment to have a common interest separate from that of the whole or of the minority; and in the 2d. place, that in case they should have such an interest, they may not be apt to unite in the pursuit of it. It was incumbent on us then to try this remedy, and with that view to frame a republican system on such a scale & in such a form as will control all the evils which have been experienced."[142]

Is this not parallel to the Bench's self-interest as it shows "*a separate interest real or supposed, & if her authority had been admitted, could have pursued that interest at our expense.*" In our case, the tense is present and *her authority* transfers to the legislature or the Bench. Our difference is that Great Britain had years of evolution to make the majority subordinate to the minority by privilege and position. In our case, our government seems to be working diligently to catch up. We note that Madison mentions republican government or system, which means, his context remains our republican principles. We may safely reside in these principles, but when we include foreign ideas or indulge innovations and accretion, we can assuredly languish in modern angst.

Section 3: Consequence of Liberty

Yet, there is a consequence, an unavoidable consequence, of liberty, as Madison records of Alexander Hamilton in his notes.

An Inequality in Property:

> "He professed himself to be as zealous an advocate for liberty as

> any man whatever, and trusted he should be as willing a martyr to it though he differed as to the form in which it was most eligible. He concurred also in the general observations of [Mr. Madison] on the subject, which might be supported by others if it were necessary. It was certainly true: that nothing like an equality of property existed: that an inequality would exist as long as liberty existed, and that it would unavoidably result from that very liberty itself. This inequality of property constituted the great & fundamental distinction in Society. When the Tribunitial power had levelled the boundary between the patricians & plebeians, what followed? The distinction between rich & poor was substituted."[143]

Section 4: Conclusion

This inequality should not come by government interference, but only by one's ability to accumulate property. Is our judicial department pawn to this tendency to level the majority to accommodate the rich or the corporate interest? Liberty carries the burden that the educated and naturally gifted prosper, indubitably, more so than the general population. Is it unfair that our government lends its power to aid those more fortunate or to aid itself by taxing the property of those with little income? Is this a republican virtue? Is it the Judiciary's place to make the majority subservient to the developers? It seems government finds the middle class targets for schemes of the rich. Do you remember the Indians' trail of tears?

Our Framers were concerned with commerce. In his representation of the United States overseas, Jefferson laboriously studied business practices in several countries. Most of the Framers read as much as they could. They shared their findings on all subjects, commerce being but one. They expressed concerns over a national bank and banking practices, speculators, and paper money. The middle class does not need its government to take away its hard-earned property to benefit corporate advancement when the people do not want to give up their homes, in my understanding of republican principles. Just as a rope drawn so taut that its fibers fray, so this union frays under the strain of taut party politics and the ideology of redistribution in its various guises. In this case, it is reverse distribution. To whom or to what shall we call upon to unite this nation? I do not ignore Glenn Beck's call to unite under his triad of love, hope, and charity. As he claims there is no political answer, I hope he will embrace the political ideas of republicanism that embrace faith, virtue, and our republican political system. I, too, believe that these Christian values relate and pertain to republican principles, but our current governmental attitudes can accept the less offensive republican terminologies. I agree with him that community organization is the answer both for political and social advancement. We may yet reverse this inconvenience of secularism.

We enjoin every power on earth and in heaven to give us resolve, but we fail to understand our differences. We cry out in the name of rationalism, socialism, liberalism, capitalism, or conservatism—all to no resolution. Do we possess the resolve to unite for self-preservation? Are political objectives adverse to our Republic so profound that we will destroy our Union for them? Does the light of the American Enlightenment grow dim? Its commonality was its vision and hope for liberty and justice for all. Do any of our above principled philosophies strive against these objectives? I think it is not our philosophical aspirations, but I do believe it is our means that frays the fibers of our Republic.

Chapter 7:

On Representation

Section 1: Federal Convention, 1787[144]

Madison's records of the constitutional debates show the Framer's concerns on representation and the separation of powers. In this section, we sample views on the national legislature, which assembles representatives from the state legislatures. The delegates discuss first the House of Representatives, then the Senate. Listen in.

Mr. Madison as scribe includes his own words as part of the transcript in third person.

> "...considered the popular election of one branch of the National Legislature as essential to every plan of free Government. He observed that in some of the States one branch of the Legislature was composed of men already removed from the people by an intervening body of electors. That if the first branch of the general legislature should be elected by the State Legislatures, the second branch elected by the first—the Executive by the second together with the first; and other appointments again made for subordinate purposes by the Executive, the people would be lost sight of altogether; and the necessary sympathy between them and their rulers and officers, too little felt. He was an advocate for the policy of refining the popular."[145]

Mr. Madison confirms that representation of at least one branch of the national legislature should be by popular vote, that is, by the people. He is in agreement with Jefferson and Washington. Washington turned the vote to fewer representatives, 30,000 rather than 40,000, so more representatives per population would constitute the House.[146] The Convention decided that indirect representation was best suited as a barrier against self-interests. The people should elect the representatives to the House, Article 1, Section 2; the state legislatures should select the Senate; Article 1, Section 3. The following quotes are a record of their discussion.

Madison acts as scribe and lists each speaker in turn who addresses the Convention.

Mr. Wilson …

> "…contended strenuously for drawing the most numerous branch of the Legislature immediately from the people. He was for raising the *federal pyramid* to a considerable altitude, and for that reason wished to give it as broad a basis as possible. No government could long subsist without the confidence of the people. In a *republican government* this confidence was peculiarly essential."[147]

> "He also thought it wrong to increase the weight of the State Legislatures by making them the electors of the national Legislature. *All interference between the general and local Governments should be obviated as much as possible.* On examination it would be found that the opposition of States to *federal* measures had proceeded much more from the officers of the States, than from the people at large."[148]

In their discussion, they address *popular* as meaning the people, who voted in their state legislative representatives. I point this out to underline that in democracy *popular* means the whole citizenry. As these representatives get to know one another, they provide the safest alternative to choosing the fit characters for Senators. If we find a way to restore faith in our state officials would this be our choice for choosing Senators. Madison argues that the people do not elect the Senate, so the people should elect the House of Representatives.

Mr. Madison …

> "…considered the popular election of one branch of the National Legislature as essential to every plan of free Government. He observed that in some of the states one branch of the Legislature was composed of men already removed from the people by an intervening body of electors."[149]

> "He thought too that the great fabric to be raised would be more stable and durable, if it should rest on the solid foundation of the people themselves, than if it should stand merely on the pillars of the Legislatures."[150]

Mr. Gerry evaluates the British experience and discovers what we have learned. Mr. Elbridge Gerry, Constitutional delegate from Massachusetts, states that he…

> "…did not like the election by the people. The maxims taken from the British constitution were often fallacious when applied to our situation, which was extremely different. Experience he said had shewn that the State legislatures drawn immediately from the people did not always possess their confidence. He had no objection however to an election by the people if it were so qualified that men of honor & character might not be unwilling to be joined in the appointments. He seemed to think the people might nominate a certain number out of which the State legislatures should be bound to choose."[151]

Mr. Gerry recommends a compromise. Let the legislature choose a pool from which the people elect their representatives.

Mr. Butler, delegate from South Carolina…

> "…thought an election by the people an impracticable mode. On the question for an election of the first branch of the national Legislature by the people."[152]

Mr. Spaight, delegate from North Carolina, opines regarding the Senate,

> "…contended that the 2d. branch ought to be chosen by the State Legislatures and moved an amendment to that effect. Mr. Butler apprehended that the taking so many powers out of the hands of the States as was proposed, tended to destroy all that balance and security of interests among the States which it was necessary to preserve; and called on Mr. Rand the mover of the propositions, to explain the extent of his ideas, and particularly the number of members he meant to assign to this second branch."[153]

Mr. Randolph, delegate from Virginia, reflects how a Senate might help. He said…

> "If he was to give an opinion as to the number of the second branch, he should say that it ought to be much smaller than that of the first; so small as to be exempt from the passionate proceedings to which numerous assemblies are liable. He observed that the general object was to provide a cure for the evils under which the U. S. laboured; that in tracing these evils to their origin every man had found it in the *turbulence and follies of democracy:* that some check therefore was to be sought for

> agst. this tendency of our Governments: and that a good Senate seemed most likely to answer the purpose."[154]

Mr. Randolph advocates a small Senatorial body in order to protect against democratic influence, which is to say the passions of the people. He would avoid this with a small number in the Senate, which would act as the guard against such passions.

Mr. Madison, delegate from Virginia, again objects. He

> "...considered an election of one branch at least of the Legislature by the people immediately, as a clear principle of free Govt. and that this mode under proper regulations had the additional advantage of securing better representatives, as well as of avoiding too great an agency of the State Governments in the General one. He differed from the member from Connecticut [Mr. Sharman] in thinking the objects mentioned to be all the principal ones that required a National Govt. Those were certainly important and necessary objects; but he combined with them the necessity of providing more effectually for the security of private rights, and the steady dispensation of Justice."[155]

The Framers resolved that the legislatures would possess the greater knowledge of the character of these individuals from working together. We must ensure that the best characters go to Washington to represent our state and our national interests. What standard shall we use to evaluate character? Our question is, are our representatives too distanced from the people's rights by privilege of office that they do not relate to our needs?

In our discussion on the Seventeenth Amendment, I said that our Framers placed in our Constitution the preference for the state legislatures to choose our Senate. While Madison and Mason favored a popular vote, the majority chose to put this power in the hands of our state legislatures. While they expressed their intent constitutionally, the people chose to change it. If we understand that popular means people rather than democratic, we might understand the stance of our Framers and accept our form of government as superior to a democracy. If the people find this change provides them with some comfort without sacrificing safety, then we benefit from both sides of the argument. Our question is whether either works, at least, in our experience? It might be an implementation problem or it may be a human nature issue or a combination of each of these or others. What our experience teaches us is that representatives do become corrupt. Our question is, how do we manage to detect it and discipline it in a decisive and timely manner? Is limited tenure the best answer?

Col. Mason, delegate from Virginia, addresses the Executive branch and mentions that the people favor democracy. He notes that in spite of democracy's evils, the people favor it. He says that,

> "Notwithstanding the oppressions & injustice experienced among us from democracy; the genius of the people is in favor of it, and the genius of the people must be consulted. He could not but consider the federal system as in effect dissolved by the appointment of this Convention to devise a better one."[156]

Col. Mason understands the democratic influence in the States and believes the Convention should consider it in granting appointment power to the Executive. Madison faithfully reports that the people want to possess sovereignty, but many believe that sovereignty means democracy. Democracy does mean popular rule, which means directly by the people. The Framers structured our republican system to protect us against self-interests of politicians, majority factions, and from our passions, while making the people sovereign over both national and federal governments.

We see this tension between direct and indirect representation with experienced eyes of time. Our dilemma continues for neither presently works perfectly, but can we claim that republican government is the best of all? What is our solution to corrupt government? Hamilton thought corruption made government work. His view, reported by Jefferson in "*Travelling notes for Mr. Rutledge and Mr. Shippen*", June 3, 1788, alienated him more so from the majority in the Convention. Is the real issue the nature of humans? If so, is the solution to teach virtue and reward it and our other republican principles while taking hold of those who violate our republican principles. The people are sovereign, but our representatives govern directly. How do we manage these representatives without devolving to mob rule when Congress fails to act? The Framers gave the people suffrage to change players should they displease them. However, how do the people respond to corruption that is immediate and harms the nation? The Framers' answer is impeachment or recall.

Section 2: American Representation

> "The difference most relied on, between the American and other republics, consists in the principle of representation; which is the pivot on which the former move, and which is supposed to have been unknown to the latter, or at least to the ancient part of them. The use which has been made of this difference, in reasonings contained in former papers, will have shown that I am disposed neither to deny its existence nor to undervalue its importance. I feel the less restraint, therefore, in observing, that

> the position concerning the ignorance of the ancient governments on the subject of representation, is by no means precisely true in the latitude commonly given to it. Without entering into a disquisition, which here would be misplaced, I will refer to a few known facts, in support of what I advance.
>
> "In the most pure democracies of Greece, many of the Executive functions were performed, not by the people themselves, but by officers elected by the people, and *representing* the people in their *Executive* capacity."[157]

Mr. Madison points out that ancient popular indirect representation was limited to the executive. He notes the confusion over indirect representation. The *demos* chose to give power to an executive, in some cases. Since the Framers limited our Executive's power through Congress, we see another example that they viewed our form of government as the best for protecting the people from power shifts from the people to strong leaders. Yet, our recent history argues that Congress may become lax. Our question is, have we the people become lax as well? Should we use our sovereign power to control effectively the branches themselves from power shifts? Would our republican principles provide the springboard to ensure clarity for what the people voted for the candidate to do? Each candidate's platform represents his or her action plan of government. Our question is, will we demand it, use it, and follow through to enforce it?

Section 3: Superior Principle of Representation

> "From these facts, to which many others might be added, it is clear that the principle of representation was neither unknown to the ancients nor wholly overlooked in their political constitutions ...
>
> "The distinction, however, thus qualified, must be admitted to leave a most advantageous superiority in favor of the United States. But to insure to this advantage its full effect, we must be careful not to separate it from the other advantage, of an extensive territory. For it cannot be believed, that any form of representative government could have succeeded within the narrow limits occupied by the democracies of Greece."[158]

Madison shows the weakness in ancient representation, so the new government of the United States leads with a "*most advantageous superiority*". Our question is how do we improve this representative advantage and ensure that our constitutional principles remain pure?

Section 4: Due Responsibility

> "I add, as a *sixth* defect the want, in some important cases, of a due responsibility in the government to the people, arising from that frequency of elections which in other cases produces this responsibility. This remark will, perhaps, appear not only new, but also paradoxical. It must nevertheless be acknowledged, when explained, to be as undeniable as it is important.
>
> "Responsibility, in order to be reasonable, must be limited to objects within the power of the responsible party, and in order to be effectual, must relate to operations of that power, of which a ready and proper judgment can be formed by the constituents."[159]

Does Madison advise the representatives to hold each other responsible to the people due to the representatives' election by the people? If election obligates a representative to the people, then is it reasonable that their responsibility is commensurate with the "*objects within the power of the responsible party*" and for it to be effective, it must "*relate to operations of that power*". If we accept this, then so must our representatives. If we believe this, then we might ask how we ensure it. Our question is, is it reasonable to expect our republican principles to be sufficient to effect it?

Section 5: Senate on Passionate Haste

> "As the cool and deliberate sense of the community ought, in all governments, and actually will, in all free governments, ultimately prevail over the views of its rulers; so there are particular moments in public affairs when the people, stimulated by some irregular passion, or some illicit advantage, or misled by the artful misrepresentations of interested men, may call for measures which they themselves will afterwards be the most ready to lament and condemn. In these critical moments, how salutary will be the interference of some temperate and respectable body of citizens, in order to check the misguided career, and to suspend the blow meditated by the people against themselves, until reason, justice, and truth can regain their authority over the public mind?
>
> "In this spirit it may be remarked, that the equal vote allowed to each State is at once a constitutional recognition of the portion of sovereignty remaining in the individual States, and an instrument for preserving that residuary sovereignty. So far the

> equality ought to be no less acceptable to the large than to the small States; since they are not less solicitous to guard, by every possible expedient, against an improper consolidation of the States into one simple republic."[160]

Our question is whether the people grant to any branch absolute power over policy once in office? The reason we ask is to ensure that policy cannot ignore our republican principles. The Framers felt it unnecessary for our representatives to seek wisdom from the people on all issues. Our question is, does experience teach us to honor this idea or to honor their intent and ensure our representatives know what we the people choose? If not, then what course of action do the people possess to intercede to correct the matter before destructive policies do great harm to our freedoms, national security, and our allies? I believe the answer is in adopting our republican principles as the means to evaluate a candidate's platform with an action plan that is the candidate's written contract to implement the majority will, if elected, or some more specific and viable way to link pledge to performance.

Section 6: Improper Acts of Legislation

> "Another advantage accruing from this ingredient in the constitution of the Senate is, the additional impediment it must prove against improper acts of legislation. No law or resolution can now be passed without the concurrence, first, of a majority of the people, and then, of a majority of the States. It must be acknowledged that this complicated check on legislation may in some instances be injurious as well as beneficial; and that the peculiar defense which it involves in favor of the smaller States, would be more rational, if any interests common to them, and distinct from those of the other States, would otherwise be exposed to peculiar danger. But as the larger States will always be able, by their power over the supplies, to defeat unreasonable exertions of this prerogative of the lesser States, and as the faculty and excess of law-making seem to be the diseases to which our governments are most liable, it is not impossible that this part of the Constitution may be more convenient in practice than it appears to many in contemplation."[161]

We must carefully watch legislation for the same reason as our vigilance over any of the other two branches of government. Our question is, what is the meaning of this statement that, "*No law or resolution can now be passed without the concurrence, first, of a majority of the people, and then, of a majority of the States*"? If this means a Constitutional Convention, how can its scope be no law or resolution? Combine this statement with Section 4's insight that community prevails over the government, and then we must ask, what is the extent of power the voters possess over the operation of the government, especially the federal? If we remain in scope of constitutional principles, should we rely upon those principles as our authority to intervene when our elected officials introduce policies that undermine our Constitution's protection of our life, liberty, and our happiness, which the latter may include our national security? I refer to policies that adversely effect our economy, our peaceful relationships with other nations, and our national security in any detrimental manner. Our question is, should we the people permit devastating policies to continue while our country crashes under their weight? If not, what is our recourse to action? The options seem to be recall, impeachment, and censorship, which might mean a petition to Congress for impeachment or disciplinary action. Should a referendum by the people push forward the will of the majority? Likewise, would we not be incited to action if political action is clearly unrepublican? Then, what action is available to the people if Congress is deadlocked? Can an invasion occur without any public way for the public to defend itself if Congress ignores our constitutional provisions?

I see the previous above quote as the Framers' intent to ensure that legislation by itself cannot alter the Constitution. Any legislation outside the limited government of the Constitution is unconstitutional. This piece supports all the other elements as an intended defense for the states against federal legislation. In effect, it prevents any of the three structures from altering our form of government.[162] I believe this is the ground for reviewing and ensuring that all law supports our republican principles in light of excess law making. Our question is, how does the Uniform Law Commission[163] operate?

I see that this also confirms that America is not a democracy because she is unique in the world and no democracy reflects this type of representation or structured form of government. Therefore, America is an extended republic in that her territorial extent, which is greater than a democracy permits and in her representational scheme, which representatives exercise in a bicameral legislature that also mitigates Executive powers. Our representation is *indirect* in the manner of Congressional arrangement, that is, with a constitutionally *limited indirect* representation, whose legislative limits should not range outside the Constitution itself. Our question is, why do we equate our American Republic with its focus on constitutional principles with European democracies? Our republican constitution controls the nature of democracy and its principles through republican principles. Thus far, I see nothing in democracies that reminds me of our republican constitution, which we shall continue to exhaustively attempt to differentiate from democracy.

Section 7: Not Popular Assemblages

> "Experience & reflection may be said not only to have exploded the old error, that republican Governments could only exist within a small compass, but to have established the important truth, that as representative Governments are necessary substitutes for popular assemblages; so an association of free communities, each possessing a responsible Government under a collective authority also responsible, by enlarging the practicable sphere of popular governments, promises a consummation of all the reasonable hopes of the patrons of free Govt."[164]

In this section I see the following ideas, which are:

1. Republican government can operate over large areas
2. Representative governments substitute for popular assemblages
3. States each with its own government, all under a collective national authority that operates in this sphere, which is our expansive territory
4. Popular governments can provide the elements for a free government when the above three elements are in place.

The phrase "*association of free communities*" brings to mind our nation as state republics in which local issues receive attention from local residents, which functions with the Federal System coordinating state law in harmony with our federal contract.

If true, then our federal form of government explicitly denies democracy and democracy would not only undermine our federal contract, it would eliminate rather than propagate free government. Our question is, does a two-party system hinder the people's responsibility to manage government by mixing two opposing sets of principles that originate in the nature of those governments? I addressed the influence of democracy in Chapters 1-4, and the rest of the book draws contradistinctions between it and republicanism. Our question is, is our goal to play out in suffrage a vote between democratic or republican policies or to ensure that our representatives duly represent and protect our republican form of government through republican policies? Which is constitutional?

Mr. Madison continues.

> "But whatever opinions may be formed on the general subjects of confederal systems, or the interpretation of our own, every friend to Republican Gov. ought to raise his voice agst the sweeping denunciation of majority Govt as the most tyrannical and intolerable of all Governments."[165]

Mr. Madison defends republican government and majority will. He concludes that Majority Government is the least, not the "*most tyrannical* and intolerable of all Governments". Since our Framers agree in majority, then how can democracy be the best form we export? Why do we continue advocating democratic policies when our Constitution incorporates democracy's limited contribution to government, its focus on the people, and nullifies its most grievous contributions, which are its steady decline to mob rule that opens the door to tyranny or despotism?

Section 8: Majority v. Popular Majority

Mr. Madison continues.

> "It may be objected to majority governments, that the majority, as formed by the Constitution, may be a minority when compared with the popular majority."[166]

I find a distinction between popular will in Jacksonian ideas and the Framers' constitutional ideas of majority will. We saw above that popular governments require a framework of protection. Madison recognizes that our votes may not produce a popular victory by constitutional regulation. Therefore, those who argue in favor of popular elections, desire to change our elective process without a Constitutional Convention. Neither the national legislature nor the USSC should decide this matter. The USSC should simply advise that it is unconstitutional to attempt to change it through policy or legislation and advise that these are improper acts. The fear is,

> "This is likely to be the case more or less in all elective governments. It is so in many of the States. It will always be so where property is combined with population in the election and apportionment of representation. It must be still more the case with confederacies, in which members, however unequal in population, have equal votes in the administration of the government."[167]

The majority will may be less than a popular vote, but suffrage gives States an equality based on our national legislature whose numbers dictate State electors. The Senate represents the states, each of which sends two Senators to Congress. The House of Representatives receives one representative per thirty thousand citizens in each state. The Electoral College combines these two totals to derive the number of electors each state rates, which might result in one or both of two events. First, it ensures that interested parties participate and secondly, voters elect principals indirectly rather than popularly, as Article II of our Constitution permits.[168] We find here why we want to be careful of democracy's emphasis on popular government. You might review Chapter 2, Section 2 for specifics.

Section 9: Constitutional Majority

Madison continues,

> "In the compound system of the United States, though much less than in mere confederacies, it also necessarily exists to a certain extent. That this departure from the rule of equality, creating a political and constitutional majority in contradistinction to a numerical majority of the people, is certain; and in modes and degrees so oppressive as to justify ultra or anti-constitutional resorts to adequate relief is equally certain."[169]

Madison explains that a constitutional majority is preferential to a numerical or popular majority. Shall we hear the voices of our past and give ear to their wisdom? Some still push for a popular majority, a democratical idea of Jacksonian vintage, over against our republican majority rule. Our question is, to whom do you trust the posterity of our nation?

We previously quoted Cicero on the three types of government. In footnote 74, is a reference to Polybius (6. 4. 8), which states,

> "where he mentions..., and of democracy to decline into Ochlocracy."[170]

Cicero is speaking of a popular democracy. He is speaking of the people possessing absolute power, which is not the form of government that we possess in America, which is shared and limited power. Our sovereignty is in our suffrage, in our Constitution, which prevents a change in our structure of government except by its amendment.

Constitutional Majority is Our Law:

> "Still the constitutional majority must be acquiesced in by constitutional minority, while the Constitution exists. The moment that arrangement is successfully frustrated, the Constitution is at an end."[171]

Popular government is contrary to our compact where majority will finds acceptance by the "*constitutional minority*", which exists by electoral vote. Our question is, do we value our form of government over a democracy?

Section 10: Subversion

> "The only remedy, therefore, for the oppressed minority, is in the amendment of the Constitution or a subversion of the Constitution. This inference is unavoidable."[172]

Some interpret freedom of speech in this way, *if you do not like the Constitution, then you can subvert it.* If one does, then it is, by definition, treason, because we undermine our republican form of government, which protects the minority from oppression by the majority. We must protect the minority as our Constitution provides. If we do not protect them, we have violated our oath of allegiance to protect and defend our Constitution and to live by its law. Shall we divide by class? How shall we govern by the will of the majority when it does not protect the minority? Our question is, do we permit the subversion of our Constitution or do we maintain rule of law?

> "While the Constitution is in force, the power created by it, whether a popular minority or majority, must be the legitimate power, and obeyed as the only alternative to the dissolution of all government.
>
> "It is a favorable consideration, in the impossibility of securing in all cases a coincidence of the constitutional and numerical majority, that when the former is the minority, the existence of a numerical majority with justice on its side, and its influence on public opinion, will be a salutary control on the abuse of power by a minority constitutionally possessing it: a control generally of adequate force, where a military force, the disturber of all the ordinary movements of free governments, is not on the side of the minority."[173]

Here I find that we authorize each branch of government to operate by constitutional minority, but a numerical majority with justice siding with it will have a beneficial effect in the midst of a constitutional minority, unless a military force is on the minority's side. Policy, legislation, and adjudication must originate by republican principle by which the people evaluate and elect their representatives. I understand that some do not believe that the above thought is status quo thinking, but is it our Framers' intent. Our question is, what form of government do we know in our world that changes government so frequently and remains so stable? If we are to possess *legitimate power*, then our constitution must remain in force. Our question is, does it?

Section 11: Best Government

> "The result of the whole is, that we must refer to the monitory reflection
>
> -that no government of human device and human administration can be perfect;
>
> -is the least imperfect is therefore the best government;
>
> -that the abuses of all other governments have led to the preference of republican government as the best of all governments, because the least imperfect;
>
> -that the vital principle of republican government is the *lex majoris partis*, the will of the majority;
>
> -that if the will of a majority cannot be trusted where there are diversified and conflicting interests, it can be trusted nowhere, because such interests exist everywhere;
>
> -that if the manufacturing and agricultural interests be of all interests the most conflicting in the most important operations of government, and a majority government over them be the most intolerable of all governments, it must be as intolerable within the States as it is represented to be in the United States; and, finally,
>
> -that the advocates of the doctrine, to be consistent must reject it in the former as well as in the latter, and seek a refuge under an authority master of both."[174]

I believe that we can now comprehend why Madison explains why we should not turn to a popular majority over an electoral majority. In doing so, Madison makes it clear that any such change would destroy our Constitution. In addition, majority will is the "*vital principle of republican government*", not of democracy, which is *popular majority. Black's Law Dictionary* defines the electoral process as "*the method by which a person is elected to public office in a democratic society.*" as its primary definition. Its secondary definition is "*the taking and counting of votes*". I hope that by now we understand that our society is not a democratic society, but one that is substantially greater.[175]

We can see and tremble that this seems to be what some are attempting to do, but they seem not to fear that their plotting is an unwitting attack on our Constitution and is at least a breach of their citizen responsibility or oath of office and, in my opinion, an impeachable offense. Our question is, can we accept that they are only doing what they think is right and be comforted? Is not the proper course to ensure that our vote signifies our intent by harmonizing policy with our republican principles? When the people vote, their voice is clear and the majority will is what our representatives implement. Party politics is not the Framers' answer to free government, but they gave us their set of republican principles that unite the Union and provide we the people with the tools of free government. Our question is, should our endeavor be to ensure these principles remain our stalwart standard?

Section 12: Inconveniencies of Democracy

> "The great advantage of representatives, is their being capable of discussing affairs; for this the people collectively are extremely unfit, which is one of the greatest inconveniencies of a democracy.
>
> "It is not at all necessary that the representatives, who have received a general instruction from their electors, should wait to be particularly instructed on every affair, as is practised in the diets of Germany. True it is, that by this way of proceeding, the speeches of the deputies might with greater propriety be called the voice of the nation: but, on the other hand, this would throw them into infinite delays; would give each deputy a power of controuling the assembly; and on the most urgent and pressing occasions, the springs of the nation might be stopped by a single caprice."[176]

I find here another objection to direct representation, where the people of the United States are too many to meet and govern directly. An indirect system elects a representative for every thirty thousand citizens. Our experience with representatives flies in the face of this faith in our representatives. What a representative does is not always pursuant to the purpose of our government. Likewise, our government takes upon itself to accomplish things contrary to our principles and this is rampant in our history. Our question is, how do we ensure that our government follows policies and purposes that coincide with our republican principles and our majority will? Our Framers concurred that,

> "The people ... the common superior of the state governments, and the general government."

We the people vote for individuals to implement the majority will of the people, which is sovereign. Are our republican principles the standards by which we elect and evaluate our representatives? Do rival principles confuse issues? The two-party system arose after the first five Presidents who served as warriors and gave their wisdom to form our government. It is true that the

Federalists and the Republican parties existed among some less prominent denominations, but once the Convention wrote the Constitution and the States ratified it, there was only republicanism that incorporated federalism as our structured government.

> "The people at large are the common superior of the state governments, and the general government. It is reasonable to conclude, that they will avoid interferences for two causes—to avoid public oppression, and to render the collections more productive."[177]

Madison's quote is from his speech on *Direct Taxation*, which by context defines his meaning of *collections*. Madison acknowledges that the people at large are superior to both the national and the federal governments. With this power, the people can avoid oppression and the unproductive use of taxes.[178] Since the people are the common superior of both state and general (federal) governments, then we can control our delegated authority by consent of majority over any act or law that is unconstitutional, that is, one to which we will not consent. Our question is, do we know our Constitution and its developmental history well enough to challenge our governmental branches? Do we possess the moral courage to do so?

Section 13: Power of Taxation

> "In the third place I shall consider, whether the power of taxation to be given the general government be safe: and first, whether it be safe as to the public liberty in general."[179]

Evidently, he proved his point. Originally, Jefferson suggested a tax to pay the interest annually and the principal within nineteen years.[180] Our question is, how has Madison's safety net failed as to permit our present indebtedness?

Section 14: National over the Federal

> "But it is urged, that its consolidated nature, joined to the power of direct taxation, will give it a tendency to destroy all subordinate authority; that its increasing influence will speedily enable it to absorb the state governments. I cannot think this will be the case. If the general government were wholly independent of the governments of the particular states, then indeed usurpation might be expected to the fullest extent: but, sir, on whom does this general government depend?"[181]

Unfortunately, it seems that the federal is slowly taking command of the States. Our question is, why are the States losing their constitutional ground?

Section 15: Delegation of Power

> "It derives its authority from these governments, and from the same sources from which their authority is derived. The members of the federal government are taken from the same men from whom those of the state legislatures are taken."[182]

Since the people, at this time, elected state legislatures and the state legislatures chose the State Senators, then the authority rests in the people. Our question is, have the States actually lost any constitutional jurisdiction retained by them or any not delegated to the Federal system? Some believe so, but the same federal courts who may usurp also say whether they have or have not.

Section 16: Means to Avoid Usurpation

> "If we consider the mode in which the federal representatives will be chosen, we shall be convinced, that the general, will never destroy the individual, governments; and this conviction must be strengthened by an attention to the construction of the Senate. The representatives will be chosen probably under the influence of the members of the state legislatures: but there is not the least probability that the election of the latter will be influenced by the former. One hundred and sixty members represent this commonwealth in one branch of the legislature, are drawn from the people at large, and must ever possess more influence than the few men who will be elected to the general legislature."[183]

Whether the people vote directly for Senators or not, our history informs us that neither the Senate nor the House of Representatives avoid corruption. I think they are vulnerable because the electorate reelects them beyond the limits of constitutional tenure. Our question is, should we consider changing this popular practice?

Section 17: Structured Government

Madison shows us how our structured government designs to block our human nature and the factions men create. The popular interests, the House, check the aristocratic interests, the Senate.

> "Thus it has been all the world over. So it will be among us. Reason tells us we are but men: and we are not to expect any particular interference of Heaven in our favor. By thus combining & setting apart, the aristocratic interest, the popular interest will be combined against it. There will be a mutual check and mutual security."[184]

The Framers structured Congress to balance itself. The House of Representatives represents smaller groups of voters, while the two Senators from each state represent the peoples' interest in their State's national and federal relationships. The House with the greatest number of representatives finds a check by the Senate with the least and vice versa.

Section 18: Conclusion

Indirect representation is the unique American ingredient to modern government. It encompasses the idea that the whole of our constitutional society operates our confederated government. Our representatives are responsible to the people who by republican principle are the people's voice. The Framers' structural designs in government are to provide a barrier to corruption. The people's problem is that this barrier is permeable. Our representatives seem not to understand their role in government. The people seem to vacillate from election to election due to interest in personalities rather than to focus on character and on how they will use republican principles to keep government limited. Our question is, if the European democracies are progressing even today toward constitutions that protect citizens, are they closer to America's variety as Madison observed? If they have a better plan, what is? If not, should we recapture our status as a republican constitutional government? If they do, then how is European democracy better than our republican form of government?

CHAPTER 8:

Founders of America's Republics

Madison declares this:

> "The founders of our republics have so much merit for the wisdom, which they have displayed, that no task can be less pleasing than that of pointing out the errors into which they have fallen. A respect for truth, however, obliges us to remark, that they seem never for a moment to have turned their eyes from the danger to liberty from the overgrown and all-grasping prerogative of an hereditary magistrate, supported and fortified by an hereditary branch of the legislative authority. They seem never to have recollected the danger from legislative usurpations, which, by assembling all power in the same hands, must lead to the same tyranny as is threatened by Executive usurpations."[185]

Madison recognizes some errors that we might use to guard against dangers to our liberty through government usurpations. We might view the principles of our Republic as guards. I find two things quite essential to understanding and implementing these principles, which Madison points out in the above quote. First, he shows respect for truth. A free government stands upon truth and freedom of speech. Secondly, they implemented tenure to overcome hereditary longevity, to protect us from corruption. Have we the people disarmed this protection by repeatedly voting the same individual back to power, which creates perpetuity, similar to a heritage, that tempts the strongest of character? Our question is, will we trust them? I have discussed many of our republican principles and created a table in which to list some of the most important principles. Two things, at least, remain. First, add any missing principles. Secondly, match the term to the behavior or expected outcome. Some are self-defining, others Johnson helps us to understand, and some only context can open its meaning. This project is for the many.

Section 1: A Republic Protects Its Citizens

Madison points out, two methods against majority versus minority interests:

> "It is of great importance in a republic not only to guard the society against the oppression of its rulers, but to guard one part of the society against the injustice of the other part. Different interests necessarily exist in different classes of citizens. If a majority be united by a common interest, the rights of the minority will be insecure. There are but two methods of providing against this evil:
>
> "the one by creating a will in the community independent of the majority that is, of the society itself;
>
> "the other, by comprehending in the society so many separate descriptions of citizens as will render an unjust combination of a majority of the whole very improbable, if not impracticable."[186]

Our society is diverse, but its diversity is becoming a unification problem. As Scripture and Lincoln's paraphrase of it predicts, "*every kingdom divided against itself will be ruined, and every city or household divided against itself will not stand*".[187] In order to protect ourselves, we must have core values that unite us, yet enable us to align our perspectives. Self-honesty, by conscience, is the way to act on what we believe. Core values inform us what to believe and how to behave. Often, we assimilate extrinsic values and form our beliefs from them. This is personal choice. We have from our constitutional principles from our Framers those merits of society that sustain it through its moral fiber, its just laws, and its common sense. As we live our republican principles, we test them, which enable us to change our behavior, our laws, and our ideologies, by which we strengthen our Union. In this fashion, we build faith in our values, which is little different from developing faith in general. I believe it is for this reason that the public square serves as the market place of ideas, where Truth speaks and wisdom prevails when we are faithful to our beliefs and principles. Our government should be silent, while the people reasonably argue for the values that they decide will undergird their conscience and guide our representatives. Truth is no friend of timidity; freedom no refuge for false ideas. The best governments stand upon the solid rock of the best moral philosophy.

Madison continues, civil rights protected by diversity of citizens as are religious rights protected by sects. We might take note that here he refers to our Union as a federal republic. How many adjectival descriptors do we have to have for our Republic before we understand that we are not a democratic representative republic?

> "The second method will be exemplified in the federal republic of the United States. Whilst all authority in it will be derived from and dependent on the society, the society itself will be broken into so many parts, interests, and classes of citizens, that the rights of individuals, or of the minority, will be in little danger from interested combinations of the majority. In a free government the security for civil rights must be the same as that for religious rights. It consists in the one case in the multiplicity of interests, and in the other in the multiplicity of sects".[188]

Madison equates rights as being on two levels, secular and religious. Jefferson also addresses this idea. If so, then our secular level is the government that must be separate from our worship, rather than how religion is to be separate from government. The Judiciary's idea of neutrality is an innovation for it is certainly not present in the Framer's mind-set. Madison explains this interplay as virtue in principle and secular in practice, which makes us secure. An established religion has the right of law on its side to punish those who stand apart from it. Our Framers experienced this. Even among colonial sects, opposing groups killed each other. Some opposing sects hung individuals from different sects. We must discipline human nature through civil law and moral teaching. While we compare two distinct groups, we cannot summarily dismiss their similarity in strength and purpose toward unification. We see why the Framers were concerned with toleration. Both play a separate role in maintenance of both governmental and personal limits, which together synergistically play a grand role in the maintenance of our freedom and citizen commitment to monitor our government. Our question is, can we tolerate our differences in these areas and unite ourselves by our republican principles?

> "The degree of security in both cases will depend on the number of interests and sects; and this may be presumed to depend on the extent of country and number of people comprehended under the same government. This view of the subject must particularly recommend a proper federal system to all the sincere and considerate friends of republican government, since it shows that in exact proportion as the territory of the Union may be formed into more circumscribed Confederacies, or States oppressive combinations of a majority will be facilitated: the best security, under the republican forms, for the rights of every class of citizens, will be diminished: and consequently the stability and independence of some member of the government, the only other security, must be proportionately increased. Justice is the

> end of government. It is the end of civil society. It ever has been and ever will be pursued until it be obtained, or until liberty be lost in the pursuit. In a society under the forms of which the stronger faction can readily unite and oppress the weaker, anarchy may as truly be said to reign as in a state of nature, where the weaker individual is not secured against the violence of the stronger; and as, in the latter state, even the stronger individuals are prompted, by the uncertainty of their condition, to submit to a government which may protect the weak as well as themselves; so, in the former state, will the more powerful factions or parties be gradually induced, by a like motive, to wish for a government which will protect all parties, the weaker as well as the more powerful."[189]

Our question is, whether we the people will guard our security by making our governors responsible to the people and more immediately so when they clearly obstruct the principles of our Republic? If in a republican government the rule of law is justice, then our sectional differences must remain free of governmental intrusion as long as we are peaceful. Our question is, does every difference of opinion mandate a legal settlement?

Section 2: Extensive Republics

Madison clarifies that republics can operate within greater territories by electing representatives who can travel and by using republican principles to choose representatives. He notes this:

> "The effect of the first difference is, on the one hand, to refine and enlarge the public views, by passing them through the medium of a chosen body of citizens, whose wisdom may best discern the true interest of their country, and whose patriotism and love of justice will be least likely to sacrifice it to temporary or partial considerations. Under such a regulation, it may well happen that the public voice, pronounced by the representatives of the people, will be more consonant to the public good than if pronounced by the people themselves, convened for the purpose. On the other hand, the effect may be inverted. Men of factious tempers, of local prejudices, or of sinister designs, may, by intrigue, by corruption, or by other means, first obtain the suffrages, and then betray the interests, of the people. The question resulting is, whether small or extensive republics are more favorable to the election of proper guardians of the public weal; and it is clearly decided in favor of the latter by two obvious considerations:

In this section, Madison suggests our representatives should help us to understand the true interests of our country. Is this a form of citizen education by our representatives on issues at hand? In doing so, he makes explicit exception to the popular assemblage, which is the democratical function. I take this to demonstrate the Convention's attempt to distance our indirect national representation from democratical popular assemblages. Our question is, why do our representatives tend to address their constituents rather than the entirety of their district? Does this latter custom represent our republican principle of representation of the whole who decide by suffrage the will of the majority?

He continues by pointing out how some representatives may misuse their office. Our question is, do we the people agree with his conclusion that "*republics are more favorable to the election of proper guardians of the public weal*"? He follows his answer with two considerations, the first of which is,

1. First Consideration: Representatives based on Population:

   "In the first place, it is to be remarked that, however small the republic may be, the representatives must be raised to a certain number, in order to guard against the cabals of a few; and that, however large it may be, they must be limited to a certain number, in order to guard against the confusion of a multitude. Hence, the number of representatives in the two cases not being in proportion to that of the two constituents, and being proportionally greater in the small republic, it follows that, if the proportion of fit characters be not less in the large than in the small republic, the former will present a greater option, and consequently a greater probability of a fit choice.

We note that the method of deciding is not democratic, but it is republican. America is a large country, so it meets the criteria of an extensive republic, but our question is, do we, because of our vast territory, produce fit characters from which we choose fit representatives? How well can we know someone through rhetoric? We must follow this question with another, would our republican values hinder or promote Madison's expected outcome by enabling the populace to understand both the values represented and the method of implementation? I see, in our present context, that we have an example where rhetoric does not match our republican principles in implementation.

2. Second Consideration: Representatives chosen by Large Number of Citizens:

   "In the next place, as each representative will be chosen by a greater number of citizens in the large than in the small republic, it will be more difficult for unworthy candidates to practice with

> success the vicious arts by which elections are too often carried; and the suffrages of the people being more free, will be more likely to centre in men who possess the most attractive merit and the most diffusive and established characters."[190]

I hope Madison is correct in his assumption. Our question is, have we the people wisely understood how representative government promotes identifying and voting for the fit person? Our question is, what does *fit* mean in the context of our republican principles?

Section 3: Extended Republic

According to James Madison, the United States is an *extended Republic* where the General Government divides *et impera, (and rules)*, to ensure an even balance between the factions of the particular States, and be, at the same time, sufficiently restrained by its dependence on the community from betraying its general interests.[191] We noted above that representatives focus on constituents rather than the interests of the nation. Since we choose representatives by ballot, we are a republic by Madison's definition above. He confirms that the public mind and the public voice govern the governing. Our question is, can we do better in electing representatives if we follow the tenure rule and measure general government representation by its interest in national rather than local concerns?

1. Republican Principle: the Ultimate Decision is the Will of the Majority:

Mr. Madison says,

> "It may be asked how private rights will be more secure under the Guardianship of the General Government than under the State Governments, since they are both founded on the republican principle which refers the ultimate decision to the will of the majority, and are distinguished rather by the extent within which they will operate, than by any material difference in their structure."[192]

How does the *"will of the majority"* operating across the United States protect private rights? If the federal is limited to *"enumerated objects"*, then private rights must be in that enumeration. It must be there because it is an *"extended republic and the multiplicity of factions"* work to ensure that we protect private rights, because the general government incorporates the Union and the latter incorporates its population, while the federal governs by delegated limited authority from the National Union. We recall that the federal touches the citizenry in their political and social capacities as constitutionally enumerated. In Barron v. Baltimore 7 Peters 243 (1833), Chief Justice Marshall in the 7-0 Supreme Court decision said that,

> "The Constitution was ordained and established by the people of the United States for themselves, for their own government, and not for the government of the individual states.
>
> "If these propositions be correct, the fifth amendment must be understood as restraining the power of the general government, not as applicable to the States."[193]

I believe he is correct on both counts. What confuses me is the focus on the Fifth Article. I have not read his argument, if there is one, so I ask a few questions. Since our Constitution enumerates the jurisdiction of the general and the States retain all rights not therein delegated to the federal, is this not the great divide between national and general. So, restricting his observation to Article V seems to be an attempt to leave jurisdiction questionable in all the other amendments. Why does he do this?

I fall back to his first paragraph as clearly and demonstrably true. So, our questions are as follows: Does not the Bill of Rights adamantly ensure that the general government does not itself ignore our natural and civil rights? Does Marshall correctly see the relationship between the states and the Federal (General) and State republics? Does he overlook the express enumeration as limitations on the general government and those reserved expressly to the national, that is, the States?

The Heritage Guide to the Constitution has a quote from Charles Warren, which states,

> "however the Court may interpret the provisions of the Constitution, it is still the Constitution which is the law, not the decisions of the Court."[194]

I believe the Constitution and the Framers' intent makes this clear. Therefore, the people can override by sovereign right any interpretation that transgresses these limits. How do the people do this is the question to motivate a process plan, since Constitutional Conventions are difficult to implement. Does it matter if the answer lies in the Framers' records of intent?

Madison makes it clear that limits on the general government reduce its involvement to codification of law rather than the overwhelming adjudication of law. Our question is, which is the focus of the Bench?

Madison believes that,

> "In every State there have been made, and must continue to be made, regulations on this subject which will, in many cases, leave little more to be done by the federal legislature, than to review the different laws, and reduce them in one general act."[195]

Our question is, is this being done? The Framers' intent is to make the people the sovereign governing force, which means the states must be sovereign and supreme over the federal system except by specific constitutional fiat. I remind the reader that I am speaking of intent and not the practice of law, except as practical law may serve as an exception to intent and a call to alarm. I believe that where a possible disparity exists between intent and practice there exists a break in the fabric of our constitutional structure that threatens our security.

> *"Sublato fundamento, cadit opus."*
>
> When the foundation has been removed (or demolished), the structure collapses.[196]

2. Constitution is to Secure the Union:

> "A second observation to be made is that the immediate object of the federal Constitution is to secure the union of the thirteen primitive States, which we know to be practicable;...."[197]

In this case, how liberally should we take "*secure the union*" in terms of branch responsibilities? Is any breach in use of powers of office against foreign invasion, disturbance of national peace, or to prosecute any federal violation of law by residents or nonresidents enforceable against the sitting government by impeachment? When the federal fails to act constitutionally, then it is a threat to the State republics. Our question is, can political policy trump constitutional responsibility?

Section 4: Compound Republic of America

Madison states the following regarding "*two distinct governments*":

1. Two Distinct Governments:

> "First. In a single republic, all the power surrendered by the people is submitted to the administration of a single government; and the usurpations are guarded against by a division of the government into distinct and separate departments. In the compound republic of America, the power surrendered by the people is first divided between two distinct governments, and then the portion allotted to each subdivided among distinct and separate departments. Hence a double security arises to the rights of the people. The different governments will control each other, at the same time that each will be controlled by itself."[198]

I believe the above quote is clear, but I am not sure how its intent is presently realized. Are our two governments balancing one another as outlined above? How does bureaucracy enhance or undermine this control?

2. Senatorial Representation:

Madison says that Senatorial representation is a compromise between the larger and smaller states that ensures incorporation of all states into one nation. This gave equal representation, or a proportional share, in government to all districts regardless of size. The United States became a compound republic with both a national and a federal character. Thus, he states that our government is unique.

3. Proportional and Equal Representation:

In Madison's words:

> "The equality of representation in the Senate is another point, which, being evidently the result of compromise between the opposite pretensions of the large and the small States, does not call for much discussion. If indeed it be right, that among a people thoroughly incorporated into one nation, every district ought to have a *proportional* share in the government, and that among independent and sovereign States, bound together by a simple league, the parties, however unequal in size, ought to have an *equal* share in the common councils, it does not appear to be without some reason that in a compound republic, partaking both of the national and federal character, the government ought to be founded on a mixture of the principles of proportional and equal representation.
>
> "In this spirit it may be remarked, that the equal vote allowed to each State is at once a constitutional recognition of the portion of sovereignty remaining in the individual States, and an instrument for preserving that residuary sovereignty. So far the equality ought to be no less acceptable to the large than to the small States; since they are not less solicitous to guard, by every possible expedient, against an improper consolidation of the States into one simple republic."[199]

Madison thus clarifies that our form of government is unique to that of democracies.

4. Representative Republic:

Technically, the United States is a representative republic, but *democracy* has come to represent any form of free government that springs from the people. This influence is from the nineteenth and twentieth century, which does not represent seventeenth and eighteenth century thought, therefore, it is contrary to our Framers' intent.[200] Our form of government did spring from the people, but it did so by Convention that gave it a unique structural form. I also note that modern democracies provide no barriers to inherent evils of democracies, so it actually incites the people to violence to this day. As we witness in the East, take-over ploys leave opposing factions to garner power, which may not be in the people's interests. If one negative replaces another, the people have no gain. The people's best hope lies in a republican form of government wherein improvements over our own form may provide greater security to our freedom. If the United Nations feels a need to succor the people, let them approach the reigning government at the behest of the people and diplomatically negotiate a change. Foreign intervention has not resolved differences or provided a government for the people. Therefore, our question is, why should we advocate for democracy over our form of government? The only justification for democracy is its violent break from tyranny through revolution. The world may find it a better way to gain power, but it is not the best form of government. Since the United Nations advocates democracy, maybe they should provide the resources to topple undemocratic regimes, hopefully nonviolently. For the United States, we can influence leaders and heads of state. Of course, the U.S. should not mandate our form, but it definitely should not be advocating democracy. Our question is, does our Constitution authorize the federal government to declare war upon a nation that is at peace with us? I mean, of course, no Congressional declaration. Our next question is, how does this square with the people's consent through elected representatives?

I would like to add a footnote. If our Constitution is a document of consent, it must totter upon the government's performance by it. When the government breaks our agreement, the people can only clamor for justice. Our question is, how do we enable the people to act against government breaches if our representatives cannot balance the power?

Section 5: Federal Republic of the United States

A federal republic derives its power and dependence from society. Madison clarifies why we call our government a federal republic. He says the following:

> "The second method will be exemplified in the federal republic of the United States. Whilst all authority in it will be derived from and dependent on the society, the society itself will be broken into so many parts, interests, and classes of citizens, that the rights of individuals, or of the minority, will be in little danger from interested combinations of the majority."[201]

I find a definition for *federal* in Samuel Johnson's dictionary.

a. Federal: means *relating to a league or contract.*

b. Federate: means *Leagued; joined in confederacy.* [202]

I see now that all of these terms attempt to link the confederated states with the changes in our new federal system. They incorporated and modified ancient forms based on the special conditions of our vast territory. Our division into sovereign states and our two forms of government, they divided into branches with a structure that ensures the people's liberties, its governments' jurisdictions, and our representatives' duties to the majority will. Our government is a new creation. Our new government relies upon the majority of states that ratified our Constitution, so it is federal. In this view, I see another difference between our Republic and a democracy. If we are to have factions, then we use them to protect the minority from the majority as opposed to majority exploitation, mob rule, chaos leading to revolution or to despotism. Our question is, can we agree that our form of government is the best form of compounded republican government?

1. Free Government:

> "In a free government the security for civil rights must be the same as that for religious rights."[203]

I treated this relationship earlier in Chapter 7, Section 1. Since our form of government is unique in structure, we need to understand its uniqueness in spirit. We usually conduct the war of words regarding separation of church and state between secular and religious sects as hostile forces. In our present usage, the battlefield is over the maxims and rules of interpretation. Our Framers saw the compatibility between moral beliefs and moral behavior, which have no moral boundaries, whether secular or spiritual. Their focus is on good government, good behavior, and the common good. All of these they address through the concept of virtue, which we must and will investigate a bit later. I see this played out in our States' failure to be responsive to Black issues that caused an *Emergence of Civil Rights as a National Issue.*[204] This in turn invited the federal government to intervene albeit reluctantly. Our question is, why the states fail to respond to their citizens and why does the majority not protect the minority? Do we the people "not want virtue, but they are the dupes of pretended patriots"?[205]

2. The Great Desideratum:

> "The great desideratum in Government is, so to modify the sovereignty as that it may be sufficiently neutral between different parts of Society to control one part from invading the

> rights of another, and at the same time sufficiently controlled itself, from setting up an interest adverse to that of the entire Society."[206]

Since the intent here is to replace absolute sovereignty with a modified version through structure, then we find that neither our power nor our freedom is absolute. If our general government is to protect everyone's rights *and* to have government control itself, why, in the latter case, do we not manage government by constitutional and republican principles rather than as legal issues or cases? Principles are broader than laws and less restrictive. Once we define them, they are less subject to manipulation and exploitation. Create a law and you create a black hole, a vortex from which not even light escapes. In law it appears that language is everything, which makes its meaning obscure and subject to manipulation. A simple example is the use of *take* and *bring*. When I take my child to school, the action is away from me; when I bring home the bacon, the action is toward me. Of course, I am addressing ancient history. Today, we mingle the two resulting in no specificity. I have to agree with C. S. Lewis that language must retain meaning. In other words, laws do not tend to solve problems, but they become the jousting grounds of modern combat. Like the police force, they get involved only after something goes awry. Principles are teachable and widely applicable. They give law something to judge. Our Constitution is our compact between citizens of each state to establish a federal government, to which we the people delegate limited powers. Is there a correlation to this in history? As much as some refuse it, there is, and that is the Christian philosophy. God's government changed from national religious legalism to universal love, he defined it through principles. Once we understand that the Ten Commandments are laws and God's fulfillment of Old Testament prophecy introduced his universal call from all nations those who would hear his voice, i.e. the principles of love, we see this innovation in his relationship with humanity. As this is the case, then love is the highest form of self-government. Human nature requires an intermediary between it and society. Do we need the federal government to manage all of us? Law attempts to do that, but principles permit freedom until someone steps beyond jurisdictional limits that we delegate constitutionally to secular law. Law is subservient to the people and then if law breaches our contract the governing guilty may be impeachable. We the people are not its stooges or servants or victims, although we pledge to obey our Constitution, we still govern the governing, who are subject to the laws, as they are subject to rules of society. Does this clarify why colonial schools focused on the Biblical studies?

From such knowledge of intent, which itself is a condition of "*extent of power*" as a republican principle, we the people must object when the USSC's rulings ignore it and amend it with ideological views.[207] I believe a great deal of chaos in society and law will be swept away when governing becomes republican in its practice in all three branches. Should we the people vote *no* on the government's strategy of nullifying the Framer's intent? Robert Yates predicted an issue with the USSC, which I mention in Chapter 1, Section 7. Jefferson gives us an example.

> "You request me confidentially, to examine the question, whether the Supreme Court has advanced beyond its constitutional limits, and trespassed on those of the State authorities?"[208]

He states that Judge Roane did make such an investigation. He goes on to say,

> "On the decision of the case of Cohens vs. The State of Virginia, in the Supreme Court of the United States, in March, 1821, Judge Roane, ...wrote for the Enquirer a series of papers on the law of that case. I considered these papers maturely as they came out, and confess that they appeared to me to pulverize every word which had been delivered by Judge Marshall, of the extra-judicial part of his opinion; and all was extra-judicial, except the decision that the act of Congress had not purported to give to the corporation of Washington the authority claimed by their lottery law, of controlling the laws of the States within the States themselves. But unable to claim that case, he could not let it go entirely, but went on gratuitously to prove, that notwithstanding the eleventh amendment of the constitution, a State *could* be brought as a defendant, to the bar of his court; and again, that Congress might authorize a corporation of its territory to exercise legislation within a State, and paramount to the laws of that State. I cite the sum and result only of his doctrines,...This doctrine was so completely refuted by Roane, that if he can be answered, I surrender human reason as a vain and useless faculty, given to bewilder, and not to guide us. And I mention this particular case as one only of several, because it gave occasion to that thorough examination of the constitutional limits between the General and State jurisdictions, which you asked for."[209]

He continues citing other writers who addressed the issue of the court's usurpation "on the State jurisdictions".

I believe the Framers' intent was for us to use republican principles to govern. As the public speaks through its elected representatives, the people must express precisely their position in order to instruct the representative(s) of their course of action. Our representatives' conscience is not the consultant of their elected office, but rather the majority will that motivates their vote and their conscience is that of the national majority. Majority, therefore, cannot be nebulous. It must be clear, precise, and agreed upon between candidate and public. Should we design debates to draw out how a candidate agrees with republican principles and how their method of implementation demonstrates success in resolving the current issue? Should we continue to permit factions that each representative responds to as a voting pool for their own special interest group? Does this latter process correspond to our constitutional election process or to political party methods? Each representative is a minority within their personal conscience unless she or he agrees with the majority will. If not, she or he must vote the will of the majority. Polls do not represent the voice of the people, which we individually speak at the ballot box. Again, this is the majority will and not the popular will. We must remember that the majority vote for a representative and their articulated republican platform, delegates our power to those we vote for, as does a proxy signature. A constituency that is not the majority will is a special interest group. It is or should be the district in or jurisdiction for which a candidate runs for office. A constituency has no voice in government after the election. We are all individuals after the election. I think this is why the Patriot Party finds acceptance. Although the danger is, it begins to assume a party mentality rather than acquire a republican mentality. Election to office is neither freedom to change agendas nor permission to deviate from republican principles. Election *by the people* is our instruction by the majority for the representative to perform her or his stated platform *for the people.* Our republican principles are the only standard by which *we the people* can evaluate whether a representative is *for the people,* and functions in office for the benefit *of the people* as elected and intended *by the people* to so act. If not, our question is, can we more explicitly observe this failure if the electorate uses republican principles to evaluate representatives?

Likewise, an election platform makes representatives answerable to the people as a fiduciary promise. As their word is a fiduciary pledge to the people based on virtue, then it becomes their fiduciary responsibility to vote the people's will. If not, then they breach their pledge and they are not acting within good behavioral standards. At present, our two-party system permits antagonistic performances rather than unified focus on the real national issues. Our question is, would the nation prosper more if the people elect individuals who present the best plan of action to resolve current issues staying within limited government jurisdiction? If the people themselves do not act in the spirit of our Constitution, then the representative should so inform them and explain an alternative that follows our Constitutional principles. We can reduce this when we educate our children about our government. If one is displeased with the republican principle at hand, then they take to the public square to sound an alarm. The majority decides if something needs to change and may use recall or other republican measures to correct the problem. In light of this, should we investigate how we can utilize referendums to keep the people informed, involved, and linked to their representatives? If a representative possesses knowledge that the public needs to decide their position, then should not the elected representative express the facts in black and white for them? A referendum would work although it carries negatives in its implementation. However, are closed-door politics more serious negatives? In a republic, our representatives must recognize the citizenry as peers and themselves as subject to the law of the land. Polls are appropriate to gauge the public pulse. Should they measure public understanding rather than the emotive response? Education is our republican principle, not emotive manipulation. Our representatives need to discipline rogue members rather than protect them. Limited tenure would work to deter established entrenchment of representatives. Our question is, do we love our freedom or our representatives more? Our anchor of stability is our bedrock of republican principles. If Drew Westin is correct, we must understand our principles of republican government and ensure that we base all decisions on them. It is not our feelings that should guide our thinking, but our knowledge of the nature and principles of our form of government. Feelings like pain attract our attention, but then we use our minds to decide upon a remedy. Our representatives have no reason to ignore the voters as if we were all a Mr. Stevens, the unknowing butler in the movie, *Remains of the Day*. I introduce Mr. Stevens in Chapter 12. Our cause for action is consistent with the public good when we know and understand the issues.[210]

I recall an appropriate quote in John Adams that speaks to factions.

> "In republics founded upon the equality of all the citizens, and as if establishing different orders of men was not a source of divisions and disputes."[211]

When our representatives begin to view us as equals rather than as voters to appease and or to manipulate, then we can find unification. Yet, in this quote, we find that a republic views equality of personhood as a right rather than as a government gift. If we are knowledgeable, then appeasement does not work. Our nature is a complex association of feelings and thinking, which we can learn how to manage, as Dr. Westin's message warns us that we must do if we desire to be leaders rather than political pawns. It is another educational deficit.

3. Confederate Republic and Federal Authority:

Hamilton speaks of a Confederate Republic. How does he define it? He says this,

> "The definition of a Confederate Republic seems simply to be *an assemblage of societies*, or an association of two or more

> states into one state. The extent, modifications, and objects of the federal authority are mere matters of discretion. So long as the separate organization of the members be not abolished; so long as it exists, by a constitutional necessity, for local purposes; though it should be in perfect subordination to the general authority of the union, it would still be, in fact and in theory, an association of states, or a confederacy."[212]

Hamilton's *"assemblage of societies"* informs us that we are too large for democracy to work. Our nation requires a structured government that permits indirect representation. Our question is, do we understand that local issues should remain in communities, not advanced to our general government, except by legislative action agreeable to the people?

4. Madison's Confederated Republic:

> "It may be suggested, that a people spread over an extensive region cannot, like the crowded inhabitants of a small district, be subject to the infection of violent passions, or to the danger of combining in pursuit of unjust measures. I am far from denying that this is a distinction of peculiar importance. I have, on the contrary, endeavored in a former paper to show, that it is one of the principal recommendations of a *confederated republic.* At the same time, this advantage ought not to be considered as superseding the use of auxiliary precautions. It may even be remarked, that the same extended situation, which will exempt the people of America from some of the dangers incident to lesser republics, will expose them to the inconveniency of remaining for a longer time under the influence of those misrepresentations, which the combined industry of interested men may succeed in distributing among them."[213]

A Confederated Republic is a federal compact between the national (sovereign states) and the federal (the three branches of the people's government). I note that the Framers designed our Republic to protect the people from their House of Representatives and themselves by incorporating a Senate. I believe the separation of powers is his meaning of *"auxiliary precautions"*. The Senate balances the House and when necessary it balances the people. This provision requires mature and informed leadership. I know Madison thought the Senate important in foreign relations and in domestic relations. He hoped it would act this way,

> "The cool and deliberate sense of the community as it ought, in all governments and actually will, in all free governments, ultimately prevail over the view of its rulers: so there are particular moments in public affairs, when the people, stimulated by some irregular passion, or some illicit advantage, or misled

by the artful misrepresentations of interested men, may call for measures which they themselves will afterwards be the most ready to lament and condemn."[214]

Does Drew Westin see *"cool and deliberate sense of the community"* as a weakness or does he see it at all among the common people? We know from experience that an uninformed and disrespected citizenry is fair game to the influence of unrepublican principles and to politicians who are without virtue. We do not need party politics to guide us, but we, I hope, long for virtuous leaders who understand our form of government. Yet we the people possess the sword of discipline, so far sheathed, but is it time for a call to arms? We the people possess the arms through our republican principles. Our question is, shall we improve our system to maintain sovereignty, peace, and our liberty and remain the hope of the world?

Hamilton on the science of politics and representation and their great improvement, adds the following:

5. Science of Politics:

"But it is not to be denied that the portraits they have sketched of republican government were too just copies of the originals from which they were taken. If it had been found impracticable to have devised models of a more perfect structure, the enlightened friends to liberty would have been obliged to abandon the cause of that species of government as indefensible. The science of politics, however, like most other sciences, has received great improvement. The efficacy of various principles is now well understood, which were either not known at all, or imperfectly known to the ancients.

"-The regular distribution of power into distinct departments;

- the introduction of legislative balances and checks;

-the institution of courts composed of judges holding their offices during good behavior;

-the representation of the people in the legislature by deputies of their own election:

"these are wholly new discoveries, or have made their principal progress towards perfection in modern times. They are means, and powerful means, by which the excellences of republican government may be retained and its imperfections lessened or avoided. To this catalogue of circumstances that tend to the amelioration of popular systems of civil government, I shall venture, however novel it may appear to some, to add one

> more, on a principle which has been made the foundation of an objection to the new Constitution; I mean the *enlargement* of the *orbit* within which such systems are to revolve, either in respect to the dimensions of a single State or to the consolidation of several smaller States into one great Confederacy. The latter is that which immediately concerns the object under consideration. It will, however, be of use to examine the principle in its application to a single State, which shall be attended to in another place."[215]

We have three phrases that inform us that our government is an innovation. These are:

1) species of government,
2) list of four innovations,
3) amelioration of popular systems of civil government.

His list of improvements is succinct, but his comment that "*their principal progress towards perfection in modern times*" testifies to the newness or uniqueness of this new form of American government. Our question is, is our republican form of government more or less inclusive than any ancient or modern democracy? If any American can pledge allegiance to any other constitution based on its merits, then he must believe he is living under an inferior constitutional rule of law. I suggest he take Justice Wilson's advice.

Section 6: Is it Strictly Republican?

> "THE last paper having concluded the observations, which were meant to introduce a candid survey of the plan of government reported by the convention, we now proceed to the execution of that part of our undertaking. The first question that offers itself is, whether the general form and aspect of the government be strictly republican. It is evident that no other form would be reconcilable with the genius of the people of America; with the fundamental principles of the Revolution; or with that honorable determination which animates every votary of freedom, to rest all our political experiments on the capacity of mankind for self-government. If the plan of the convention, therefore, be found to depart from the republican character, its advocates must abandon it as no longer defensible."[216]

Does he refute those who think the Framers would today name our form of government a democracy? Would we contend that any known modern democracy is a better form of government than a strictly American republican government? Shall we hear, perceive, and respond to Madison? Does he voice our sentiment toward government today? If not, our Republic crumbles at the hands of those who change it without resistance from we the people. If he does, then our Republic shall stand. Our Republic stands upon republican principles and its nature is more mature than any modern democracy or other form of government. It only takes the will of the majority to resuscitate the vigor that our Framers breathed into it. Jefferson in his letter to Justice William Johnson relates that the republican idea is that nature endows man with rights. The Convention's intent was to,

> "...maintain the will of the majority of the convention, and of the people themselves. We believed, with them, that man was a rational animal, endowed by nature with rights, and with an innate sense of justice; and that he could be restrained from wrong and protected in right by moderate powers, confided to persons of his own choice, and held to their duties by dependence on his own will. We believed ... that wisdom and virtue were not hereditary ... the cherishment of the people then was our principle ..."[217]

If anything is co-opted, it is democracy's *demos* as a republican principle. Our government is so distant from a democracy that to attempt to fit it into a democratic shoe is to feel the pinch of corruption of the nature and principles of our Republic. I note that the quote above offers an opportunity to challenge such "*innovations*". We ensure "...the forms of government under which the compact was entered into, should be *substantially* maintained." The federal guarantees to the national a republican form of government.

Jefferson goes on in the same place to say that ...

> "I believe the States can best govern our home concerns, and the General Government our foreign ones. I wish, therefore, to see maintained that wholesome distribution of powers established by the constitution for the limitation of both; and never to see all offices transferred to Washington, where, further withdrawal from the eyes of the people, they may more secretly be bought and sold as at market."[218]

Jefferson speaks of the new republican form of government, so his reference concerning the people testifies to majority government. Yet, he notes that local government by the states is separate from the general government. If their intent was to minimize government, our question is, should we permit federal government to expand into local districts?

Section 7: John Quincy Adams

Dr. Rakove said that Dr. Shklar quoted from the Memoirs of John Quincy Adams, which I cannot locate in his memoirs. However, I did find a quote that refutes the implication that America by the Framer's intent is any type of democracy. John Quincy Adams in his 1833 Memoirs says this,

> "The discourses of John Locke concerning government demolished while they immortalized the work of Filmer, whose name and book are now remembered only to be detested. But the first principles of morals and politics, which have long been settled, acquire the authority of self-evident truths, which, when first discussed, may have been vehemently and portentously contested. John Locke, a kindred soul to Algernon Sydney, seven years after his death published an elaborate system of government, in which he declares the 'false principles and foundation of Sir Robert Filmer and his followers are detected and overthrown.' Subsequently, he published an essay concerning the true original extent and end of civil government. 'The principles,' says Mr. Adams, 'of Sydney and Locke constitute the foundation of the North American Declaration of Independence; and, together with the subsequent writings of Montesquieu and Rousseau, that of the constitution of the Commonwealth of Massachusetts, and of the constitution of the United States.' Neither of these constitutions separately, nor the two in combined harmony, can, without a gross and fraudulent perversion of language, be termed a *democracy.* They are neither democracy, aristocracy, nor monarchy. They form together a mixed government, compounded not only of the three elements of democracy, aristocracy, and monarchy, but with a fourth added element, *Confederacy.* The constitution of the United States when adopted was so far from being considered as a democracy, that Patrick Henry charged it, in the Virginia Convention, with an awful squinting towards monarchy. The tenth number of the *Federalist,* written by James Madison, is an elaborate and unanswerable essay upon the vital and radical difference between a democracy and a republic. But it is impossible to disconnect the relation between names and things. When the anti-federal party dropped the name of Republicans to assume that of *Democrats,* their principles underwent a corresponding metamorphosis; and they are now the most devoted and most obsequious champions of Executive power—the very life-guard of the commander of the armies and navies of this Union. The name of democracy was assumed because it was discovered to be *very taking* among the multitude; yet, after all, it is but the investment of the *multitude* with absolute power. The constitutions of the United States and of the Commonwealth of Massachusetts are both the work of the people—one of the Union, the other of the State—not of the whole people by the phantom of universal suffrage, but of

> the whole people by that portion of them capable of contracting for the whole. They are not democracy, nor aristocracy, nor monarchy, but a compound of them all, of which democracy is the oxygen, or vital air, too pure in itself for human respiration, but which in the union of other elements, equally destructive in themselves and less pure, forms that moral and political atmosphere in which we live, and move, and have our being."[219]

He mentions Executive power as an identifier to mark the change. Jackson became president in 1829, four years before Adams wrote his Memoirs. Some contend Adams was angry over his loss to Jackson, so he harbors some animosity. Maybe, but his history confirms my research. I would garner from his reaction, a justified abhorrence over the acute change between Jackson and the Framers. I know I feel the emotion based on my knowledge of history. Our question is, are we ready to reclaim the fundamentals of republican government?

Section 8: Our Downhill Journey

I know that capitalism is neither moral nor immoral, but man chooses whether he is virtuous or not. I recall Jefferson's dire words.

> "Religion is well supported; of various kinds, indeed, but all good enough; all sufficient to preserve peace and order: or if a sect arises, whose tenets would subvert morals, good sense has fair play, and reasons and laughs it out of doors, without suffering the state to be troubled with it. They do not hang more malefactors than we do. They are not more disturbed with religious dissensions. On the contrary, their harmony is unparalleled, and can be ascribed to nothing but their unbounded tolerance, because there is no other circumstance in which they differ from every nation on earth. They have made the happy discovery, that the way to silence religious disputes, is to take no notice of them. Let us too give this experiment fair play, and get rid, while we may, of those tyrannical laws. It is true, we are as yet secured against them by the spirit of the times. I doubt whether the people of this country would suffer an execution for heresy, or a three years imprisonment for not comprehending the mysteries of the Trinity. But is the spirit of the people an infallible, a permanent reliance? Is it government? Is this the kind of protection we receive in return for the rights we give up? Besides, the spirit of the times may alter, will alter. Our rulers will become corrupt, our people careless. A single zealot may commence persecutor, and better men be his victims. It can never be too often repeated, that the time for fixing every essential

> right on a legal basis is while our rulers are honest, and ourselves united. From the conclusion of this war we shall be going down hill. It will not then be necessary to resort every moment to the people for support. They will be forgotten, therefore, and their rights disregarded. They will forget themselves, but in the sole faculty of making money, and will never think of uniting to effect a due respect for their rights. The shackles, therefore, which shall not be knocked off at the conclusion of this war, will remain on us long, will be made heavier and heavier, till our rights shall revive or expire in a convulsion." [220]

Jefferson is not neutral. He understands that religion is a necessity in society for it is the external good that soothes man's human nature through internal commitment. Madison sees property in religious belief. They all understood the tenuous character of liberty, the tenacious encroaching creep of government, and the tenuous nature of humanity. Hope mingled with reality spurs caution, safeguards, and vigilance. Until recently, he was right on in his anxiety. Today, a spirit of revival sweeps among our people. The double-edged sword of truth we wield; the light of hope dawns. We the people unite to reclaim our life and liberty in order to pursue our happiness. We are a republic that should function by our republican principles that underwrite our Constitution. May God bless America and in his providential wisdom may He unite us under his aegis, his Royal Law.[221]

Section 9: Conclusion

Madison believes that a republic is both the best state and the best form of government. A republic by indirect representation is the best state and form of government. A Federal Republic extends representation across a vast territory that is indefinite in extent and peopled by a diversity that calls for a new order of government. Our government confederates the individual sovereign states into a nationally authorized federal government that expresses itself in three balanced branches. Our Republic strengthens all three of the ancient forms, which the United States introduces as a new republican form of government and new world experience that introduces representation bolstered by separation of powers as the new idea of modern government. Since our republican form of government is unique, and compound, it cannot be simply designated a democracy, but it contains positive democratical elements. The interaction of the nature and principles of our Federal System raises the people to a more secure form of government. A republican form of government entails and justifies the idea that government rests in the constitutional authority of the people, but a republic also binds itself to rule of law through its constitution rather than popular will. Further, the United States distinguishes its republic through representation.[222]

Does the complex plan and shared power of the European Union (EU) possess such maturity and reliance upon the sovereignty of the people? Does it construct barriers to representatives' usurpation of power of the people? All may have a constitution, but none possesses our framework to stay the sway of the evils in the three known types of government. The EU's structure is convoluted and redundant with tiers of bureaucracy. The EU is admittedly, a democracy of states.[223] In the European Union (EU), federalism is the belief that any national entity must follow the principle of *subsidiarity.* Federalism in the European Union is a rule that a nation state must comply with the EU's rules of law over its own.[224] A nation-state operates under the supreme laws of the European Union. *Subsidiarity,* in this context, seems to mean that nation states are subsidiary (*subordinate; under another's control*), which means subordinate to the EU.[225] How is federalism in the United States' different from the European Union's form of federalism? When our politicians change our views of the nature of our government from a republic to a democracy, they also change our government's principles. Our question is, does this modern meaning set up all governments to one day be subsumed under some form of world government? This question leads us to ask, what guarantees does a world government give to the people as to its form? If it is a democracy, then our Framers forewarn us that it is not the best for the people, except in a small city, if then. How then, can it serve a world population? A world government is a mystery compounded when one realizes that proponents of modern democracy do not provide us with a clue how a modern democratic regime operates.

Chapter 9:
Jefferson's First Inaugural Address

President Jefferson died on July 4, 1826, twenty-five years after his First Inaugural Address that represents his mature testimony of his creed and purpose.

Section 1: Sum of a Good Government

In his First Inaugural Address, on March 4, 1801, President Jefferson lists fourteen principles of what he terms "*the sum of a good government ...*" And what he deems as "*the essential principles of our Government*", which are:

1. Equal and exact justice to all men, of whatever state or persuasion, religious or political;
2. peace, commerce, and honest friendship with all nations, entangling alliances with none;
3. the support of the State governments in all their rights, as the most competent administrations for our domestic concerns and the surest bulwarks against antirepublican tendencies;
4. the preservation of the General Government in its whole constitutional vigor, as the sheet anchor of our peace at home and safety abroad;
5. a jealous care of the right of election by the people—a mild and safe corrective of abuses which are lopped by the sword of revolution where peaceable remedies are unprovided;

6. absolute acquiescence in the decisions of the majority, the vital principle and immediate parent of despotism;
7. a well-disciplined militia, our best reliance in peace and for the first moments of war till regulars may relieve them;
8. the supremacy of the civil over the military authority;
9. economy in the public expense, that labor may be lightly burthened;
10. the honest payment of our debts and sacred preservation of the public faith;
11. encouragement of agriculture, and of commerce as its handmaid;
12. the diffusion of information and arraignment of all abuses at the bar of the public reason;
13. freedom of religion;
14. freedom of the press, and freedom of person under the protection of the habeas corpus, and trial by juries impartially selected.[226]

Historians say that Jefferson founded the Republican Party in 1792, which others reformed in 1854 as an anti-slavery coalition and since strives for the restraints the Constitution … *"imposes on the main parties contending for office"*.[227] I find the following three issues embedded in this proposition. First, we mistakenly take it as a political party as we know them today, as national committees. Johnson defines party by distinguishing eight definitions with the first being "a number of persons confederated by familiarity of designs or opinions in opposition to others; a faction and four a "side; persons engaged against each other". This innovation comes with President Jackson's Democratic Party. Secondly, Jefferson by letter and deed advocates the totality of republicanism for the protection of the people from government. Thirdly, it justifies the two-party system. The signers of the Constitution were republican-federalists. Jefferson's friendship with Madison yields letters that demonstrate their conciliation of ideas. Jefferson spoke of all being of the same mind toward their views of government. The conflict with Hamilton was due to his favoritism toward the British form of monarchial-aristocratical government and his financial ideas and the national bank of the U.S. Jefferson remained a federal-republican while Hamilton became a monarchial-federalist. These were positions on principle, not parties. Jefferson explains that differences are about principle and this was one of principle.[228] Jefferson, Madison, and the majority of Framers disagreed with Hamilton and Adams, but most agreed that the framework of government was republican.[229] As far as democratic tendencies in the Constitutional Debates, voters replaced democrats with republican-federalists by the 4th election.[230]

We see that the main idea in the republican character as applied to person and government by Madison, are these, it is essential in that it derives all its power either

1. directly—majority of votes by state or
2. indirectly—by elected representation to state legislatures and to House of Representatives and to the Senate elected by each state in proportion to population, and the Executive directly elected from the great body of people.

In these ways, the people elect representatives and the people retain supreme authority over government. This harmonizes with Madison's definition of a republic and with his distrust of democracy. It is sufficient because administrators are persons holding their offices during pleasure, that is:

1. for a limited time, a constitutional limitation, or
2. during good behavior.

The Executive is impeachable at any time during term; the Judiciary "*during the firm tenure of good behavior*". I find it interesting that the Bench struggles with the meaning of "*good behavior*".[231] In addition, Prakash and Smith look at original intent and declare that the Framers relied upon,

> "a generic tenure that could be granted to anybody with respect to any item that might be held (e.g., jobs, licenses, land). The phrase meant that the holder could be deprived of the item only through a judicial proceeding establishing misbehavior."[232]

These authors go on to say that if impeachment was the Framers only answer to remove a sitting judge, then our Constitution should inform us that it was breaking with centuries of good-behavior tenure. It does not, so one concludes, they were not. This process lies outside the impeachment process. Madison makes clear the Framers' intent that Judges are subject to impeachment. Our problem is the reluctance of our representatives to challenge Judicial decisions and personal conduct. Is this reluctance a symptom of corruption? When we default to our republican principles, we stand on firm moral ground whose scales weigh the facts. If one doubts the conclusion above, we ask does the separation of powers permit the Bench to decide what *good* means in their conduct? Our question is, should this be a legislative function, may be for the Ethics committee? Our republican principles are decisive in terms of values by principle, but we can only solve moral issues when we understand the Framers' call for morality by the standards of the Christian philosophy.

In Chapter 5, we examined this promise,

> "...both under the federal and the State governments; and in its express guaranty of the republican form to each of the latter."[233]

The Constitution guarantees a republican form *to each of the latter.* I take the phrase "*to each of the latter*" to reference the "the state governments". If true, then any political party or any representative directly elected to office or indirectly appointed to office is accountable to our Constitution for maintaining the republican form of government. As many attempt to alter this form by usurping powers directed by the Constitution to these established offices and its limited powers, we must conclude that they fail to uphold the public trust to protect our Constitution, which provides us our republican principles. Should we the people advocate for impeachment of any representative for failure to uphold the Constitution's guarantee of a republican government?[234] Our question is, do we fail to do it because some pundits note that we all love our representatives and blame *your* representatives for the Congressional mess? Madison sees the republican principles as a defense against innovations.

Section 2: Republican Form

Jefferson draws a distinction between the principles of the Monarchists and the Republicans. The Monarchists failed to establish a monarchy in America, so they attempted a consolidated government, which also failed. Next, they tried to eliminate "the rights reserved by the constitution to the states as a bulwark against that consolidation, the fear of Republicans in Congress...." He then says,

> "Ours, on the contrary, was to maintain the will of the majority of the convention, and of the people themselves."[235]

A republic, we learn, is a state accountable to its citizens. If our government fails *substantially* to maintain our contract, we should intervene.

> "To the second question, it may be answered, that if the general government should interpose by virtue of this constitutional authority extends no farther than to a *guarantee* of a republican form of government, which supposes a preexisting government of the form, which is to be guaranteed. As long therefore as the existing republican forms are continued by the states, they are guaranteed by the federal constitution. Whenever the states may choose to substitute other republican forms, they have a right

> to do so, and to claim the federal guarantee for the latter. The only restriction imposed on them is, that they shall not exchange republican for anti-republican constitutions: a restriction, which it is presumed, will hardly be considered as a grievance."[236]

Do we see that our States are to maintain a republican form of government? I failed to grasp this early on. If so, can we permit democracy to creep into our system? We know that we have democratical ideas in our form of government and in our Democratic Party? Only those elements that our Constitution embraces are constitutional. Our Republic is neither a democracy nor any form of a democracy. Therefore, we must not infuse other governmental forms or ideologies as though they were constitutional. No state can change our republican form, then how can the Federal government that guarantees to the states that it will remain a republican form, exchange its republican form to an anti-republican form? How is it that our representatives believe that they can fundamentally change our government when our nationally ratified federal Constitution can only change by amendment? Our answer must lie in how our branches interpret our Constitutional principles.

Some words that confuse the issue and that describe different points of view are as follows, Democrat, Libertarian, Progressive, Left, Right, Centrist.[237] Should we not use the one word that our Framers applied to these principles, republicanism? Can one be right or left of republicanism? If we rally around republicanism, then we could use one set of rules and standards for governing. As it is, the term democracy invites such a broad infusion of ideas that they confound us. Anyone can advocate for anything, but a change of government is the people's decision by republican processes guaranteed by our Constitution.

Section 3: A Republican Form of Government

> "A government in the republican form; specif., a government by representatives chosen by the people."[238]

Does this statement challenge our ideas that vie for democracy? We the people are the government and you, our representatives, are our voice, our hands, and our productive minds. Our voice today is discordant, but we can unify our voice through our republican principles. Interpretation is not by political association, but rather by understanding the roots of our liberty that reside in the firm meaning of our Constitution known by the principles that undergird it.

Section 4: A *New* Creation

> "Our political system is admitted a new Creation—a real nondescript. Its character therefore must be sought in itself; not in precedents, because there are none; not in writers whose comments are guided by precedents ... What can be more preposterous than to say that the States as united, are in no respect or degree, a Nation, which implies sovereignty; altho' acknowledged to be such by all other Nations & Sovereigns, and maintaining with them, all the international relations, of war & peace, treaties, commerce, &c, and on the other hand and at the same time, to say that the States separately are completely nations & Sovereigns; although they can separately neither speak nor harken to any other nation, nor maintain with it any of the international relations whatever and would be disowned as Nations if presenting themselves in that character."[239]

How can we confuse the meaning of "*new creation*"? If new, then how do we fall back to an old and dangerous concept such as democracy? If our political system is a "*new creation*", then how can our system be related to an old system known to be riddled with tenets that lead to evil outcomes for the people.

Madison quotes Jefferson from his "Notes on the State of Virginia" in the following,

> "THE Author of the "Notes on the State of Virginia," quoted in the last paper, has subjoined to that valuable work the draught of a constitution, which had been prepared in order to be laid before a convention, expected to be called in 1783, by the legislature, for the establishment of a constitution for that commonwealth. The plan, like everything from the same pen, marks a turn of thinking, original, comprehensive, and accurate; and is the more worthy of attention as it equally displays a fervent attachment to republican government and an enlightened view of the dangerous propensities against which it ought to be guarded. One of the precautions, which he proposes, and on which he appears ultimately to rely as a palladium to the weaker departments of power against the invasions of the stronger, is perhaps altogether his own, and as it immediately relates to the subject of our present inquiry, ought not to be overlooked."[240]

All of these adjectives plainly point out that a new creation defines our Constitution and its republican principles.

Let us repeat this clear denunciation that America is a form of democracy, "*...turn of thinking, original, comprehensive, and accurate; and is the more worthy of attention as it equally displays a fervent attachment to republican* *government and an enlightened view of the dangerous propensities against which it ought to be guarded."*

Section 5: Madison's Call for Convention

> "...that whenever any two of the three branches of government shall concur in opinion, each by the voices of two thirds of their whole number, that a convention is necessary for altering the constitution, or correcting breaches of it, a convention shall be called for the purpose."[241]

Does this confirm that no one can dismantle our form of government by policy, ideology, mixing concepts, ignorance, design, or otherwise?

Section 6: Madison's Answer to Churchill

Madison says,

> "...it is a misfortune incident to republican government, though in a less degree than to other governments...."

I think he includes democracy in *other governments.*

1. A Senate:

> "...3. First, it is a misfortune incident to republican government, though in a less degree than to other governments, that those who administer it may forget their obligations to their constituents, and prove unfaithful to their important trust. In this point of view, a Senate, as a second branch of the legislative assembly, distinct from, and dividing the power with, a first, must be in all cases a salutary check on the government. It doubles the security to the people, by requiring the concurrence of two distinct bodies in schemes of usurpation or perfidy, where the ambition or corruption of one would otherwise be sufficient. This is a precaution founded on such clear principles, and now so well understood in the United States, that it would be more than superfluous to enlarge on it. I will barely remark, that as the improbability of sinister combinations will be in proportion to the dissimilarity in the genius of the two bodies, it must be politic to distinguish them from each other by every circumstance, which will consist with a due harmony in all proper measures, and with the genuine principles of republican government.[242]

> "4. Thirdly. Another defect to be supplied by a Senate lies in a

> want of due acquaintance with the objects and principles of legislation. It is not possible that an assembly of men called for the most part from pursuits of a private nature, continued in appointment for a short time, and led by no permanent motive to devote the intervals of public occupation to a study of the laws, the affairs, and the comprehensive interests of their country, should, if left wholly to themselves, escape a variety of important errors in the exercise of their legislative trust. It may be affirmed, on the best grounds, that no small share of the present embarrassments of America is to be charged on the blunders of our governments; and that these have proceeded from the heads rather than the hearts of most of the authors of them. What indeed are all the repealing, explaining, and amending laws, which fill and disgrace our voluminous codes, but so many monuments of deficient wisdom; so many impeachments exhibited by each succeeding against each preceding session; so many admonitions to the people, of the value of those aids which may be expected from a well-constituted Senate?
>
> "5. A good government implies two things: first, fidelity to the object of government, which is the happiness of the people; secondly, a knowledge of the means by which that object can be best attained. Some governments are deficient in both these qualities; most governments are deficient in the first. I scruple not to assert, that in American governments too little attention has been paid to the last. The federal Constitution avoids this error; and what merits particular notice, it provides for the last in a mode, which increases the security for the first.[243]

I find a most important explanation of tenure in item 4, which is "*continued in appointment for a short time*". I am not sure where the custom derived to send representatives repetitiously back to Congress, but our experience proves it an unwise custom. I have heard that it developed because seniority begets the best committee heads. All of these items work to explain the uniqueness of our republican form of government. Therefore, we can use them for Madison to dispute Churchill's claim for democracy's supremacy. He points out another plug in the dam that holds back the tides of bad government, namely, our Constitution ensures the happiness of the people, the object of government, and provides the means to attain that end, structured government. Where in the history of democracy is it clear that this is the object of democracy? At the top of the list, our Constitution provides protection from those who would "*forget their obligations to their constituents, and prove unfaithful to their important trust*". When did custom nullify this by practice?

2. Contemporary View:

This comment on February 21, 2011 from the Huffington Post's Gary Hart praises democracy,

> "Meanwhile, in Washington and Madison, and soon in many other state capitals around the country, we are seeing democracy in action with street demonstrations that don't look all that much different from Cairo and other cities. Democracy is easy when the economic pie is growing. It begins to creak and crack, however, when the pie is shrinking."

That is the case for democracy, but for our republican form, it is not, for it is stronger, more viable, and less brittle than democracy alone. Our Framers knit our Constitution with the best of the fabrics of the ancient triad and its sinew is its American experience.

This article on March 16, 2011 from Lew Rockwell's web site states,

> "Democracy is not 'the worst form of government except for all those others that have been tried.' Democracy is the worst form of government ever tried, period. Democracy ranks among the gravest threats to individual rights and individual liberty in human history. Democracy is, in certain respects, even worse than absolute monarchy. Ignorant and arrogant modern day 'champions of democracy' need to get a clue."[244]

In other words, we are very confused about the benefits of democracy. Is our confusion because of party lines? Shall we hear the Framers' words that inform us that the best form of government is compounded of democracy, Monarchianism, and aristocracy to form the fourth and best form, which is a compounded republic?

3. Mixed Government:

> "6. My design is more extensive than barely to shew the imperfection of Mr. Turgot's idea. This might be done in a few words, and a very short process of reasoning: but I wish to assemble together the opinions and reasonings of philosophers, politicians, and historians, who have taken the most extensive views of men and societies, whose characters are deservedly revered, and whose writings were in the contemplation of those who framed the American constitutions. It will not be contested, that all these characters are united in Polybius, who, in a fragment of his sixth book, translated by Edward Spelman, p. 291 at the end of his translation of the Roman Antiquities of Dionysius Halicarnassensis, says: —'It is customary to establish three sorts of governments; kingly government, aristocracy, and democracy:

> upon which one may very properly ask them, whether they lay these down as the only forms of government, or as the best; for in both cases they seem to be in an error, since it is manifest, that the best form of government is that which is *compounded of all three.'* This is founded not only in reason but in experience, Lycurgus having set the example of this form of government in the institution of the Lacedemonian commonwealth.
>
> "Six kinds of government must be allowed: kingly government and monarchy, aristocracy and oligarchy, democracy, and the government of the multitude."[245]
>
> "The generation and corruption of governments, which may in other words be called the progress and course of human passions in society, are subjects, which have engaged the attention of the greatest writers; and whether the essays they have left us were copied from history, or wrought out of their own conjectures and reasonings, they are very much to our purpose, to shew the utility and necessity of different orders of men, and of an equilibrium of powers and privileges. They demonstrate the corruptibility of every species of simple government, by which I mean a power without a check, whether in one, a few, or many. It might be sufficient to shew this tendency in simple democracy alone, for such is the government of one assembly, whether of the people collectively or representatively: but as the generation and corruption of all kinds of government have a similitude with one another, and proceed from the same qualities in human nature, it will throw the more light upon our subject, the more particularly we examine it. I shall confine myself chiefly to Plato, Polybius, and your namesake Sir Thomas Smith."[246]

4. Representative Suffrage:

John Adams records from history the need to consolidate ideas that are good and filter those that are evil to prosper a good government. He and all the Framers concur that this is what our Constitution accomplishes. They call it republican because our Republic is subject to the will of the people through suffrage, which rule of law guarantees, whereas the others tend to some evil end that ends the sovereignty of the people.

Section 7: Conclusion

If our Republic stands, it stands upon those elements that form a good republican government. As we traverse our place in history, shall we pledge allegiance to our form of government? If we choose to honor our frame of government, then we must understand what comes next, which is our republican principles embedded in the writings of our Founders and Framers. We must use knowledge by education girded by virtue.

CHAPTER 10:

Republican Principles

Section 1: Majority Rule or Rule by a Lesser Number

Madison speaks:

"General question must be between a republican government in which the majority rule the minority, and a government in which a lesser number or the least number rule the majority.

"Those who framed and ratified the Constitution believed that as power was less likely to be abused by majorities in representative Gov^{t}. inferred also, that by dividing the powers of Govt. and thereby enlarging the practicable sphere of government, unjust majorities would be formed with still more difficulty, and be therefore the less to be dreaded, and whatever may have been the just complaints of unequal laws and sectional partialities under the majority Govt. of the U. S. it may be confidently observed that the abuses have been less frequent and less palpable than those which disfigured the administrations of the State Govts. While all the effective powers of sovereignty were separately exercised by them ... It has been said that Govt. is an evil. It would be more proper to say that the necessity of any Govt is a misfortune. This necessity however exists; and the problem to be solved is, not what form of Govt. is perfect, but which of the forms is least imperfect; and here the general question must be between a republican Governt in which the majority rule the minority, and a Gov^{t} in which a lesser number or the least number rule the majority.

The Framers agree that popular government is the most imperfect. Their corrective answer is the body of fundamental principles in our Constitution. Majority Rule is one of the first principles. They achieve it through a representative republic.

I separate this section for emphasis.

Our Fundamental Principle: All Principles in Our Constitution are Fundamental:

> *"If the republican form is, as all of us agree, to be preferred, the final question must be, what is the structure of it that will best guard against precipitate counsels and factious combinations for unjust purposes, without a sacrifice of the fundamental principle of Republicanism.*

The Framers answer this question with our constitutional structure of our three branches of government that share power. One reason for their decision is to protect the people from self-interests gained through abuse of power.

> "Those who denounce majority Govts. altogether because they may have an interest in abusing their power, denounce at the same time all Republican Gov^{t} and must maintain that minority governments would feel less of the bias of interest or the seductions of power."[247]

Madison speaks for the majority's agreement that majority rule and the republican form of government is best. Our following question is, what is a minority government? Monarchy, oligarchy, aristocracy, despotism are all minorities. Is democracy a minority government? Democracy is a form that may devolve into one of the minorities, such as autocracy, so it is one of the lesser choices in its pure or uncombined form. For these reasons, our Framers developed our republican form. Our question today is, what structural problems do we see in our form of republican government? Let us repair our bulwark against the corruptions of human error, pride, prejudice, and evil designs rather than attempt to undermine our form through subtle manipulations of ideas and attempts to seduce by passionate appeals. Since democracy fails the test of least imperfect form of government and it provides no security or stability for any extended period, the Framers move past it to develop the least imperfect form, *their* American Republic. I say "*their*" because *ours* is progressively more imperfect.

Section 2: Sources of Powers

If some believe the federal and the national are synonymous, I break out the composition of the national and federal systems as Madison explains them in the table, *Sources of constitutional authority and powers*, see Appendix B: Table of Government Powers.

> "The proposed constitution, therefore, even when tested by the rules laid down by its antagonists, is, in strictness, neither a national nor a federal constitution; but a composition of both."[248]

Madison says our "*mixed*" Constitution extends across the whole of our Republic. It is unique to America and is a composition of national and federal characteristics. Madison hails America as a "*representative republic*".[249]

We have discussed majority will as the principle he addresses, but our indirect representation, our three-branch government with a bicameral legislature are also fundamentals. A republic becomes our Republic because our form of government is a new creation.

Madison:

> "In framing a government, which is to be administered by men over men, the great difficulty lies in this: you must first enable the government to control the governed; and in the next place oblige it to control itself. A dependence on the people is, no doubt, the primary control on the government; but experience has taught mankind the necessity of auxiliary precautions."[250]

Madison delivers fair warning in the above quote that all the branches of government are under the scrutiny of the people and, should our structures for protection fail, the people are to reinforce it. We have human nature to guard against and experience to guide us to maintain and improve these "*auxiliary precautions*".

Section 3: Separation of Powers

Separation of Powers:	Shared Term	Impeachment[251]
1. Executive	X	anytime during tenure for *failure of good behavio*r
2. House of Representatives	X	ditto
3. Senate	X	ditto
4. Judiciary	X	ditto

Madison on the republican form of government says this:

> "*Majority interests* and *minority interests* must receive attention without the minority being oppressed."[252]

Our republican principles *in toto* serve to defend the people from representative changes to our form of government and from any other source, even ideological encroachment. Our most serious breach is the laxity of Congress to attend to republican principles as they govern. All political ideologies carry a form of government in them and if those forms do not derive from republican principles, they collide with them and create confusion that may lead to a violation of oaths to protect our republican constitutional form. Our question is, did the people comprehend this historic fact when they accepted the Democratic Party? I focus on the nature and principles of democracy as it collides with our republican nature and principles of government. Therefore, all pretensions are discoverable by determining whether any principle is hostile to the United States Constitution and, as such, it is a declaration of intellectual war against its people and their republican form of government that our Constitution commands. I am led to the conclusion that all laws of the land must conform to these principles as a strand in the constitutional web of law and, if not, should be declared null and void for they are a breach with our Constitution.[253] I am chary of our common law that seems to evade constitutional governance due to ideological persuasions that influence interpretation. Our question is, can the common law circumvent Constitutional law? I respect our leaders and I pray for them, as did Jefferson. However, we humans are susceptible to error and it takes the majority to correct the minority. Yet, the majority must possess the tool kit of knowledge to do so. We cannot rely upon the history of law alone for it is too narrow to encompass the sphere and expanse of our republican principles, especially if the Bench considers them irrelevant in their intent, which they deem their right to determine. Since James Wilson found so many errors in Blackstone and our system incorporates English common law into our system, then our question is, does English common law skew our constitutional principles? Like an administrator, a judge must be a generalist to grasp the depth of meaning that lies within the verbiage of our Constitution. While our Founders were lawyers, for the most part, they also were philosophers and historians. The Framers' drew moral standards from the Christian philosophy, which was a further safeguard against human nature. I must emphasize that Christian sects were and are plentiful. Our Framers understood this diversity and Jefferson counted its diversity as another guard against government and minority suppression that required tolerance. While faith is a personal decision, citizens have a history lesson about humanity's failure to learn that moral corruption results in political corruption that ends in societal destruction. I believe knowledge of law alone is like sex among relatives, it corrupts the gene pool. My purpose herein is to give all patriots reason for reflection, thoughts for constitutional action, and hope for union in understanding and applying these principles to ourselves and to one another, if we are to evaluate the constancy of our constitutional obligations to guard them against corruption by whatever means or designs.

Section 4: Checks and Balances

I recall John Adams's overview of the state of government in 1776 in which he says the following regarding progress and the checks and balances of republican governments:

> "The arts and sciences, in general, during the three or four last centuries, have had a regular course of progressive improvement. ... The checks and balances of republican governments have been in some degree adopted by the courts of princes. By the erection of various tribunals, to register the laws, and exercise the judicial power—by indulging the petitions and remonstrances of subjects, until by habit they are regarded as rights—a control has been established over ministers of state, and the royal councils, which approaches, in some degree, to the spirit of republics. Property is generally secure, and personal liberty seldom invaded. The press has great influence, even where it is not expressly tolerated; and the public opinion must be respected by a minister, or his place becomes insecure. Commerce begins to thrive: and if religious toleration were established, and personal liberty a little more protected, by giving an absolute right to demand a public trial in a certain reasonable time—and the states invested with a few more privileges, or rather restored to some that have been taken away—these governments would be brought to as great a degree of perfection, they would approach as near to the character of governments of laws and not of men, as their nature will probably admit of. In so general a refinement, or more properly reformation of manners and improvement in knowledge, is it not unaccountable that the knowledge of the principles and construction of free governments, in which the happiness of life, and even the further progress of improvement in education and society, in knowledge and virtue, are so deeply interested, should have remained at a full stand for two or three thousand years? According to a story in Herodotus, the nature of monarchy, aristocracy, and democracy, and the advantages and inconveniences of each, were as well understood at the time of the neighing of the horse of Darius, as they are at this hour. A variety of mixtures of these simple species were conceived and attempted, with different success, by the Greeks and Romans. Representations, instead of collections, of the people—a total separation of the Executive from the legislative power, and of the judicial from both—and a balance in the legislature, by

> three independent, equal branches—are perhaps the three only discoveries in the constitution of a free government, since the institution of Lycurgus. Even these have been so unfortunate, that they have never spread: the first has been given up by all the nations, excepting one, who had once adopted it; and the other two, reduced to practice, if not invented, by the English nation, have never been imitated by any other except their own descendants in America. While it would be rash to say, that nothing further can be done to bring a free government, in all its parts, still nearer to perfection—the representations of the people are most obviously susceptible of improvement. *The end to be aimed at, in the formation of a representative assembly, seems to be the sense of the people, the public voice: the perfection of the portrait consists in its likeness.* Numbers, or property, or both, should be the rule; and the proportions of electors and members an affair of calculation. The duration should not be so long that the deputy should have time to forget the opinions of his constituents. Corruption in elections is the great enemy of freedom. Among the provisions to prevent it, more frequent elections, and a more general privilege of voting, are not all that might be devised. Dividing the districts, diminishing the distance of travel, and confining the choice to residents, would be great advances towards the annihilation of corruption."[254]

Adams gives us a prime reason why our republican form of representation is distinct from a democratic representation. He uses the phrase, "*Representations*", instead of, "*collections of the people*". I find in this quote words that answer our modern dilemma of how to deal with a government that turns from our republican principles, whether one or all, and how to treat any citizen who undermines them in any manner whatsoever. The answer is to recall them from office as soon as possible. As for the individual or group that threatens our form of government, they commit treason against the people, if treason still maintains its place as a viable weapon in the arsenal of freedom. Freedom of speech must prevail, but if we do not know that our republican form of government is not a democracy, how can we voice a defense against speeches that propose to undermine or fundamentally change it by some unrepublican policy or ideology? Would Madison commend the European countries in their approach to our republican spirit if democracy were what he intended? When one uses words manipulated for a purpose, we must understand the purpose to understand the twist. One can best engineer subterfuge by commandeering his opponent's words and ideas to his own cause. We the people must beware of maneuvers to do this. Some of the books I recommend do inform us of these schemes. These weapons of mass mind manipulation pierce the mind, heart, and soul of a united nation to make islands of discontent. We each must be vigilant against subtle influences that open our nation to invasion whether by ideas or actions from within or without, which undermine our ratified constitutional principles.

I formulate a question for your consideration, which is, does the Jackson Democracy correlate with the Framers' *intent* and with the *spirit* of our republican Constitution? When I compare Jacksonian Democracy with the Framers' idea of democracy, I have to answer in the negative.

Section 5: Doctrines of Europe

> "The doctrines of Europe were, that men in numerous associations cannot be restrained within the limits of order and justice, but by forces physical and moral, wielded over them by authorities independent of their will."[255]

Why do we desire democracy? Do we believe we cannot govern ourselves? Do we long for government to lord it over us as potentates their followers? Is this not another insight to the Framers' meaning of a barrier between man and established authority? The Greeks modeled constitutions after four types, which are: democracy, oligarchy, aristocracy, and monarchy. They describe a democratic constitution as "*one in which offices are distributed by lot....*"[256] *Demos* means *the people*, but its practical meaning includes direct representation as the Framers understood it, while Jefferson considers one of our two anchors to be indirect representation.[257]

Section 6: Conclusion

I conducted a survey of the Convention Debate's Notes. What I uncovered suggests that democracy unmixed is not part of the spirit of our Constitution, but *pure* democracy introduces evils that the Framers testify the spirit of our Constitution remedies. Yet, a blend of democratical ideas with other forms mitigates the evils of democracy in its *pure* form, thus we have our Constitution that creates our republican form of government, which blends the other forms as well.[258]

My labors bring me to understand that declaring our form of government a democracy loses the meaning for the Framers' structure of our form of government. It invites the idea that a democracy can embrace the safeguards of our Republic without the dangers that open the doors of confusion that exist in our society today. We cannot mix our republican principles with democracy and expect to live by the nature and principles of our Constitution.

We must revisit Montesquieu's distinctions and remember that each form of government has its nature and its principle. Our economic Republic is vastly different from an economic democracy. Our mixed form of government tames the three forms of government known in eighteenth century, which are democracy, monarchy, and aristocracy with each degenerating into an evil form. Separately, democracy and republicanism are antagonistic because democracy lacks the balance that our Constitution provides. Maybe that is the ploy. We invite a collision of principles that open to parties a smorgasbord of ideas foreign to our republican principles—that, in fact, our republican principles bar constitutionally from implementation. Is this not subterfuge? Is it intentional or unintentional?

When one tenders democratic ideas under the misperception that they are authentic because they are *popular*, then we invite anarchy. We can only live by one set of principles because a government's form dictates its nature and principle. Our republican form of government falsifies the nature and principles of unrepublican principles. We have the voices of the past to testify to this truth. We have the words of the past to guide our ideas of today to rectify our misdirection.

CHAPTER 11:

Republican Form Today

Section 1: The Character of Our Constitution

> "Our political system is admitted a new Creation—a real nondescript. Its character therefore must be sought in itself; not in precedents, because there are none; not in writers whose comments are guided by precedents ...[259]

The voices of our past remind us that the nature of our Republic is its original structure. In it rests our assurances against all forms of man's contrivances to usurp our unalienable rights and to twist positive law into the bonds of slavery. If we detect weaknesses, we can amend it rather than condemn it.

Section 2: Compact Should Be Substantially Maintained

> "The more intimate the nature of such an union may be, the greater interest have the members in the political institutions of each other; and the greater right to insist, that the forms of government under which the compact was entered into, should be *substantially* maintained."[260]

We add that we must defend the system against modern democracy and especially globalization that desires to equalize all persons and peoples. Such a state must be republican, monarchical, or despotic, as Napoleon. Our Framers eliminated two of these, and then laid waste to democracy as a standalone government. We have only one viable solution and that is the American experiment. Our Republic stands the test of time. Our two foes are the corruption of our representatives and the disinterest of our citizens. We have a course of action if we have the character to self-govern. We must take our Framers' advice and modify our Republic, if necessary. However, a more direct form of action is less desired than an exercise of constitutional sovereign power. We can use recall, referendums, and impeachment to stabilize our government in an emergency when a politician refuses to resign by popular demand. Should we not do so based on violation of our republican principles rather than by angry reaction whenever we disagree? Our control over those who labor to destroy our ratified government of the people, for the people, and by the people, is our law, by which we ensure our government remains "*substantially*" the same. Such a popular uprising is unconstitutional as a method to change our government. We best manage by our interest in our representatives' activities. Since Jefferson warned against standing armies and our Framers made the Executive dependent upon Congress, should we the people intervene now to place in Congress all authority to commit our armed forces to any kind of military action? We must reexamine The War Powers Act of 1973 (Public Law 93-148) since Presidents have ignored its authority. In our history Major General Smedley Darlington Butler, USMC, functioned as liaison for corporate purposes on three continents, so we should be, in my opinion, alerted. The old head, *interests of the United States,* is too broad for the people to grasp why our government commits our armed forces to invade a country in support of one side against another. I find no support in the Framers' writings to support such an engagement or an aggressive action such as preemptive strikes. Again, the idea of amoralism creeps into our consciousness. If our enemy does not directly attack us either in principle or in action, then should we engage in military action? If free speech can persuade passionate action, then we must be passionate about our principles in order to speak against those who are against our Republic. If we are a country of law, then our principles must be our bulwark against undeclared war. However, formal declaration is not the strategy of modern enemies, so we must understand our republican principles in order to combat aggressors within and without our borders. We find complications in globalism and transborder capitalism when other nations call upon the United States for defense. Our cause is not to fight all wars on request, but to defend ourselves and to be a refuge for liberty. Our republican principle is to treat with other nations. We cannot export democracy as a ruse to equalize the peoples of the world. Either the United Nations is the place for appeal or it is not. The nations must decide what they want. Factions fracture and no one knows the will of the majority. If disgruntled minorities can rise up and involve the U.S. in conflict by declaring themselves democratic rebels, then the world is in chaos. The cost of such wars in human and material resources is unsustainable. Our question is, who is on whose side and what is their goal?

Section 3: Madison's New Creation

Madison says the following as his introduction to his explanation:

> "Our political system is admittedly a new Creation—a real nondescript. Its character therefore must be sought in itself; not in precedents, because there are none; not in writers whose comments are guided by precedents ...[261]

Madison's argument against precedents is as valid today as it was in his day, but it has different premises. Today, we still have the Framers' fears of innovations and human nature. We have questionable precedents in law today because of our two-party system and because judges may use unconstitutional ideologies that set precedents for new interpretations. An example is the rulings around the New Deal. If our confusion about democracy is so blatantly real, then how do we know if our laws are really in *pursuance* of our Constitution? Judges biased by political motivations interpret law by those interests or ideologies. We witnessed a heated election involving two State Supreme Court Justices in Madison, WI with differing political stands. The public was highly interested in which would win, and the public was divided along party lines. Shall we the people sheepishly accept such undermining of our form of government that in turn undermines our ability to maintain *"substantially"* our republican government? Democracy's principle and character affects our ideas and character as a nation, if Montesquieu and our history are accurate. We must see our reality in order to contribute to healing our nation's crisis by ensuring that republican principles operate throughout it without obfuscation from unrepublican ideas. The argument from comparative political science for a two-party system states that only in single party countries is found "genuine political conflict". In a democracy , some believe, such conflict is necessary. However, our Constitution provides for freedom of speech, which is truly embedded as a fundamental principle that anyone can speak their mind and heart-felt opinion without fear of imprisonment. The public square is the republican forum for republican debate as the Federalist Papers and the Anti-federalist Papers printed and circulated publicly demonstrated that the public possesses the ability to digest and respond rationally and passionately to debate issues.

Section 4: Some Considerations on Substantially Maintained

A. Intermixture:

Madison uses the word *Intermixture*[262] that leads me to define it. Madison explains his position.

> "This conclusion becomes irresistible, when it is recollected, that the constitution cannot be supposed to have placed either any power legislative in its nature, entirely among Executive powers, or any power Executive in its nature, entirely among legislative powers, without charging the constitution, with that kind of intermixture and consolidation of different powers, which would violate a fundamental principle in the organization of free governments. If it were not unnecessary to enlarge on this topic here, it could be shown, that the constitution was originally vindicated, and has been constantly expounded, with a disavowal of any such intermixture."[263]

I locate the word *intermixture* and find that its definition is:

1. "A mass formed by mingling bodies.
2. Something additional mingled in a mass."[264]
3. Black's conjoins intermixture with goods. It defines an intermixture of goods with the phrase confusion of goods, which means "*the mixture of things of the same nature but belonging to different owners so that the identification of the things is no longer possible*".

If our national legislature owns the making of law, then our Executive should not have power to make law. Is Madison's usage, in context, in agreement with our Constitution and our republican form of government? *Black's* definition goes on to allow that if there is common consent, then both are owners in common. Nevertheless, if one willfully acts alone, then the lone actor loses all rights and the recipient gains all rights. I offered a quote earlier that is apropos here, so, I am taking liberties with *Black's* definition, but my intent is to demonstrate that if such liberties are in law, then they become precedent. We seem to accommodate it, but the reality is this procedure admits extension and abuse of power. So, why do we have such laxity in constitutional compliance? The original intent is greater than this innovation. Our question is, have we the people given constitutionally explicit consent or passive submission without understanding the effect of this practice?

I see the word *entirely* refers to the separation of Executive and legislative powers, such as in Article II, Section 2, "*with the advice and consent of the Senate, shall appoint Ambassadors*", et al. If so, then it applies to the legislature as sole authority for the budget, so, sharing budgetary responsibility is intermixing. Does not this violate the rule of clear and defined responsibility? Madison in his Amendments speech says,

> "The powers delegated by this constitution are appropriated to the departments to which they are respectively distributed: so that the legislative department shall never exercise the powers vested in the Executive or judicial; not the Executive exercise the powers in the legislative or judicial; not the judicial exercise the powers vested in the legislative or Executive departments."[265]

If we view such legislative action in these terms, does it violate Congressional budget responsibility? Do we permit our legislature to intermix branch responsibilities if our Constitution intends to block it? If it does, then it violates our republican principle of separation of powers. My point is that we do have precedents today. As Jefferson warns us, the government encroaches upon the people's security and puts it at risk for deficits that threaten our common security and tranquility at all levels, personally, nationally, and federally. Precedents of past Presidents also give too much power to the Executive, which the Framers feared could lead to a monarchy or oligarchy or despotism. Does the current practice of czarism suggest this power extension is empowered by budgetary independence? Does Congress impart to the Executive such regulatory authority as administrative law in spite of intermixture restriction? The Constitution does assign to Congress the "*payment of Debts*" and the "*general welfare of the United States*" and the power "*to borrow Money on the credit of the United States*". Does this violate the rule that with responsibility must go the power to manage it? Of course, we do transfer power, which is unconstitutional. Congress constitutionally is responsible for all monies incoming and outgoing. In this sense, Congress is responsible to ensure the people's financial, domestic, and national welfare. Our question is, how does the Fed depend upon Congressional legislation for its existence and operation? While the people clamor for a *balanced* budget, Congress dodges the responsibility and its *intermixing* of functions contributes to an unbalanced budget, not to mention its political rhetoric and evasion. If we the people hope to re-establish our Constitution, to reclaim our rights by it and to its provisions, and to honor its principles, should not we the people question precedents based on this insidious erosion. Should we ignore vigilance over such behavior? Hear Madison again,

> "That the people have an indubitable, unalienable, and indefeasible right to reform or change their government, whenever it be found adverse or inadequate to the purposes of its institution."[266]

B. Purposes of Government:
Madison answers,

> "That government is instituted, and ought to be exercised for the benefit of the people; which consists in the enjoyment of life, liberty, with the right of acquiring and using property, and generally of pursuing and obtaining happiness and safety."[267]

C. Article VI:

> "This Constitution, and the Laws of the United States which shall be made in Pursuance thereof; and all Treaties made, or which shall be made, under the Authority of the United States, shall be the supreme Law of the Land; and the Judges in every State shall be bound thereby, any Thing in the Constitution or Laws of any State to the contrary notwithstanding."

The phrase "*in pursuance thereof*" should alert us to the fact that all law must be constitutionally appropriate. I understand this article to make the people's scrutiny of all government decisions another of our highest citizen duties. As Congress rubber-stamps the Executive's budget, it relinquishes its oversight responsibility by legislative ruling that seems incompatible with intermixture. However, its legislative act seems to be a breach of faith with our republican principles. An appropriations bill, by its delineation of all expenditures and its support for the need, negates Congress's reliance upon the Executive's notification to Congress, which is the only legal obligation the Executive, by the Framers' intent, owes to Congress. Congress can never obtain a budget with legislative enforcement as long as the Executive possesses spend-at-will freedom that it uses to ignore *limited* government. Does not Madison state that the Constitution intends that the legislature be *the* lawgiver? He says,

> "The essence of the legislative authority, is to enact laws; or in other words, to prescribe rules for the regulation of the society. While the execution of the laws and the employment of the common strength, either for this purpose, or for the common defense, seem to comprise *all* the functions of the Executive magistrate."[268]

All legislative law must conform to all of our applicable republican principles. If the above does *comprise all the functions of the Executive magistrate* and Madison's response in Helvidius 1 demonstrates effectively the intent of the Framers, then it argues that Executive function is the execution of legislative law and it is not intermixable with legislative functions. When we apply the concept of original intent, which the USSC says is impossible, and hedging their claim that no one person speaks for all the Framers, we find that the intention of the Framers is possible to grasp. What is difficult to grasp is the current state of Congress's inability to grasp the constitutional republican principles that balance the powers of our Republic. Is this by intent, ignorance, or deceit? In any case, the representative is the one responsible to the people by re-election, recall, censure, or impeachment based on either fiduciary compliance or negligence, and that according to our republican principles. These principles are objective, comprehendible, and comprehensive.

Our government tampers with the meaning of our Constitution while expanding all branches, their functions and budget while neglecting the most obvious of its purposes, viz., they are to run the government for the benefit of national, i.e., the states and its citizens' common interests in order to harmonize the *United* States without abridging the liberties of the people. Can the average citizen understand our republican principles? I believe they can. Our question is, by understanding will they be able to see through pressed interpretations that really do not correspond to intent? All branches of government are subject to the scrutiny of public opinion, so no branch is above the sovereignty of the people. The USSC seems to believe that the *supreme* in its designation over law means it is supreme over the people and can dictate what they must accept, while their activism rescinds our Constitution and breeches our tranquility, not to mention our unalienable rights, at least in some cases. If the USSC waits for someone to make a matter a case for their wise interpretation, then we must make our case so sound that their intellectualizations and politicalizations are so obvious that the people retain their final arbiter rights as sovereign rulers. The Constitution of our Founders is clear, but it is subject to "*ingeniously devised*" and "*innovating constructions*", Madison says. The voices of our past give us this warning. If the Constitution is the law of the land, then the republican principles at stake are too important to our life, liberty, and our pursuit of happiness.

D. Stare Decisis et non Quieta Movere

If *stare decisis et non quieta movere* stands, then the court reduces the people's sovereignty to submission. The above phrase means,

> "Literally, to stand by previous decisions and not to disturb settled matters. To adhere to precedents, and not to depart from established principles."[269]

Our question is, which principles, constitutional or precedential? We know the USSC has reversed course with the change of times, which in most cases was the republican thing to do. What about those rulings that remain?

E. Article 1, Section 1 of our Constitution:

> "All legislative Powers herein granted shall be vested in a Congress of the United States, which shall consist of a Senate and House of Representatives."[270]

What does *all* mean? What does it *modify*? What does *vested* mean and to what does it apply? If English is plain, then the legislature cannot delegate this function even by law. It is by being a fundamental republican principle, i.e., it is governed by our Constitution, it is trumped by a superior principle of our Constitution. Hence, all such legislation is *null and void*, which means all such laws are invalid; they are not the law of the land. No branch of our government can act as a tyrant over the people. Therefore, we the people can and should change the system and the law to agree with our Constitutional Republic's nature and principles. We will have to argue the question when our minds shed unrepublican ideas and grasp those that are *strictly* republican.

F. Executive Orders and Appropriation:

Black's defines *appropriation* as a legislative act that sets aside monies for a public purpose.[271] If so, then Congress is responsible for the contents of Appropriation Bills. Then how does it oversee the Executive spending that occurs through Executive Orders? How does the legislature hold the Executive responsible to the holders of the public's purse strings in the interest of their common good? Obviously, the intent of a policy against *intermixing* functions serves to separate powers and to give to Congress budgetary controls in harmony with levying taxes. If so, we thus unveil another area that distances the citizenry from governmental control. I see an application to Madison's quote earlier used, which is this:

> "To say then that the power of making treaties, which are confessedly laws, belongs naturally to the department which is to execute law, is to say, that the Executive department naturally includes a legislative power. In theory, this is an absurdity—in practice a tyranny."[272]

Human nature strives for its self-interests, which we see served by compromise and political nest building. However, lazy legislation seems to be a common virus among our *elected* representatives in today's reality. Executive Orders should pertain only to the extent of constitutionally granted functions to the Executive power, i.e., its own departments and not be extended to the public. When the Constitution vests the legislature with an undistributable power of making laws and only permits a specific bifurcation when making treaties, etc., Congress cannot give to the Executive any legislative power without amendment from the States to do so.[273]

It is not within the power of the Judiciary to overrule the Constitution. Recently, the Judiciary intervened and commanded the Executive to authorize leases for drilling oil in the Gulf. I think this type of proactive advisory behavior is necessary, especially when it is obvious that our economy is in need of jobs and our national security is in jeopardy, and we lease drilling permits to non-national interests. To my mind, this is a no brainer because our republican principles warrant this action without case law invocation as an intervention to protect the people's common good and national security. I am not sure of the Bench's reasons for its actions, but I applaud it. If the executive action is unconstitutional and it ignores the Bench, then the States should bring a case to the USSC. Is it necessary for the Legislature to pass a law or the Bench to adjudicate? If the Constitution addresses the issue in principle, why not just clarify the meaning. Madison attacks heresy with much enthusiastic encouragement from President Jefferson. I recall Jefferson's urgent plea to Madison in the former's letter of July 7, 1793. The following letter to Justice William Johnson in 1823 notes that ...

> "Laws are made for men of ordinary understanding, and should, therefore, be constructed by the ordinary rules of common sense ... I believe the States can best govern our home concerns, and the General Government our foreign ones. I wish, therefore, to see maintained that wholesome distribution of powers established by the constitution for the limitation of both; and never to sell all offices transferred to Washington, where, further withdrawn from the eyes of the people, they may more secretly be bought and sold as at market."[274]

The Bench says, *there must be an ultimate arbiter somewhere.* True, there must be. Of course, they mean the Bench. The ultimate arbiter is the people of the Union, assembled by their deputies in the Legislature, in convention, at the call of Congress, or of two-thirds of the states. Let them decide to which they mean to give an authority claimed by two of their organs, especially when the decision is biased, politically motivated, or in any other way unrepublican.

G. Seriatim Opinions:

Jefferson proclaims that seriatim opinions,

> "Besides ascertaining the fact of his opinion, which the public have a right to know, in order to judge whether it is impeachable or not, it would show whether the opinions were unanimous or not, and thus settle more exactly the weight of their authority ...
>
> "But, our general objects are the same, to preserve the republican form and principles of our constitution and cleave to the salutary distribution of powers which that has established.

> These are the two sheet anchors of our Union. If driven from either, we shall be in danger of foundering. To my prayers for its safety and perpetuity, I add those for the continuation of your health, happiness, and usefulness to your county."[275]

H. The two sheet anchors of our Union:

   a. preserve the republican form and principles of our constitution and

   b. cleave to the salutary distribution of powers

Can we justify intermixing responsibilities against constitutional separation of powers where legislative power is constitutionally limited to Congress?[276]

Section 5: Our Destiny

What mode of communication best enables the people to use our republican principles? I provide a table of some of the republican principles to help answer this question. In this book, lie most, if not all, of these principles. If we have twisted democracy into our republican form of government, what else have we done to confound ourselves, or worse, to permit others to obstruct our duty as citizens to be the final arbiters of our justice, our freedom, and our conscience? Do not our leaders rely on the parties? What do parties offer us? They set an agenda. They give us a platform of promises. After we vote, they give us the shuffle, by mixing their donor constituency with the will of the majority. Is it a problem that we do not set the agenda? Should we set it? Are parties not an obstruction between the people and the candidates? If republican principles are our rules of government, should we orchestrate our issues to conform to the principles of our form of government? Since these questions challenge the status quo, we ask do they make sense in a republican government.

What is wrong with the current picture? Party platforms emphasize only certain causes or current interests and these become the sole subject of the campaign. I believe the remedy is to ensure that all of our republican principles are the subject of our candidates and the emphasis may be a response to a particular situation. The best remedy encapsulates all republican principles to the degree necessary for all to be congruent. For instance, when the USSC invites corporations to compete with the voice of the people, how is its ruling congruent with the sovereignty of the people? If it permits those with a stake in profits, it establishes a faction at odds with the common good. If a corporation lobbies for its own agenda, it narrows the whole of our federal and state system. Is this at odds with our republican principles? In this case, a corporate Executive has, at the least, two votes and an abundance of money that serve a special interest that hires lobbyists who have direct contacts in government. How does this tie into the sovereignty of the people? How does it relate to fair wages?

The federal is to coordinate state affairs in order to codify and to enforce the laws without prejudice for or against any state. A corporation has a *vested* interest in yielding a profit for its investors, says the USSC. That is fine, but we saw in Chapter 5, Section 3.a. that corporations with an eye toward profit become greedy. If our Constitution protects property, should it be more the citizen's property rather than the right of the business to take property? Our compact with the government is for the people, of the people, and by the people that we establish constitutional government, says Warren, with whom our republican principles agree. Does our Constitution elevate anything above the people? A commercial republic operates for the people overall. A commercial republic must use competition wisely to prevent it from competing with our common good, which we see manifested through greed and international and national rape. If the republican form of government is the best, then it must be extendible to any other nation. We have an interest in convincing our neighbors that a republican government protects them better than any other form of government. Our behavior is our proof of our virtue in honoring our principles. Corporations have neither an intrinsic nor an external motive to comply with our form of government as globalized or internationalized entities that exist for profit only. Certainly, this applies to foreign nations. How are their interests compatible with our tranquility or security or economic interests when profit is their sole motivator? Jobs are important, but they must serve the purpose of government in our nation, i.e., to constitutionally protect our life, liberty, and pursuit of happiness. Therefore, corporations that unite to influence our leaders to address their partnered self-interests rather than the common well-being of the United States are at constitutional odds with the people. Can anyone argue that this has not occurred in the past? If you think you can, then I refer you to the history of Major General Smedley Darlington Butler, USMC, whom I introduced in Section 2. His exploits did serve our government to protect corporate America. Does not our Constitution address individual rights rather than foreign nations, except in treaty? The Executive makes treaties with nations in harmony with Congress for the common good of peace and domestic tranquility. If corporations can act out of an interest in profit with other nations or their businesses, is our Executive and Congress out of the loop with commercial agreements, which one might see as treaties? Can we get Congress back in the loop with the Executive to control transborder impacts upon the public? Such agreements are at least transborder partnerships not unlike interstate commerce, which the federal system coordinates. Under the present system, how many republican principles do we disregard? In addition, we ask, how does our government control these outside players? It cannot any more than it can control rogue governments. How effective are embargoes? If not these, then how can we manage unknown private multination corporate agreements that take away American jobs and taxpayer funds? Please, do not invoke the taxation issue here. It may be a problem, but it is not the cause for corporations to exploit the resources of other nations. Another problem is that it invites the United Nations (UN) to arbitrate and unify international law. The United States becomes a subsidiary of the UN. Our laws honor other national laws, as is the mode since philosophers wrote the laws of Nature and Nations.[277]

If we are bewildered about managing our domestic affairs, how can we manage this intermix of our representatives and big money players and foreign interests not governed by our system of government and often in opposition to both our form of government and our domestic tranquility? Are not corporations by nature and law artificial persons and not natural born citizens? Most often, the USSC waits for a case in law to inform the Executive that it violates its oath of office to defend our borders when illegal immigrants, especially drug lords, swarm our land. If our government cannot or more believably will not defend us, then why should we succumb to this tyranny by branch inaction, under action, and at times over reaction? Our republican principles inform us of the appropriate action. What part of *self-*government does the federal system not get? How difficult is the word *limited* to get? Our government extends and contracts its tentacles inappropriately, which seems to be in unconstitutional ways seen through the spectacles of our republican principles.

Are the people at the helm of their destiny? In order to direct our leaders we must be in control of agenda setting. The future belongs to the people only when the people own the present and the political process. In order to accomplish this, should we relegate the two-party system to the museum of antiquity? The lesson learned is that the only people who can protect our unalienable rights are those who govern the system. The question is whether these basic freedoms are enough to protect our lives, sustain our liberty, and enable our pursuit of happiness. Do they motivate us to protect them? Do we recall the voices that advise us that a parchment cannot alone protect us? The people must remain sovereign through voter participation.

When we give our monies to a party, the party leadership wins. If we were to select a candidate and contribute to his or her campaign directly, we the people control that candidate's destiny. If he or she fails to follow pledges, we immediately cut off our contributions and we begin to lobby for a recall. We can best manage our local governments through suffrage more directly. We eliminate his or her dependence upon and allegiance to a party rather than to the people. We ensure that our agenda is their focus. We also curtail the power of a national committee and negate its intermediary status that makes its interests prior to the people's interests. The reality is our system encourages power brokers and special interests in spite of our Constitution's declaration that the government is of, by, and for the people. From what corner does this influence come?

The only core beliefs that we must all share as participants in republican government are the principles of our Republic. If this resolution is to work, we must examine the system of government our Founding Fathers established to understand how they wove it to guard us against governments' and human nature's revealed weaknesses to reinforce its strengths. Did not Madison answer the Anti-Federalists by answering their concerns in his *Federalist* Papers? During the development of the U.S. Constitution, he took notes on the debates. History accepts his notes as accurate and official. How could they not be a resource for interpretation? Even though Madison adamantly insisted that the Constitution itself was the source of self-explanation, can we rely upon interpretations to be "*in pursuance*" of our Constitution. He knew what the convention meant, but we have lost touch with their beliefs, knowledge, and experiences. In this latter wisdom, we possess the experience of modern interpretation and its innovations. Nevertheless, we possess the experience that the Framers knew, that man is a confounded creature who confounds the simplest of ideas.

I think Madison is a resource. Man is the cause of the Constitution's weakness. Politics is the means of encroachment. The national crisis with Great Britain offset individual interest by the urgency of self-preservation. What is our national urgency today? Is it not the threat of using unconstitutional principles to overthrow the republican principles of our Constitution? Does that not endanger us? As immigrants flow into America, should we not accept them as knowledgeable citizens by educating them about our republican principles? How can we not see that antirepublican doctrine can ever be consistent with republican principles? The very collision of principles declares war against the people who have elected representatives to protect our Constitution. Would it not be a breach of their oath of office for any party or person in government to break faith with our republican principles?

The Framers quoted many ancient writers and philosophers of their time. They also complained of some whose use of rhetoric seemed to ignore the Greek warnings against rhetoric. Plato argues that rhetoric misleads the people in order to persuade them to an opinion that lacks justice.[278] A joke about an international horse race is an example of rhetoric at work. The United States and Russia agree to compete. The U.S. wins. The USSR newspaper headline reads, "USSR places second; U.S. comes in next to last." Facts are one thing; truth is everything.

A present example of such a usage is common in the legislative branches. The greater the rhetoric representatives use to present their case, the further they lead the people from rule by debate and law to rule by unrepublican principles. Rhetoric distorts both fact and truth, which leads to the need for clarification by our Judiciary. When we understand the use of passion to persuade, then we may understand how manipulation overrides the citizens' self-interest. Is there a parallel when the Bench decides the meaning of a law? Should Congress pass laws clearly related to our republican principles? The case is the argument. An argument based on rhetoric combines propositions to make a conclusion that sounds logical, but it is deceptive. Does this technique sound similar to that of the kitsch? The major characteristic in argumentation is the character of those who offer the argument. In the current discussions over the economy, the obvious lack of information about our economic system relegates the citizen to the corridors, awaiting the great double doors to open, so the decision-makers can inform the people of their decision while ignoring their arguments for their decision.

How does modern capitalism effect our destiny? Is our capitalist system in harmony with republican principles? Our system cannot support unrepublican principles and maintain the sovereignty of the people. Therefore, we have a dilemma. How do we manage our economy without destroying our form of government? Montesquieu provides our answer and his answer is inherent in our republican principles. (See Chapter 1, Section 5 on commercial democracy and compare it to Chapter 11.) However, the USSC seems to have negated republican principles while international capitalism exploits their breadth of separation from our constitutional principles. Is this the way that our Framers arranged things? They accepted capitalism, but their form bases itself upon republican principles of commerce. Do our republican principles stand the test of time? A clash between mercantile interests and propertied interests occurred as agrarian gave way to western expansion. In Europe, the clash between aristocrats and everybody else was the issue. Today, we experience expansion to foreign countries and we find some of the same events that our plains Indians suffered. How do we control corporations that operate from foreign shores that give it absolution from our form of government? How do we hold offshore financial institutions accountable? Should corporations like people pledge allegiance to a country rather than act as rogue entities with no ties to any government? Can citizens compete with such unbounded organizations?

Our Framers also believed future generations would have to apply the lessons of history to their own present situation. The U.S. Supreme Court interprets this wisdom as meaning that the U.S. Supreme Court by reading society can revoke its values and institute whatever wisdom the court deems as appropriate. The problem with this course of action is blatant. The U.S. Supreme Court's decision-making forces its opinions upon the majority because their rhetoric says that the Bench seeks the *common good* of the people. Do they deny *majority will* since they are unelected representatives? However, we the people carry the duty to decide what should be the *good* that we the people make *common* to all our citizens through our laws of the land. The U.S. Supreme Court should ensure that the lower courts interpret in context of our republican principles, and not by precedent, at least if precedent fails to guide law by our republican principles. If they do, then our laws of the land will become congruent with our republican principles. Therefore, the people must unite under some-thing greater than party allegiance or judicial decision-making. For our Founding Fathers, it was God. Deism is not the issue because the Declaration of Independence makes the *God of Nature* the source of its authority for our freedom and their God was of Judaeo-Christian heritage. Such a God is trustful, is powerful, is providential, and is personal. I do refute deism as their faith in my article, *Deism Examined*.[279] If we the people decide to render God as dead as most secularists desire, then we must comprehend that we give up the bedrock upon which our unalienable rights stand. When we make our decision, it shall be for our prosperity for many of us shall not live long enough to see the total outcome. If our Republic falls, it most likely will come through despotism set up by mob violence or incorporation into some form of world government. A major lesson of the Enlightenment was that people are free only when they are free to think. Our common law must base its sandy soil upon the solid rock of our republican principles. It is more obvious to me today that our society is so nonplused about our origins that our laws are made by Judiciary interpretation fortified by referenced precedents far from our natural rights.[280]

The Founding Fathers expressed the culmination of freedom to thinking of the philosophies as the sacred qualities of right of life, liberty, and the pursuit of happiness for all human beings as unalienable because the God of nature gives them to humanity. That is their unalienability. Without the God of Creation, we possess only positive law. Did not the Framers consider a republic to be *an empire of laws and not of men*?

If I have correctly distilled these ideas here, then the people have the duty and freedom to reorganize themselves. A republican citizen must be knowledgeable. We should acquire knowledge of our system of government through self-education until we clean up our misinformation mess, or is it disinformation? A successful republic must ensure that the people maintain their power by educating their children. If we live in such a society, truth is open for discussion. In a society where we present ideas rhetorically, that is politically, we cannot persuade, only obey. Contra Karl Raimund Popper, a scientific theorist, who made a great impact on science and knowledge, absolute Truth does exist. Popper does not treat absolute Truth that I can find, but he uses the nondescript phrase *profound truths*. However, he shares with Kant the idea that "we must not accept the command of an authority, however exalted, as the basis of ethics."[281] As Popper and all of science is limited to physics, he can only claim a relative application that metaphysics is "not expected of methodology". As science stalls in micro- and macro-physics at singularity, science is unable to claim for itself absolute authority over knowledge. Man's god of the gaps is not the God of nature as revealed in Judaeo-Christian history. In any case, now or later, we must accept Truth as beyond falsification. In Popper's open-society, skepticism may be the modus operandi that resists "*definitive truths*", but we cannot accept this as a philosophy for moral behavior. It may find in physics a case from probability, but that exists only when science finds physical examination exhausted and turns to theoretical physics, as is the case with modern physics.[282] Popper can reject inductive logic as it falls within the realm of falsifiability, but it is not sufficient for belief in the real world. Faith in black holes is another such example. How does one examine a black hole? So, Popper can neither disprove nor prove all physics, he cannot touch revelational Truth if he chooses to disbelieve it.[283] That black swans exist is now a scientific fact even though it was a practical fact long before science saw with its own eyes a black swan swimming.[284] Scientific skepticism did not prove their existence. Their observation of them did not prove their existence, but it only confirmed the witness' report. Revelation as Truth is Jesus in the world of facts, which some believe and some do not. Jesus presents us with a moral dilemma, which the Framers accepted as the best moral philosophy available to humanity. They understood that Jesus touched one's life that changes one's perspective. James Wilson's discussion of belief and knowledge demonstrates the importance it bears upon understanding constitutional law. Jesus did not speak rhetoric. His speech was life lived without deceit. In rhetoric, the people hear a view usually from some charismatic personality who relies upon slanting the evidence to make his story sound reasonable and his personality to make it acceptable. Should we not reconsider our system of faith that we use in our decision-making? Since we are interested in our common good, should we examine the status of our society and its underlying workings with and without virtue?

Politics is a method of influencing that often uses strategies that are contrary to our common good and our ability to think and to decide based on truth. The one ingredient that our secular idea of separation of church and state removes from the common good equation is the common good character of the citizen, since character development is a personal decision of any supposedly common good ideology. If so, then we have isolated another breach with our Framers' republican principles, which is we are at odds with the principle of virtue. So, we must decide what ideology presents itself as the *best* character building ideology. Do we side with our Framers or with some other form of thought? Is it supportive of republicanism? How does it contribute to our destiny?

A. Virtue, Human Nature, and Republicanism:

I see George Washington as a prime example of a virtuous person in our republic. He said this:[285]

> "Observe good faith and justice tow(ar)ds All Nations. Cultivate peace and harmony with all. Religion and morality enjoin this conduct; and can it be that good policy does not equally enjoin it? It will be worthy of a free, enlightened, and, at no distant period, a great Nation, to give to mankind the magnanimous and too novel example of a People always guided by an exalted justice and benevolence. Who can doubt that in the course of time and things the fruits of such a plan would richly repay any temporary advantages w(hi)ch might be lost by a steady adherence to it? Can it be, that Providence has not connected the permanent felicity of a Nation with its virtue? The experiment, at least, is recommended by every sentiment which ennobles human Nature. Alas! Is it rendered impossible by its vices? ...
>
> "While I reiterate the professions of my dependence upon Heaven as the source of all public and private blessings; I will observe that the general prevalence of piety, philanthropy, honesty, industry, and economy seems, in the ordinary course of human affairs, particularly necessary for advancing and conforming the happiness of our country. While all men within our territories are protected in worshipping the Deity according to the dictates of our consciences; it is rationally to be expected from them in return, that they will be emulous of evincing the sanctity of their professions by the innocence of their lives and the beneficence of their actions; for no man, who is profligate in his morals, or a bad member of the civil community, can possibly be a true Christian, or a credit to his own religious society.
>
> "I desire you to accept my acknowledgments for your laudable endeavors to render men sober, honest, and good Citizens, and the obedient subjects of a lawful government."[286]

In the above quote, George Washington explicitly states that he believes in God who acts in history for the benefit of men, society, and government when they possess the proper moral thought and conduct, unless they are not a "*true Christian*". He recommends to the people a hope based firmly in his belief. Our question is, have we followed his plan? This man of character who made history and whose reputation was without equal in his day understands the importance of moral-based behavior. He also comprehends that our nation needs a moral ground. Is he alone among the Framers in believing this? When we understand the connection between virtue and grace, it becomes clear to us that there is a link between character and government. Grace is God's favorable influence on the human mind that has the effect of virtue. When we associate secular and grace, we discern the likely meaning of separation of church and state. Church is always an organized and established religion that interferes with the liberty of individuals to worship God as their conscience reasons. The government is freed from established religion to operate for the common good rather than to support the established religion.

Mr. James Wilson compares monarchial honor to that of a republican government.

> "For the possession of this honour—vicious in its practice, and, even when right in its practice, vicious in its principle—a republican government will not, I presume, contend. But to that honour, whose connexion with virtue is indissoluble, a republican government produces the most unquestionable title. The principle of virtue is allowed to be heirs: if she possesses virtue, she also possesses honour. I admire the fine moral and political instruction, as well as the elegant architectural taste, exhibited by the justly framed structure, in which the temple of honour was accessible only through the temple of virtue."[287]

Washington as president is not *neutral* about religion, which is faith. James Wilson, a Supreme Court Justice, is not neutral about religion's benefits. Does the USSC justify its decision of *neutrality* based on faith or on a lack of faith; on established religion or religious practice? Either way, the question is whether the Bench is neutral. One can have no faith, no belief, no practice of worship. Delusion believes in something that does not exist. It is false, irrational belief whose origin lies in emotional needs that rejects proof.[288] Proof is of two kinds, faith and experiment. Faith is our companion all day long; experiment mostly in the laboratory, which must rely upon faith for its acceptance by those who cannot duplicate it. No matter how many scientists swear an experiment is duplicable, you must have faith that their word is, at least, factual. Science demonstrates Einstein's theory that light should bend around objects to be a fact, but science now suspects his theory of relativity.

In fact, singularity throws the whole of physics into doubt because it brings mathematics to a halt. I do not doubt that science can solve the problem. My point is that man is not all knowing, not infallible, and not without need of moral guidance. Our question is, what is the common good of our society—virtue or laxity of morals? The moral person relies upon religious faith; the scientist upon faith in method. What is their difference? The Framers labeled laxity of behavior as *libertine.* Which of these is the republican principle of behavior, virtue or libertine? Absolute freedom is dangerous at all times. The question is this, why does the Bench fail to find this meaning? If Washington presents the Christian philosophy as contributing to the common good and to our system of law, why does our Supreme Court interpret *secular government* as necessarily neutral rather than *virtue* as actively necessary? Since Congress may suffer corruption by greed and self-interest, then a source of moral influence that builds moral conscience in government seems necessary.

Within our system of government, we have two ideas we need to examine: the branches of government and the fabric of government. We all know that the three branches of a republican government are the Executive, the Legislative, and the Judiciary.[289] These basic identifiers do little to enable us to know their full purpose and protocol. How do we know who influences who and how do their interests support the common good, which is always the "*will of the majority*"? Republicanism considers "*will of the majority*" to be a fundamental principle. The individual states must bend to the majority of votes in an all or nothing contest toward their opinion of the Constitution.[290] The common good is that which serves the national interests of the confederated states. Madison supported Montesquieu's separation of powers into the three branches because separation provides a safety net for the people. They called this type of government federal, which they took from a 1645 treaty as a covenant between God and an individual and they adapted it in 1707 to pertain to a government of independent states formed on the earliest sense of treaty.[291] If we are to defend our moral values, then we must present our case in the public square. Political correctness is political suicide in a free society. Political correctness is another form of belief that bullies truth out of the public arena. It like democracy deteriorated over time into *thought crimes.*[292] While many ideologies vie for acceptance, we must meet them with a defense of our way of life. If we are not allowed or we are too afraid to make our presentation, maybe we should surrender and be assimilated.

B. Virtue and Religion:

If citizenry is the "*standard of merit*", then it is also a republican principle that opinion is at least as great as other property. Like our natural resources, your opinion is a natural right property. The First Amendment rests upon this right. In *Unfurl the Flag*, I argued that the USSC established a religion, atheism, as a national religion due to its ruling that a "*strongly held belief*" equals a religion based on the USSC's proclaimed neutral position on religion. If the Bench is neutral, then why so broadly define religion? Our question is, does atheism provide the religion of choice for *disinterested* persons? (See *Establish* in the Glossary) Atheism does not worship the theistic God. Worship and religious practice require an object of adoration. Our question is, does neutrality in religious faith necessarily result in neutrality of thinking? If neutrality demands impartiality, how does one set aside strongly held beliefs? If a disinterested person is truly impartial and takes no personal advantage, then that person must possess the will to examine both sides of the issue to such a depth as to possess understanding, its consequence, and its fit with republican principles. If one does, then one develops a strong belief that weighs the findings. Therefore, neutrality commands perfect knowledge, absolute understanding, and objective decision-making. Since no human is capable of such perfection, then no human can attain either personal disengagement or a disinterested mind to the extent the USSC asks us to accept their judgments. If I bend the interpretation, do I do so any greater that the USSC bends its definition. I find it not an insignificant consequence that their ruling embraces an all-inclusive definition of belief. On Fox News in mid-December 2010, an atheist claimed that his religion was the fastest growing religion in America. If that is the case, the USSC can take much credit, for atheism is not a religion in any sense, but the Bench's misunderstanding of separation of church and state demotes and quarantines the Christian philosophy among others. The USSC's definition elevates non-religions, such as atheism; to a prominent place in the public square for its tenets easily coexist with the Bench's neutrality, in a contorted way. Does atheism represent virtue as a natural right in our republican government? Is atheism a faith in the God of Nature or a faith in the nature of man? Our Republic stands upon the solid foundation of religious belief as a defense against usurpations, corruption, and religions that advocate hostile methods of conversion. The Framers' religious belief was Judaic in origin and Christian in practice. Atheism does not value the God of creation or nature's laws due to God's creation in any sense. Therefore, it does not believe in the origin of our natural rights, which means it is not rooted in our republican principles. Does the USSC point the U.S. toward world government by their definition of religion be it intentional or not? Is their definition of religion faith or polity? Is it any part of our republican government? Is faith, as our Framers recognize opinion, a property right? Yet, how does atheism provide a moral basis of judgment to facilitate conscience? Does it do so through the idea of absolute freedom that we call liberalism? Our Framers were liberal, in terms of education that aristocracy forbid the common man to acquire. Is the Framers' liberal mindset a match with modern liberalism? They desired liberal education, liberal rights, and limited freedom and government, not liberticide.[293] The Bench's loose definition of religion mitigates our Framer's ideas about the Christian philosophy. Did not Jefferson disparagingly refer to Calvin as an atheist?[294] Our Framers' conception of religion possesses the more inclusive moral ground and the higher moral standard contra Austin Dacey, author of *The Secular Conscience.* Another writer, European, notes this,

> "There was no royal road, then, from the natural sciences to godlessness. The emergent interest in Nature was not a step outside a religious outlook, but a mutation within it."[295]

Our first question is, if the First Amendment says one thing, how does the Bench justify using its own words in case law to add flavor to our Constitution's meaning? Our second question is, if the Bench reaches beyond the intent of the Framers, should it not be by quoting their words rather than by slanting meaning to accommodate its ideology.

Some in society may clamor for progressive thought, but we should question change for its reason and seek the truth for its wisdom. For Madison, this being the case, a just government protects individuals "*in the enjoyment and communication of their opinions, in which they have an equal, and in the estimation of some, a more valuable property*". Madison says in his paper on *Property*, March 27, 1792:

> "That is not a just government, nor is property secure under it, where arbitrary restrictions, exemptions, and monopolies deny to part of its citizens that free use of their faculties, and free choice of their occupations, which not only constitute their property in the general sense of the word; but are the means of acquiring property strictly called."

Therefore, a limited government does not rule against opinion that is not in its jurisdiction. If a State community posts the Ten Commandments in its school district, the State possesses jurisdiction. The Bench's opinion that the Ten Commandments might pose a harm to its readers is a supposition unsubstantiated by time. However, time has ruled upon the Bench's decision by the state of our schools and its incidence of violence.

C. Legislation, Human Nature, and Virtue:

When we examine the methods of politics by observing their usage in Congress, then our answer should be clear. We need to encourage our representatives to write legislation with the following in mind:

No pork

No earmarks

Pass a line-item veto for the president to carve out pork and earmarks to expedite legislation

All legislation is:

- issue specific only
- meets the test of its relevance to our common good
- is written for the average citizen (lawyers can twist the words later)
- meets republican principles (the Bench can codify it)

Legislation is clear about:

- why it is needed
- its priority in the list of needed legislation
- what should be posted on the appropriate government website
- each item on the list explains why it is in its position
- when it will be effective
- date it becomes law
- date it should be rescinded, if applicable
- Where in the system it takes effect
- What department or departments
- What department's or departments' programs
- Who is the target?

How will it:

- impact the target?
- do what it is supposed to do?
- increase/decrease the budget and/or expenditures?

Arguments made respecting proposed legislation must be:

- for the common good whether pro or con
- devoid of partisan bashing
- restricted to terminology appropriate to any of the above categories only

May address partisan platforms that focus on:

- a solution
- a promise

- a new platform objective

May explain:

- conflict with another
- solution
- promise
- principle of government policy

Would this provide us a way to determine:

- what our representatives are doing?
- how effective they are?
- whether they serve the people or special interest groups?
- if they represent our common good?

This suggestion is certainly incomplete, but its purpose is to start a conversation. Speaking of special interest groups, the Framers did not expect that our government would provide special interest group fulfillment that is not for the common good. Minorities were important to them, but would the Framers support public funds diverted to political groups? They hoped to ensure that our laws of the land are for the common good of the Union, not for unions as political special interests (Copage v. Kansas, 1915) or any other such groups' self-interest, as a minority at odds with the majority will.

I see why democratization develops classes. Classes permit our representatives to divide our common interests into special interests, thereby instituting intergroup disharmony. Is this a republican principle? Classes naturally exist in as an extensive country as ours and they serve to watch out for their own interests. Do the Framers advocate the government to take the initiative? Our Framers saw factions as useful to manage special interests that combine to make the majority. Some interpret majority as the elite, but a majority derives from all voters from all the states. However, an unrepublican majority that forces its will on a minority does so unconstitutionally. Our Framers seem not to have anticipated government's powers focused primarily on minorities. The Framers gave us individual rights, not minority rights. Our individual rights protect each citizen. We develop divisions of a pernicious kind when persons in any group attempt to persuade government to provide them what the majority declines. I speak in the spirit of Jefferson and Madison who believed minority groups have republican protection. This tension between segments of society and the majority will is why there is a clamor for popular will. If popular will arouses passion, then emotion rules rather than law. In this state, no one has any security and all are equally vulnerable to the mob. From what form of government do we find this idea to descend?

It is democracy. The human condition admits many causes, which is why the Framers labored to ensure the federal government did not become the enemy of the states. In the states, we are citizens in a republic. We are responsible for its governance through each locality. In this manner, we protect ourselves first, then our community and our statehood. When we assail Washington with demands, we operate against ourselves. The federal is a coordinator of the law that binds the states to cooperate without malice toward each other. We are *the people* only when we are a *united people*. Our union is through the grace of God for only by his love of his people can we overcome our differences as we learn to embrace his character of love, compassion, forgiveness, hope, trust, etc. Except for the Judaic-Christian god, whatever god one chooses to worship, that god is not greater than our republican principles. If one believes their god authorizes civil disobedience in order to accomplish a theocracy, then our Constitution protects us from the minority, unless the people change the Constitution or submit to its overthrow, lack of enforcement, or annulment by precedent. For this reason, natural law remains fixed, absolute law. God is great and greater than man is alone contra Dawkins[296], and He is necessary when man associates, which is why the Framers prayed and acknowledged his providential care.

The larger question is a tough self-examining one, which is this: do I really desire to be united, to exercise my liberty, to be responsible and exercise my freedom? I thought I had resolved to do that, but this is really like the pig's involvement in the barnyard party. Am I committed to giving the bacon rather than just laying an egg? Our Framers established the republican principles upon the analysis of what is the *best* way to govern. Our Framers ensured that the republican framework is the solid foundation for a government of the people to exercise positive law with the greatest security to the freedom of the people. How does the United Nations' *Universal Declaration of Human Rights* fit in with our republican principles. Does not this United Nations' common standard of achievement for all peoples and all nations trump our individual citizen-state compact?[297] Whatever its purpose, our question is whether the citizens of the United States desire to dissolve our Constitution and commit the United States as a member state of the United Nations and to its universal creed? What seems certain is that if some complain that the good ole U.S.A. is hypocritical in transporting its principles, then he or she must also complain the same of the good ole UN and other countries that export their creeds. The question each citizen who realizes that America is not a democracy must ask is, why does the United States State Department advocate promoting "*... Democracy ... around the world ...*" and making it ... *central to U.S. foreign policy* and stating that it is one of "... *the values upon which the United States was founded centuries ago.*"[298] It is true that the Framers assimilated some democratical ideas, but they also included tenets from other forms. The Framers define Republicanism, as a form of government, by its wholesome fabric of principles manifested by its structure. Should we respect our Framers and refer to our government as they did? Should not we sponsor republicanism? When we understand that the meaning of *for the people, by the people, and of the people* comes directly from our republican representative form of government, then we shall salute our flag and pledge allegiance to our Constitution. How can we, the United States, support the European Commission's strategy that states "... *the best protection for our security is a world of well-governed democratic states*"?[299] The use of *world* makes their strategy inclusive of the United States. Does the ax fly to the root of our government? Our politicians who support this European strategy must work against our form of government. Shall we the people accept this overt call to destroy our American form of government?

> *"In democracies, respecting rights isn't a choice leaders make day-by-day, it is the reason they govern."*
>
> *Secretary of State Hillary Rodham Clinton* [300]

I cannot help asking myself why the United States is so confounded over our founding principles. I cannot help wondering why we the people permit our leaders to disparage our government and elevate inferior forms. If our government representatives believe that democracy is the best form of government in which to protect citizen rights, then we are indeed in a crisis. I am cognizant that in this case, a world focus is present, but the belief that any democratic state is better than our republican nation is unbelievable. I assume our Framers' research and debates did surface the best form of government under God. Maybe my problem is faith in God or is the problem with some their lack of faith in God and their disagreement with our Framers' faith in God. What faith do the states incorporate throughout East and West democracies? From the voices of our government, we hear some who rhetorically subscribe to this allegiance who do not explicitly proclaim it. Such a democratic method is foreign to our republican principles. The word *we,* in we the people, must express the *will of the majority* through appropriate state-by-state agreement to such a proposal that culminates in the majority of states voting in its favor. The Electoral College provides for each state having a voice. The movement to vote by popular majority is a ruse to reduce constitutional majority will to popular majority. *Black's Law Dictionary* views the Electoral College as "*the body of electors chosen from each state to formally elect the U.S. President and Vice President by casting votes based on the popular vote.*"[301] Our voting system is not setup for a popular majority, but a constitutional majority based on the total of state representatives presently in Congress. Our confusion about popular government feeds the great squabble about illegal immigration. The rhetoric is that the Democrats proclaim social justice for the illegal immigrants while ignoring our republican principle of sovereignty and the federal system's constitutional obligation to protect our borders, which means our faith in our republican principles. If there is an illegal population that thinks it has a right to intrude into our constitutional system, then it incorrectly understands our system. Is such a thought a form of democratization? Can we blame them when they are encouraged by democratic principles to howl for citizenship without honoring our system or that the rights they feel they have are unconstitutional? Intruders who possess no allegiance to our principles may become internal enemies of our Constitution. When our leaders fail to enforce the laws of the land, then they jeopardize our Republic. Our nation provides immigration law to regulate entry by those who contribute to the common good and vow to honor and protect the constitution that protects them. The Republicans use the illegal immigrants as a threat to our system, which it is, but they fail to address the issue as set out above. Another, maybe more significant issue is the difference in the legal status terms of jus soli and Jus sanguinis. The fourteenth amendment grants citizenship based on the place of birth (just soli) rather than the parents place of birth (jus sanguinis). Its intent is long past its fulfillment, but it now permits aliens to enter the United States, birth a child who possesses citizenship in the U.S. Our question is, does terrorism suggest a change to this amendment when a child is raised in another country, but can come to the U.S. with full citizenship? Do they have any allegiance to their abroad country and its principles? We could settle this conundrum if parents pursue citizenship legally and swear allegiance to the United States' Constitution. It is no guarantee that either the parents or the child will emulate good citizen behavior, but it is far superior to our present situation. Why do our issues divide us? Why are we not truthful? Because, in a two-party system there must exist at least two distinct groups that vie against each other for power. In this way, the political machines function to provide the opposition against whichever side you choose. The protagonist-antagonist drama stirs our passions, which is why we see it everywhere in life. Our politics should not be about drama, but it should be about constitutional principles. Our new form of divisiveness is both political and capitalist in that it forms an audience of interested and supportive consumers, which also keeps the parties necessary. For another power to emerge, it must maneuver itself between this schism and either create enough draw of the public to declare itself a third party or like Hitler or Stalin or Napoleon or any despot who dominates all the other parties bully its way into control. By admitting democracy, we open the gates to other unconstitutional ideologies. Whether capitalist or *politicalist*, our American drama plays out in this power struggle arena of deceit and malice aforethought countered by faith and loyalty. Our solution is to reform our union by our republican principles, then, we the people measure our representatives by these standards. If we do not, are we susceptible to manipulation, division, and financial exploitation?

Parties cost a lot of money and they ensure that only the rich can govern. Politics comes from the word *polity* that means a form of government with a constitution. Its modern translation is "*the science of manipulation and disguise*". Should we return to principles and away from personality to form our vote? In addition, every candidate should support the entirety of our republican principles. Are not our republican principles and our understanding that we are not a democracy vital to our awakening? What is policy if not the direction our country needs to continue our freedom and maintain our national security? If policy is only a candidates' plan of self-interest or of destruction of our form of government, would we support it? I have to stand up and speak up as I see our governmental systems threatened from decadence within, from failure to communicate with the electorate, and from ideological differences that many do not understand. Are not these distractions symptomatic of unrepublican ideologies, which deaden us to the purpose of government? Can we be at war with one another and expect national tranquility? Can we misunderstand our goals and expect continued liberty? Can we harangue one another over partisan divisions and hope to find common ground? Can our republican principles and our faith unite us so we can compromise, not our principles, but our position on issues that drive our government? Can we unite around a platform that informs us and requires us to choose on directions that strengthen our union? Shall we return to reasoned arguments to support our issues? If our Framers searched history and modern governments for the answer and gave us our Constitution, where shall we search to replace it? Can we be supreme when we are subject to the manipulation of leaders who possess the information, the wealth, and the power to control what they want us to know? Are we willing to permit a national convention to set our American agenda? Shall we continue to guess what a candidate actually means and wonder what s/he will actually implement? Can we afford to continue business as usual when representatives so easily manipulate our system for their advantage and that of others rather than to fulfill our republican principles? Are we not tired of holding our breath from one election to the next? Shall we stay out of the fray as similar to our British butler who we meet in Chapter 12, who uniformed went about his work? Can we ensure that the processes of choice are in our hands? Can we vote for candidates and issues with full disclosure and knowledge that they will truly support our Constitution? If our government is a system of checks and balances that protects the people constitutionally and if we are the owners of the process, then why wouldn't the people insist that all branches of government be subject to these republican principles?

D. Applying the Republican Principles:
Referring again to a portion of Article VI, which states,

> *"this Constitution, and the Laws of the United States which shall be made in Pursuance thereof."*

Does this mean that our Constitution regulates all positive law whether passed by the legislative branch or by the Judiciary? Is not judicial legislation a violation of our republican principles? Does our common law yield constitutionally qualified law? It seems to be exclusively the realm of the judges as some refer to it as the judges' law.[302]

Does this section mean that ... *all Treaties made, or which shall be made, under the Authority of the United States, shall be the supreme Law of the Land* must conform to the principles of our Constitution? Does, *and the Judges in every State shall be bound thereby, any Thing in the Constitution or Laws of any State to the contrary notwithstanding,* mean that the Constitution rules state laws, but only to the limit of federal Constitutional power? Should it limit the USSC's interpretation of Congressional legislative law in the spirit of our republican principles that undergird our Constitution? If so, how do we know that the USSC's interpretation of Congressional legislative law is in the spirit of our Constitution? Is the Bench angelic contra Jefferson?

Since these fundamental and constitutional republican principles exist, then the public should know how the political candidates match campaign issues with these principles. Each candidate breaks out issues and correlates them to republican principles. I found two sources that provide some insight into this process. One works from beginning concepts as a basis of political argument in the United States. The other looks at the two-party system and draws demarcations of each by their emphasis on issues. We can draw some parallels from these two resources. If we match them to the Framers' fundamental republican principles, we can check our theory. If we find gaps, then we can reason with further analysis what republican principles will fill in the gap. We may desire to know what is being ignored and if possible why. Below, I list thirteen arguments as I found them in Howard Fineman's book *The Thirteen American Arguments*, which are,[303]

1. Who is a Person?
2. Who is an American?
3. The Role of Faith
4. What can we know and say?

5. The limits of individualism
6. Who judges the law?
7. Debt and the dollar
8. Local v. national authority
9. Presidential power
10. The terms of trade
11. War and diplomacy
12. The environment
13. A fair, "more perfect" union

How are these relevant to the list of republican principles? Are all worthy of attention? How do they relate to republican principles? Four address American identity: number 1 (a person), 2 (an American), 3 (faith), and 5 (individual as understood by the idea of individualism). The others that pertain to republican principles are these:

a. freedom of the press: #4

b. the Judiciary: #6

c. local and national authority: #8

d. presidential power: #9

e. trade: #10

f. war and diplomacy, which is split between Congressional authority as to declaration of war and presidential as supreme commander, and power of the president to receive diplomats and to appoint ambassadors of diplomacy: #11

g. one seems to be a policy issue of the president: #12 (the environment)

h. a fair and "more perfect" union seems to apply to all three branches: #13.

Jessamyn Conrad provides in her book, *What You Should Know about Politics, but Don't: A Nonpartisan Guide to the Issues*, a breakout of issues that topically sorts them according to party platforms.[304] These present us with an exercise. Associate the items in the list of issues below with the republican principle you think it best matches. Ask, does the category fit with limited constitutional government or a form of government other than republican? Does the candidate understand their connection with our republican principles?

1. Elections
2. The Economy
3. Foreign policy
4. The military
5. Health care
6. Energy
7. The environment
8. Civil liberties
9. Culture wars
10. Socioeconomic policy
11. Homeland security
12. Education
13. Trade

Carry it further and ask, which branch of government is responsible for it? Do two or more branches share responsibility for it? Can you separate them into categories of our republican principles? You might ask, do I now have a better grasp of the issues as they fit in with our form of government based on republican principles? If I know what all of these are, then I can ensure that I ignore none in my focus on the most relevant to the context. You might add some republican principles to my table. In contemporary terms, how does health care fit in with our republican principles? When tax dollars are used, how can we reconcile the use with the purpose of government? Do you remember what the Framers' considered the purpose of government to be? How does Congress authorize itself to pass a bill the people vote No on? If the elected representative believes her constituency elected her, does your representative base her belief on the majority will or on her re-election? Do our republican principles give her that last commission? However, due to our nebulous party issues in campaigns, the electorate has no singular majority voice. Therefore, we, the people find our voice interpreted in ways that confound meaning and undermine the majority will of the people. Would platform promises tied to our republican principles ensure that our representatives hear, understand, and follow the voice of the people so we can evaluate their actions in office?

Section 6: Conclusion

In our Republic, democratical ideas play a role in our freedom, but democracy is not the form of our government. The Framers built our form of government upon constitutional principles that translates their ideas into the best form. It is still a new and vibrant republican form of representation unknown to both classical thought and modern Europe. Our form of government remains the best form that republican principles can offer, but it is secure only when the people ensure it remains *"strictly republican"*. Unfettered democracy remains an evil form that our Framers agreed could never long endure. Our question is, whether our alien democratic inclusions are the flares that alert us to our jeopardy? Can we *"substantially maintain"* our Constitution to ensure our government remains in the hearts, minds, hands, and hopes of the people as the Framers defined our Republic? To my mind, Europe proves the Framers' conclusion to be accurate. As its socialist programs fall apart and it attempts to reunite as the European Union (EU), it demonstrates the failure of democracy's longevity. Democratical ideas that do not support our mixed form of government create chaos. Note the division we discussed between federal and national. Now, we come to the foundation of our Senate's role in settling disputes, not through party politics, but by coolheaded republican action. I believe Dr. West proves the validity for this structure. Do democratic ideas contribute to our modern form of government? How do democratic and republican ideas mesh? Does Wisconsin make the point? The election for State Supreme Court Justices highlighted a battle between a Republican and a Liberal. Ideologies other than republican principles in our system compromise our fundamentals of republican government. In my evaluation, the Republican Party does not at any given time capture all the fundamentals of republicanism. How could two parties become opponents unless there is a division of principles? Does a two-party system strengthen our form of government or does it simply divide the people?

At our peril, we ignore our republican principles by which we govern our governors. Our times also *try men's souls.* We place ourselves in peril of undermining our Republic by installing democracy. Two forms of government cannot co-exist. Our Framers labored intently and exhaustively to avoid a democracy, a monarchy, and an aristocracy by combining the best of all three, then adding new ideas of structure. We value democracy over our republican principles only because of the subtle, yet insidious, march away from knowledge of our past. Can you hear their voices? They are present. We can find, hear, and live their principles today. How treacherous this ignorance to our Constitution and its form of government that employs unrepublican tactics to lessen or destroy it.

CHAPTER 12:

Voices from the Past

In this Chapter, I present a scenario where science finds a reason for us to find an interest in our past. From this, we rediscover Jefferson's thoughts on our society. I then offer an analysis of his discussion in contemporary terms. The analysis uses questions to understand whether our present situation corresponds with Jefferson's thoughts.

Section 1: The Discovery

Announcer: Ralph Brown,

> "We interrupt this program to bring you breaking news.
>
> "Science has found that electromagnetic waves carry sound. As these waves follow the circular path around the globe, scientists have often encountered them. Today, scientists heard the voices of the past, and, at different organizational levels, they have isolated one of these voices. The recent past is closer than we have ever imagined.
>
> "A scientist who is a history buff found snippets of colonial history. Here is an example. In an electromagnetic band, the scientist heard Thomas Jefferson reading a letter. Jefferson is, evidently, proofreading it, but he does not mention names, so we don't know to whom the reader is speaking. However, we can listen in."

Section 2: Thomas Jefferson's Letter

"No, my friend, the way to have good and safe government is not to trust it all to one, but to divide it among the many, distributing to everyone exactly the functions he is competent to. Let the national government be entrusted with the defense of the nation, and its foreign and federal relations; the State governments with the civil rights, laws, police, and administration of what concerns the State generally; the counties with the local concerns of the counties, and each ward direct the interests within itself.

"It is by dividing and subdividing these republics from the great national one down through all its subordinations, until it ends in the administration of every man's farm by himself; by placing under everyone what his own eye may superintend, that all will be done for the best. What has destroyed liberty and the rights of man in every government which has ever existed under the sun? The generalizing and concentrating all cares and power into one body, no matter whether of the autocrats of Russia or France, or of the aristocrats of a Venetian Senate. And I do believe that if the Almighty has not decreed that man shall never be free (and it is a blasphemy to believe it), that the secret will be found to be in making himself the depository of the powers respecting himself, so far as he is competent to them, and delegating only what is beyond his competence by a synthetical process, to higher and higher orders of functionaries, so as to trust fewer and fewer powers in proportion as the trustees become more and more oligarchical.

"The elementary republics of the wards, the county republics, the State republics, and the republic of the Union, would form a gradation of authorities, standing each on the basis of law, holding every one its delegated share of powers, and constituting truly a system of fundamental balances and checks for the government. Where every man is a sharer in the direction of his ward-republic, or of some of the higher ones, and feels that he is a participator in the government of affairs, not merely at an election one day in the year, but every day; when there shall not be a man in the State who will not be a member of some one of its councils, great or small, he will let the heart be torn out of his body sooner than his power be wrested from him by a Caesar or a Bonaparte.

"How powerfully did we feel the energy of this organization in the case of embargo? I felt the foundations of the government shaken under my feet by the New England townships. There was not an individual in their States whose body was not thrown with all its momentum into action; and although the whole of the other States were known to be in favor of the measure, yet the organization of this little selfish minority enabled it to overrule the Union. What would the unwieldy counties of the Middle, the South, and the West do? Call a county meeting, and the drunken loungers at and about the courthouses would have collected, the distances being too great for the good people and the industrious generally to attend. The character of those who really met would have been the measure of the weight they would have had in the scale of public opinion.

"As Cato, then, concluded every speech with the words, *'Carthago delenda est,'* so do I every opinion, with the injunction, 'divide the counties into wards.' Begin them only for a single purpose; they will soon show for what others they are the best instruments. God bless you, and all our rulers, and give them the wisdom, as I am sure they have the will, to fortify us against the degeneracy of our government, and the concentration of all its powers in the hands of the one, the few, the well-born or the many."[305]

Now a word from our Scientist:

"We hear in the quote, *Carthage must be destroyed,*" the passion for completion. Cato the Elder meant it as a statement to complete Roman's revenge upon Carthage. Jefferson expresses his passion to 'divide the counties into wards.' Evidently, he thought smaller units govern best. We know Jefferson sprinkled his correspondence with Latin, Greek, and French phrases. However, we have to question whether this is authentic or if it is someone propagating a fraud."

Reporter asks a person in the park:

"Sir, Pardon me! Have you heard the news about sound existing in electromagnetic waves? I would like to get your opinion on this astounding new story."

Citizen in the park:

"I think it's great. To hear a voice from our past like Jefferson is exciting. I like what he said, but in our democracy, I do not think he is talking about the United States. What is a *republic* anyway?"

Reporter:

"A good question. I'm not sure either, so let's go to the newsroom for a discussion."

Narrator's voice:

"Thanks, Jack. This is Ralph Brown speaking. I have with me today Dr. Rawlings Hardstudy, who is a professor at the University of Swelling. Dr. Hardstudy, would you throw some light on the time-period of this breaking news?"

Dr. Hardstudy

"Well, as I understand it ...."

Section 3: Analysis

Jefferson wrote this letter to Joseph Cabell in 1816. My interest in the American political experiment began in college, but like many, I had to set it aside as work became my major concern. Now, my interest heightens with the events of our day sending out tremors like the rumbling earth. My desire to know drives my mind with ruminations. In the course of my studies, I have learned to use my mind to explore questions in order to test what I believe against the facts of history. Although I made a strong argument that the Founding Fathers were never deists, at least not the first five presidents or most of the Framers, I hope these insights bring a rediscovery of the great principles of the past into the modern American political drama.[306]

Jefferson addresses topics that we moderns fail to observe as did our Framers'. We find that Jefferson says that government is to be a "*good and safe government*". Secondly, Jefferson says that only a "*good and safe government*" can be trusted when you "*divide it among the many, distributing to everyone exactly the functions he is competent to.*"

Our Constitution draws these limits. The relationship today between our federal and national government is like an octopus embracing its prey. I note that Jefferson speaks of the national as separate from the state republics. The states are independent republics, but they are collectively national. Madison clearly states that the national's function is distinct from the federal's in certain respects. See Chapter 7, Section 14 and Appendix D: Table of Constitutional Powers. The federal entangles the national by the lure of funds intruding into the affairs of states and bribing away or usurping their sovereignty. Greed and politics are no strange bedfellows. If the public cries for services, the government strives to win approval. I propose questions in order to put our fingers on the pulse of government. Is it the majority public or the minority special interest public that howls for handouts? How does this partnership feed the need for convenience without increasing taxes? That old octopus must suck the funds out of public pockets. So why do we cry *big government*?

It is accretion. Like age, it slips into our lives a bit at a time until there are noticeable differences in how we look, feel, and think. Yet, we the public cannot deny our part in perceiving government as our provider rather than as our federal system to coordinate the interworking of our *United* States.

What about our state government demands? Have not they dropped the ball at times? Do not they lap up all the scraps from Congress? What do the states do about our civil rights protection? Did not Dr. King have to intercede because the states did not apply our republican principles across our society? President Kennedy, after many appeals from Dr. King, but only after his murder, eulogized Dr. King's death and efforts, which summoned the Civil Rights Bill of 1964. President Kennedy finally made it a national issue escalated by Dr. Martin Luther King. Federal intervention was positive. Nevertheless, the states' failure to protect all its citizens made them fall victim to federal laws, thus relinquishing some of their sovereign status. Our republican principles do not make the Federal the big brother over the states. It seems that our Bench simply adjudicated it and circumvented the states and our Constitution's intent. Should not the state Senators have taken this issue to their state legislatures for a state constitutional change? Why did the Judiciary not advise this action? Could it be a conflict of interest too great to honor our Constitution?

Our republican principles say the majority are not to deny the minority their rights. When we do, we open the doors for Big Brother in state business. One problem is our ideas about rights. Another is our ideas about government. I guess a lesson learned is to apply our republican principles in our local communities to keep the tentacles of that old octopus in Washington. First, we have some house cleaning to do. James Wilson provides us a maxim, which says,

> "there is not in the whole science of politicks a more solid or a more important maxim than this—than of all governments, those are the best, which, by the natural effect of their constitutions, are frequently renewed or drawn back to their first principles."[307]

If we were serious about this, we might go out on the proverbial limb and rethink our entire process. To do this, we might simply do a brain storming exercise, which permits us to consider every idea without immediate acceptance or elimination. In this venue, we play off the previous chapters in which I attempted to generate ideas to satisfy James Wilson's suggestion. On the local scene, we see today that principles out of mind are principles unpracticed. How else can we realize Jefferson's idea that state law, police, municipal administration, and all other local concerns belong to each district managing its own interests "*within itself*"? He does not say it is a federal responsibility. It is a local one.

Here are some wild thoughts.

Should state governments reach out to Washington for monies? When the federal entangles itself in the affairs of the States, central government grows. The government requires more resources, so it asks taxpayers to pick up the tab. Through this financial door enters corruption. Bureaucracy, like an octopus, has many limbs all sucking the life out of its captured prey. We seem to believe that this is a constitutionally permitted embrace, when it is simply our demands on government that authorizes itself to answer.

How do the two parties express conflict in principles? Democrats appease their constituents with social promises; the republicans advantage themselves as proponents of business and limited government. Do our Constitutional principles support or curtail such agendas? We have to ask, what does "limit" modify? It modifies "government", specifically, the federal system. What powers does the Constitution delegate to the federal system? Our republican principles settle the issue by enumerating those powers. Which branch of government ruled that commerce opens the door to federal intervention? How do some use the phrase "common good" to open other doors? What other such innovations extend the federal system? We must ask, is this tampering with our Constitution and its intent to limit government? So, "limited government" in principle applies to those enumerated powers and nothing more. Therefore, most increases in federal power come from judicial adjudication, executive expansion, legislative laxity, lobbyists, and special interest groups to name the top contenders. However, the concepts inherent in democracy that are not republican principles also enlarge government, such as socializing government. The two-party system serves only to advantage national committees, which requires great donations to support its bureaucracy.

How would we fix our system? In Jefferson's opinion, the state districts work for their citizens, the more local government meet citizen's needs, the less demands are made upon Washington. Another lesson learned from Dr. King is that we must ensure that the states do not give cause for federal intervention. Citizens can take leadership roles in local districts in any civic cause.

Should we use referendums more often to understand what the people want? Majority rule would then set the standard for local and federal opinions. If the public votes *yes* on a law, then the state legislature and the State Attorney General can review it and take appropriate action. Is not this a true contractual arrangement? It is a matter of whether the states retain their sovereignty by managing themselves. So, should each State Attorney General scrutinize all legislation for its fit with intrastate law? The State Supreme Court tests state law for its local federal fit. The United States Supreme Court rules on interstate laws that include those between citizens and states. The Federal Supreme Court codifies law for interstate fit, hopefully in "pursuance of" our Constitutional principles. The least government would be for the USSC to stay out of decision-making for the States. Is this not the intent of the Framers? In either case, the Courts rule in their respective limited arenas. Might we propose that it return the law with recommendation back to the State legislature?

If each state representative is responsible to his or her electorate, then it means the whole electorate rather than select interest groups. Promises to special interest groups as block votes violate our majority rule principle. Likewise, I strongly believe it extends to lobbying and corporate law that gives advantage to this minority group.

If the Bench would re-implement their historic, seriatim process, as Jefferson suggests, then we the people could see how each judge evaluated the case and we could understand their individual arguments and reasons. Jefferson thought this the best mechanism to decide on each judge's case and the outcome of the decision. I hope our government still has faith in the people to govern themselves, as did the Framers. Is this not an aspect of our republican principle of sovereignty of the people over government? Marshall's Judicial Review is the first time the USSC over stepped its jurisdiction to review all legislative law. Where in our Constitution do the States delegate this function to the Judiciary? I think the above proposal replaces this process and gets the USSC out of the business of extending its power and being overlord of the States.

If the districts work out their need for law, would we reduce the number of laws the State, Congress, or the Judiciary put on the books. I hope that all laws are based on republican principles, but the Framers' intent was for the United States Supreme Court (USSC) to determine if it does or does not. I cannot find Judicial Review as a constitutionally delegated power. Was it their intent for the USSC to make law based on politics or ideologies rather than on republican principles?

Could this custom answer the question why we have so many bills in the first place? It seems many bills play the numbing role of slipping in pet projects for state revenues, special interests, nest building, payoffs, etc. than for real national concerns. Why did not the USSC challenge this custom, if it wants a judicial voice to monitor Congress? If Senators watch out for their state republics, then their Congressional activities may play a significant role to limit how that ole DC octopus extends its tentacles into state provinces. If this is a fair assessment, then state laws, police, and administration are state business, such as the counties and their local concerns with each district managing its own interests "*within itself*".

If Jefferson thought that "*each state is a republic and each is divided and subdivided from the great national one, our union, down through all its subordinations, until it ends in the administration of every man's farm by himself"*, then the federal government has overstepped its constitutional limits many boundaries ago.

1. United Nations and United States Constitution:

The United Nations views all governments under their egis as member states. I find it interesting that this form of government assumes the characteristics of our Union, but places itself over all nations as Washington, DC, does over all our state republics. Is this the intent of our Framers? The states must decide unanimously to acquiesce to this global government and/or federal system. Secession must be a majority republican decision and not democratic (popular) to change our republican (representative) form of government.

2. District Governing

Now, the second aspect of Jefferson's quote is district governing. I think it is a strange concept to today's body politic to hear Jefferson's idea that this method of "*placing under everyone what his own eye may superintend*" is the intent of the Framers. Even more so that by doing so "*all will be done for the best*". He says *all* because his words correspond to our Constitution's word *limited* and to its *delegated to* phrase. What exactly could he mean by *best*? The old adage: "*the best government is the least government*". Madison said that the best government is the *least imperfect*. We ignore these sages at our peril. Our republican form is the *least government* and the *least imperfect*, in our Framers' minds. What do you believe? Our modern dilemma concerns the part legislation plays with the Judiciary and the Executive. Jefferson's words should echo through our minds to their deepest levels.

> *"What has destroyed liberty and the rights of man in every government which has ever existed under the sun?"*

Now, this question is one that we must answer, for it surely is the path to good government. His answer is,

> "The generalizing and concentrating all cares and power into one body ..."

Jefferson refers to those forms where the executive possesses all the real power. The British monarchy is one such head. Jefferson thought it heresy in America to contemplate such a system for the United States. How do we relate this to our day? Our whole system has become complacent and the separation of powers, which was a past prohibition on unbalanced power, made nugatory by new customs. Past presidents have extended the power of their office almost to the exclusion of Congress and with the appointment of justices that favor their political persuasion. Could monarchism creep out of the past and into the present? Probably not! However, some Framers thought it could evolve into despotism. As we see democratization leading to chaos, this becomes more of a threat. With the advent of the European Union (EU), we have a movement toward unification. Globalization has its elitists plying the political trade for power. Corporations hire lobbyists who use politics rather than principles to influence our representatives. Is Bolivia symptomatic of all of this and a message that natural resources are at risk of sole corporate or private ownership? Why was the World Bank so intent on establishing corporate ownership of rights to nature's bounty, rain, that the people revolted to protect themselves? What about corporate genetic engineering, which our Patent Office now approves, that might eliminate the small cattle business, grain business, ad infinitum by granting patents to corporations to own solely the DNA of these commodities. How long before these cattle replace the natural variety that the public can buy, sell, trade, and own? How do these new trends effect the idea of property of Adams and Madison? Our fear may not be genetic alterations, but the fact that only the corporation can own, harvest, and sell (to the highest bidder?), the stock and the meat, which may eliminate small business ownership and give power and profit to private ownership. The public can buy corporate stock, but is this a *free market*? How would Jefferson deal with this type of accretion that private power ownership through politics and law advances against the peoples' natural rights? How are our natural rights effected by these corporate tactics?

3. The Almighty and Self Government

I ponder the word *Almighty*. Jefferson's double negative obfuscates the meaning a bit. If I remove it, what do we have?

> *"And I do believe that if the Almighty has decreed that man shall be free ..."*

I justify the clarity by Jefferson's bracketed comment, which reads, after I remove the double negatives, and add a negative here *("and it is a blasphemy* not *to believe it").* We can rhetorically ask whether we believe that the Almighty decrees whether man ought to be enslaved. Have we ever seen slavery not tied to economics? This sage of America knows that the classical Muses are no match for the wisdom of the Ancient of Days. God does declare that man is a free being. Jefferson wrote this wisdom into the Declaration of Independence, which all the Founders assented to, and to which the whole of the confederated states agreed was the sound of their trumpet of revolution. Jefferson's conclusion that the secret for the protection of a *good and safe government* lies in man ... *making himself the depository of the powers respecting himself ...*

Do we not yet realize that men cast truth beneath their feet still today as Daniel prophesied of the Romans and the Jews? Humanity has long trampled upon the word of God as Truth. I surmise that this warrants our consideration today. My mind reels with the impact of Jefferson's phrase, *man*, his own governor, to paraphrase. If so, then it is part of those unalienable rights since man is the *Almighty's* creature, so man, by the Almighty's authority, always retains sovereignty over the powers of government, over our federal system, and over each state government. We should note that the Judaic-Christian God never relinquishes authority over humanity. We have no human intermediary between man and God.[308] I see this as the argument against man's divine right to rule over man. I make a point of this for preparation to defend our form of government from those forms that believe their God like their form of government is greater than America's. This is the new battlefield against the war on terror, which wields principle against principle.

4. Higher and Higher Orders of Functionaries

These, our elected governors, who function in our towns to our state capitols and on to our federal representatives, represent those "*higher and higher orders of functionaries*" that lie outside the competencies of most of us. In this *limited* way, we are dependent upon the virtue of our representatives whose skills and abilities recommend them for this function, or at least they should.

Let us follow through and make this realization. If government must spiral upward "*to higher and higher orders of functionaries*" in order "*to trust fewer and fewer powers in proportion as the trustees become more and more oligarchical*", then what powers must lie at the top? What is the top? The *top* is always the Executive, in this context, but our Framers warn against all power consolidated in one person or office. If despotism is the primary likelihood for the Executive, what is the probability of an oligarchy? An oligarchy is government by a few persons and a cabinet is a *few*. The Executive is at present the strongest branch politically, but the Judiciary is the silent strong actor as its opinions filtrate throughout our land. I find the answer in Cicero[309], which I provided earlier. Do not we still today speak of *elites* as a governing body? Could elites parallel Hamilton's idea of an aristocracy that he advocated should constitute the Senate? Our modern concern of these elitists emerges, as their values become public policy. Intellectuals have their influence.[310] Yet, lobbyists are the strongest voices owned by businesses with unlimited resources and direct contact with our representatives. We have Progressives in both parties who articulate values that reverse Jefferson's idea of man governing himself. They seem to conjure out of democracy the idea of a peoples' republic modeled after communism. We have conservative Democrats who protect social benefits as the democratic help to the masses as part of their political agenda. *Democracy's Discontent* by Michael Sandel explains the foundations of the Progressive movement and its intended destination. It explains why democracy is the weapon of choice to give dissent a voice. They must eliminate republican principles to establish their new order that will install democracy and its nature and principles. It appeals to the public's passion for justice. In *Democracy and disagreement*, Amy Gutmann and Dennis Thompson address topics including *deliberative democracy* that provides the platform in their opinion for moral argument. As writers infuse democracy into our republican system, they do not harmonize with our form of government, because they expand its limited role and overburden its ability to function as designed. Most of these issues belong in the States, which, unfortunately, tend to ignore civil rights and fail to protect the people from ill treatment by power brokers. Is this because we the people elect representatives from this elite pool? We must accept the minorities' right to protection under republican principles rather than encourage this right through weaker systems, which possess less moral virtue and political structure. Have we, as Thomas Sowell argues, permitted intellectuals to influence our leaders and our public opinions? Do these intellectual beliefs run counter to our republican principles? If we understand our republican principles and we despise them, then we can alter our form of government. If we do not understand why our form is the best of governments, then we might want to grasp its nature and principles that form its structure before we turn it into or allow it to become Gehenna.

We have conservative Republicans who protect free markets in the name of capitalism and smaller government in the name of republicanism for the common good as political platforms. Are these issues the extent of republicanism? Centrists operate within both parties' conservative boundaries. What values do we prefer from each group? Do we choose only republican principles from these parties? I hope we choose the principles over the parties. We have the appointed czars who are the highly educated and socially distanced few who believe they run the government, and they often do. Some czars are simply the recipients of the President's favoritism. How do czars fit in with limited government and budget controls? The more permanent fixtures of government, public servants, are the ones Jimmy Carter said prevented him for getting his policies implemented. How republican is the Washington bureaucracy? We have unionized government *servants* who receive better pay and benefits on average than their employers do, pundits inform us. Is this another political quagmire? How do these realities relate to our republican principles?

5. The Remains of the Day

My mind conjures up the distant recollection of the American in the movie *The Remains of the Day* who tells the Brits that they are amateur politicians. He suggests that they retire and let the professional politicians handle the government. I ask myself a series of questions. First, do any, all, or some of these ideas represent the government of the people, by the people, and for the people that our Framers envisioned? The answer leaps from my lips. No! Did the aristocrat's grilling of Mr. Stevens, the butler, in the movie reveal this snobbish aura? I think so. Does not his attitude denigrate the average citizen who works all day, comes home tired, and struggles to get all the chores done while trying to participate in family life? Mr. Stevens is humiliated, certainly. He knows nothing about all these issues. He remarks that to eavesdrop on the diplomats would distract him from his duties. He, evidently, cannot help feeling inferior as the taunting questions poke him. He feels his embarrassment as he turns his head and looks anxiously at the lord of the house as if to say, *rescue me*. I, along with Mr. Stevens, am irritated by the questioner's arrogance. Mr. Stevens, after the lord of the house gives approval, turns and hurriedly walks through the massive door. I felt disgust toward this aristocrat who, smiling, turns his head toward the speaker's voice and retorts, "you made your point". I hear the smug aristocrat ask sarcastically,

"And shall we leave government decisions to such as this?"

I garner from the scene that Mr. Stevens' posture falls from its edifice of dignity to the lowlands of commonality. His self-respect compresses as his composure crumbles to a humble, but elegant, gait toward the great door. He seems in a trance as though his thoughts deepen his reflection and the emotional force of the incident propels him from the room. I feel the dart's hurt as it strikes my heart as Mr. Stevens retreats through the door that shrinks his stature. Oh, how confounded is man! I follow Mr. Stevens further along as he reflects upon his ignorance and that incident among *gentlemen* in the lord's mansion. The lord who recently dismissed two Jewish girls because they were Jews, yet that incident was trivial to him then. Only now does it seem to stir him as he feels *now* somewhat as they must have *then*. I see how this incident melts the staid, controlled, and disciplined head butler. It shakes his entrenched position regarding life, his perceived duties, and his dignity. His feelings shake my emotions. If I view this scene from a perspective of time, I understand that the lord's position of superiority over the girls is a response that the Nazi ideology manifests. If Mr. Stevens' focus on daily responsibilities blinds him to this creeping danger, such stealthy dangers may catch others off guard. How does one guard against such insidious progression? Shall some incident need to occur in the life of each person that affects each one that he begins to think about his participation in life, liberty, and his pursuit of happiness? I find another question following upon *happiness, is* the Framers' concept of happiness the same as our modern conception? Did they see happiness in freedom? What priority did they assign to it? What place and roles does happiness play in our life? I see its order in the Declaration of Independence is third, not first. Do we have it backward? Do we take life and liberty for granted?

Life is our highest priority. Then, our liberty follows. So, intrusion from government into one's personal conscience concerning living one's life hinders one's liberty and one's pursuit of happiness. Yet, Jefferson's concerns about government must be his primary concern about life, for government is the beast that devours the flock, at least the Framers' research into ancient governments seems to conclude. I recall Jefferson's conclusion from both ancient and recent history that the three ancient forms always devolved into an evil. How subtle was Nazism in its day. Do the political differences of Chamberlin and Churchill and the public's response to their stands answer this question?

6. An Idea of a Republic

My mind jumps to the recent past. If the Executive acquires more power, then what is the concern of President Carter who saw *bureaucracy* as the greatest hindrance to his getting his job done?[311] Bureaucracy is another head of the beast that forms a barrier between the people and their representatives.[312] Jefferson's thoughts are powerful.

I turn my mind to the idea of republics.

> "The elementary republics of the wards, the county republics, the state republics, and the republic of the union, would form a gradation of authorities, standing each based on law, giving each one their delegated share of powers, and constituting truly a system of fundamental balances and checks for the government."

If Jefferson is serious, then we may want to rethink his statements. Is Jefferson democratic or republican in spirit? I find that the Pledge of Allegiance forms on my lips as I recall "*to the Republic for which it stands*" and that singular use of the word *republic*. So, I wonder, *Why do the Framers speak of republics?* John Adams made a defense of the Constitutions of the United States, which seems strange in that we have one Constitution. No! Each state has its own constitution. Jefferson informs us that each part of the state is a republic. I gather from Jefferson's letter that the states are to possess the authority for civil rights. Prior to the Constitution, each state operated with a preference for democratic principles.[313] These practices revealed some concerns that the Framers ensured our federal Constitution prevented. Is this why our Constitution guarantees a republican form to the states?

The thought ebbs away as I grabble with my concern about limited government. I know that Madison discussed republics in his *Federalist* articles.

I feel the power of Jefferson's next section. Is it a call to arms? Or is it a patriot's salute to patriotism? Is it a foreboding voice from the past hailing the future to beware of the iceberg before the unsinkable ship of state. I hear Jefferson's words.

> "Where every man is a sharer in the direction of his ward-republic, or of some of the higher ones, and feels that he is a participator in the government of affairs, not merely at an election one day in the year, but every day; when there shall not be a man in the State who will not be a member of some one of its councils, great or small, he will let the heart be torn out of his body sooner than his power be wrested from him by a Caesar or a Bonaparte."

I recall that the tyrant Napoleon is a wispy recollection and a warning signal that an ambitious man is a threat to freedom as Napoleon was to the Corsican republic, which was the first republic.[314] I shudder as Jefferson's words and the events of modern history commingle. My mind concentrates on the word *participant.* I should be a participant. I should get involved in what the representatives who represent me are doing in agreement with good government. *I will be a participant.* I realize that Jefferson is talking about all the states coexisting in agreement because of Great Britain's failure to represent the colonies by their constitution. I am but a single voter. Am I a disenfranchised voter when my party is out of office? I feel that I am as soon as I cast my vote. I do not feel Jefferson's enthusiasm in the letter below in my situation.

> "How powerfully did we feel the energy of this organization in the case of embargo? I felt the foundations of the government shaken under my feet by the New England townships. There was not an individual in their states whose body was not thrown with all its momentum into action; and although the whole of the other states were known to be in favor of the measure, yet the organization of this little selfish minority enabled it to overrule the Union."

Jefferson seems to say that a minority makes a difference when it stands its ground and its ground is its organization to defend its position. He is speaking of the 1807 Embargo Act he signed that stopped colonial vessels making foreign voyages. The Napoleonic wars nullified neutral American shipping to ports in England and France. New England stood against it because it could not continue its lucrative whaling commerce. Congress repealed the Act in 1809.[315]

My ground is the Constitution whose foundation forms the principles that should guide our country. Organization must begin with a single person's decision to participate. Does the Patriot Party represent a call to community organization? Such a stand is our guard whether majority or minority *against the degeneracy of our government, and the concentration of all its powers in the hands of the one, the few, the well-born, or the many who would change our system.* Yet, Jefferson knows that we are reliant upon our rulers. Jefferson prays for his recipient and our leaders.

> "God bless you, and all our rulers, and give them the wisdom, as I am sure they have the will, to fortify us against the degeneracy of our government, and the concentration of all its powers in the hands of the one, the few, the well-born, or the many."

Jefferson's first word binds present hope to future realization to God's providential care. Faith stimulates hope as commitment stimulates action. Jefferson's words give us the answer. The Federal government overflows its banks and is now in the wards, the counties, the municipalities, so the voter has little influence in not only these republics, but not even within his family. I shockingly realize that change is subtle and the government spreads its insidious tentacles across its constitutional boundaries as it entangles itself in state business and the citizen's personal business affecting even one's conscience regarding one's beliefs. What is the answer to curtail this floodgate of intrusion?

Each citizen must stand in his republic for its principles of self-government and a limited federal government. I hear an emphasis in the sound of Jefferson's voice as it pronounces the phrase *divide the counties into wards.* This strategy combined with the tactic *Begin them only for a single purpose; they will soon show for what others they are the best instruments.* A form of *divide et Impera,* (divide and conquer). Well, each of us is some place. Where we are is where we best serve and as we serve, some will rise. I suppose this is what he means by the oligarchy that it is those of virtue who should rise to the highest levels when their talent, whether developed or natural, parallels their virtue. *Virtue?* I reflect upon this word. Jefferson and the Framers considered this association very relevant to government. Yet, do we see this combination in our government? Why do we permit this disconnection with our past? Why have some risen who are so different from our Framer's vision? Are our republican principles the foundation of our law of the land? If so, how can we violate these principles? If they are not the foundation of our law, would this explain our confusion. What do all these references to republics mean?

A. Which Form of Government are WE?

Recently, the news showed several persons who refer to the United States as a "democracy."[316] I had been working on this book for a year when I heard their answer and it inspired me to explore these ideas of democracy and a republic more deeply. I read in the *Heritage Guide to the Constitution* a reference to "the second was the problem of making a democratic form of government efficient and effective." This was the answer to the two "diseases most incident to Republican Government"[317], which it lists as 1) democratic tyranny and 2) democratic ineptitude.[318] I could not locate these words or phrases in any of Madison's "Federalist Papers. In my research, I did not locate them in any materials that I studied. I must assume that the author drew his conclusion from some source to which I am not privy. I have shared my report that our government is a mix of three that Madison, et al designate as monarchy, aristocracy, and democracy. My point here is that giving the nod to democracy above the others is an over statement.

Since I gave my conclusion, I shall not belabor it further. How do you distinguish a republican form of government from a democratic one? I know that the meaning of *democratical* comes from d*emocracy*, but its emphasis in Johnson's definition demonstrates its connotation, which is,

> "As the government of England has a mixture of democratical in it, so the right of inventing political lies, is partly in the people." Arbuthnot[319]

I see that George Washington discussed democratic societies with his nephew and advised him to be cautious in his association with them. Genêt was at their source in America, and he, being French, brought these popular French revolutionary ideas to American soil.[320] They were most popular in the South and revolved around the slavery issue. Europe founded representation, but America founded *unmixed and extensive republics* and its establishment of a comprehensive system of checks and balances as its innovations to government, which lessens the evils of a democratic form.[321] His use of *un*-mixed seems to mean that our Republic is not a mixture as those that pre-existed ours, since our Republic is a mix of the three ancient forms of government plus indirect representation, separation of powers, which are equal and balanced and that includes other principles that benefit both citizen and government.

The Framers' exception is not indicative of their overwhelming agreement to frame the federal government as an extended republican government for the following reasons.

Characteristics of an Extended Republican Government:

First, law is the basis of a republic.

Secondly, a republic bases its character on virtue.

Thirdly, a republic does not restrict the people from participating in governing to a limited territory as a pure democracy does.

Fourthly, a republic that extends indefinitely across a vast territory as

America provides representation by suffrage that enables representatives to travel great distances to the location of the assemblies.

Fifthly, the people in a republic govern the governing and the people retain as the voice of the majority sovereignty over the government by a Constitution and its suffrage. Their form goes beyond a democracy by establishing that sovereignty is an unalienable right established by the God of Creation and that the Constitution sets forth republican principles through constitutional law.

Sixthly, the Convention of 1787 separates powers to offset the evils of a democracy by which human nature so naturally gravitates to corruption and history proves so soon fails.

Seventhly, an economic republic's commerce is better suited to free markets than a pure democracy that limits spending to necessities and strives to equalize wealth and to create a *middling* society. All these facts make the United States not only a republic but also a unique variety of republican government.

1. On Treason

Since the Constitution represents a republican form of government, then it must be the responsibility of all representatives to protect the people's constitutional form of government from all usurpations and innovations. If representatives do not, then they are responsible to the people. How can we hold them more immediately responsible? The final draft of the Constitution stated impeachment was mandated by the House of Representatives, but the Senate must convict and that only for *high crimes and misdemeanors.*[322] Neither the Congress nor the United States Supreme Court is any real defense against a rogue president, especially when the president's party controls Congress. If this is a weakness of the Constitution and unforeseen by the Framers and their foresight provides amendments to fix such future problems, should we use it? The people might closely watch their Senators and might demand explanations of issues, then develop some republican way to voice their views. Such power also enables the people to govern rogue representatives who elected by majority will vote their own conscience or implement unrepublican policies against the majority will of the people.

2. On Conscience

Conscience is a private decision, but it operates on public issues. How do I understand *conscience*? What standard do I use to comprehend *conscience*? Literally, the word means *with knowledge*. In America, one's conscience still connotes *a moral sense of right and wrong*, but some construe it to mean *an internal conviction*. The USSC mates this idea with its definition of a *religion* as any strongly held conviction, which is akin to amoralism. Since we are exploring the concepts and intents of the Framers, then we must comprehend what *conscience* meant to them. In 1755, Samuel Johnson released his first edition of his new dictionary. In it, he defines *conscience* under six points. He utilizes descriptors such as *good, justice, knowledge, veracity, scruple,* and *reasonableness.* These in turn make use of knowledge by which we construct a judgment toward oneself as being good, honest, or just, especially toward our own behavior.[323] From this, I gather that the Framers' understanding of conscience is closer to our discussion on virtue than it is to our modern conception, which has many fathers.

As the smell of sulphur and oozing lava warns of an eruption, so too ideologies that rub against the fabric of our Constitution ignite flaming warning brands of verbiage. Like smell, we possess ears that can finely tune in meaning and its ramifications. If such flamboyant ideologies are so contrary to government by the people, why do we not see these as unconstitutional? Are we protecting free speech and overlooking treason? We simply do not understand, because we think such speech is democratic, therefore constitutional. It is constitutional to speak one's mind freely, but it is unconstitutional when it actively undermines our constitutional principles that every citizen should protect. If we understood our republican principles, we would understand that the only way to change our government is by a Constitutional Convention. Any other method, such as policies, Executive orders, or legislative law that changes it, violates our pledge to protect our form of government that is the framework of our Constitution. That is an act of treason, for it is a direct attack against our form of government and its promise to retain a republican form. I may use the term liberally, but I think a review of treason is a modern need for the war on terror and usurpation of governments. When we label something democratic, it is not automatically justified. What these democratic ideas and movements miss is that their focus should be on the States and their constitutions for they are responsible for civil rights beyond areas the Constitution does not specifically cover.

Do we not have a conundrum? How do we protect our constitutional principles from corruption when free speech of our representatives is attempting to influence radical unrepublican changes using unrepublican methods?[324] Are representatives honoring their pledge of allegiance, their implicit fiduciary trust of the people, or their oath of office? Certainly, their action of change to our form of government may not occur without a Constitutional Convention or can it subtly change our attitudes. Yet, Europe suffers from just such a fate and they call it d*emocracy.* Is this the ploy, to convince citizens that if they revolt they are lawful citizens? Yet, their modern form of democracy is young in that its birth was in the nineteenth century. This type of democracy was unknown to our Framers as it is unknowable to the present for reasons already cited. (See Chapter 1)

Section 4: Conclusion

Thomas Jefferson provides one perspective of representation in the new American republican government. While he extends the concept to local and state governments, his views are consistent with those of the 1787 Congressional Constitutional Convention. We might say that this 1816 letter is a synopsis of the 1787 convention's views. We know that Jefferson and Madison corresponded on this subject. Jefferson requested Madison to answer Hamilton regarding his views advocating monarchy and aristocratic representation. We may safely conclude that the majority of the Founding Fathers and Framers agreed on the form of government they adopted and the states unanimously ratified. We have not one voice but a majority of voices.

I use Jefferson's stratagem as a tool for considering our issues and how we might deal with them by implementing our republican principles. I ask you, the reader, to evaluate this strategy by using it.

Wrap-up

"In the last quarter of the 18th Century, there was no country in the world that governed with separated and divided powers providing checks and balances on the exercise of authority by those who governed."

Warren E. Burger, Chief Justice of the United States, 1969-1986

Chairman of the Commission on the Bicentennial of the United States Constitution

From our historical documents, we see that our Republic is a *new* addition in the progress of government. Our Framers saw the federal system as the experimental answer to societal stresses upon our lives and souls wherein virtue brought the best of humanity to the corridors of leadership.

Our Framers placed the heart and soul of government in a united people to safeguard it against encroachments of their representatives. Our nation is a nation of people who stand as a militia ready to give life and limb for their right to life, liberty, and happiness. Our nation stands upon the principles of republicanism that clear our consciences for combat against an enemy that would destroy our Republic without a Constitutional Convention. In this, all such politics is tyranny to this free people.

As I worked through the history of the development of the Constitution of the United States, I found many differences between those our country now lives by and those intended by our Framers. If I am correct, then every voting participant is the voice of government. These might find it interesting to discover what differences disagree with our Constitution should it be interpreted using the Framers' mind-set. If we did this, would the United States possess so many factions with unrepublican goals? Would everyone from private citizen to public representative comprehend our system of government?

If so, then would not the private citizen be able to assess laws and policies by the set of original intent standards? If one could, then representatives and judges would have to base their decisions on standards that we can all agree are the roots of our Republic. Would this not, at least, reduce capricious decisions?

Our law is based neither on the common law of England nor on the ecclesiastic laws of Roman Catholicism nor on those of the Church of England. The original idea of the Framers was to write ecclesiastical orders out of our government, but not the virtue of faith in God and the morals of the Christian philosophy. The Framers did not make belief in Jesus a requirement for adoption of his moral philosophy. Our Constitution is a new law weaved from republican principles that form our Constitution. Alien ideas and laws weaken our system and our common good. I would like to say to those who follow Ayn Rand that her philosophy does not parallel our republican principles. It does capture the spirit of American individualism, but her philosophy while broad is too complex for most of us to absorb. Simplicity recommends itself over complexity when laws and principles are to serve the "common man". If so, then must we wonder why we do not understand the law? I offer Wallace v. Jaffree, 466 U.S. 924 (1984) as one example. This case refers to at least ninety-nine case precedents that the court presents to sustain their conclusion. It is erudite, but is it comprehensible to the average citizen? Why must we support a cadre of attorneys who defend us against rules of which we have no idea of their existence, let alone how they apply to our everyday lives? If our laws are not those that enforce our republican principles, then our confusion is the very weapon of our enemies among us. Our domestic tranquility is awash among religious views that possess no relation to our republican principles because they are self-centered rather than universal. Our education should bring understanding of our history and of our faith, which enlightens our hope for all humanity and these give vigor to our republican government. Eliminate any one of the above or burden it with alien ideas and we undermine our government and enslave ourselves with the chains of ignorance and the shackles of confusion, which opens our minds and our shores to tyranny. As true as this is, if we continue government support of education should we not demand that our tax dollars for public education support this knowledge bank for the benefit of our prosperity. Should we not challenge the Bench's unrepublican stand on neutrality and inform them to stand down from adjudicating about our faith and directing the contents that form our personal and social conscience? If our allegiance to our Constitution is sincere, then our participation in government is our certain strength reinforced by virtue derived from religion. Our knowledge protects us from tyranny by elitists who filter what they teach in order to control what we think. If we know, then we can teach our children and we can endow them with the security of our historic truth. In addition, we can impeach our leaders for undermining our ratified government that stands upon our republican principles. Anything less is treason.

Treason in Madison's version of the Constitution as recorded in his Notes:

> "Sect. 6. ...They shall in all cases, except treason, felony and breach of the peace, be privileged from arrest during their attendance at the session of their respective houses, and in going to and returning from the same; and for any speech or debate in either house, they shall not be questioned in any other place."[325]

Madison's Federalist #43, Item3:

> "To declare the punishment of treason, but no attainder of treason shall work corruption of blood, or forfeiture, except during the life of the person attained.
>
> "As treason may be committed against the United States, the authority of the United States ought to be enabled to punish it. But as new-fangled and artificial treasons have been the great engines by which violent factions, the natural offspring of free government, have usually wreaked their alternate malignity on each other, the convention have, with great judgment, opposed a barrier to this peculiar danger, by inserting a constitutional definition of the crime, fixing the proof necessary for conviction of it, and restraining the Congress, even in punishing it, from extending the consequences of guilt beyond the person of its author."[326]

Constitutional definition

> "Witnesses to the same overt Act, or on Confession in Article III, Section 3.
>
> "Treason against the United States, shall consist only in levying War against them, or in adhering to their Enemies, giving them Aid and Comfort. No Person shall be convicted of Treason unless on the Testimony of two Witnesses to the same overt Act, or on Confession in open Court.
>
> The Congress shall have Power to declare the Punishment of Treason, but no Attainder of Treason shall work Corruption

of Blood, or Forfeiture except during the Life of the Person attainted."

Only when the majority decides that personal liberty is not worth the effort of education and participation as watch guard over our representation shall we be defeated, and that from within ourselves. Do we have modern justification for our concerns? Dr. Eric Posner informs us that "over the years the courts have reinterpreted it. Ordinary people have reinterpreted it. And its meaning has definitely changed. Some people like the way it's changed. Some people don't like the way it's changed. But, it seems pretty clear to me that the original understanding has not that much relevance to how our lives are organized today."

Dr. Posner is responding to a question from an email which questioned how we got so far from the intent of the original constitution. Dr. Posner began by saying that, "the Founders had certain expectations about how the government would work, but they really had no idea. They were gambling. There was very little precedent. Basically, no precedent. And they were hoping the government structures would work in certain ways. They were wrong. Almost immediately a party system arose which they hadn't anticipated and the party system had a lot of influence over how the government worked. Almost immediately the executive became more powerful than many of them thought. So what's happened over the years, you know things change. Technology changed. People's views changed. You know, the risk is if the Constitution is interpreted somehow according to its original understanding, it just won't catch up and it will be ignored."

These last remarks seem to grant blanket permission from the intellectuals for the court's decision to do as it will with our Constitution's meaning. This is the best example of democratization I have come across. Does his view support the history that I have documented in terms of our Constitution's irrelevance? I heartily disagree, yet he is correct that views change. I wonder how much the change is due to the influence of the court's new interpretation and its failure to support our Constitution's fundamental principles."

Epilogue[327]

During my research, I transform from ignorance, due to misinformation and lack of education, to shock, to concern, to anger, to decision, to peaceful republican. I know that I am in for a fight because many Americans will have to run the same emotional gamut regarding the true nature and principles of our Republic.

If human nature permits justification for crimes against humanity and our Framers took every precaution they could devise to defend against man's corruption, what shall we as individual persons decide to follow? When the Bench justifies abortion by its ethical standards, then our past is a mist that veils the basis of our natural rights. Truly, atheism is on the rise.

Human nature is deceptive in its motivations. Our need is to be able to see others and ourselves, but in what water or which mirror? When Narcissus gazed into the water, he saw his reflection and fell in love with himself. When we look into the mirror of ancient philosophy, we see a vision of man in love with himself above all. Only in the Judaeo-Christian God does man see his true nature and his need for a God of Truth. Man's modern philosophy has been the waters of deception as man sees himself as good and self-reliant. History challenges this perspective. If reason serves us, then it must be able to look beyond our reflection to our nature and beyond to those principles that develop our conscience.

Our form of government consists of our republican principles that begin with the Creator granting us unalienable rights through natural law. Roscoe Pound points out the difference in meaning of natural rights in antiquity and in evolutionary thought.[328] Republicanism embraces virtue. Our Founding Fathers and the Framers acknowledged God through prayer and providence. They valued religion as the source of virtue and moral behavior. Their direct experience was with the Christian philosophy, which they counted as the best available to the human soul. We find secularism is not the separation of church from state, but it is rather separation of both state and church from interfering with personal belief (and worshipful behavior). Established religion is always a form of one faith (church, synagogue, temple, mosque, etc.) that discriminates against those outside its tenets. Jefferson noted this was changing, but our political ideologies are replacing it. Jefferson's faith lay in reason and tolerance because he believed truth would win the day. I agree. Our conclusion is that limited government is not to interfere with sects as long as they are not violent to the state. Christian sects were numerous and accepted by most Framers. Islam was encouraged to commune with our government, as John Adams mentions in the Treaty of Tripoli. Religion is a vital force of good that mollifies the nature of man toward absolute self-interest, except when its goal is to govern man. When it is destructive, it is unrepublican. We cannot ignore religion as part and parcel of our republican principles through the gate of virtue. Contra the article, *American Jurisprudence, Natural Law, and Clarence Thomas*, June 30, 2011, Thomas Aquinas' natural law is not synonymous with the Framers thoughts. In 1724, William Wollaston wrote his views on *The Religion of Nature Delineated*, which John Clarke refuted in 1725 in his *An Examination of the Notion of Moral Good and Evil, Etc.*, which is closer to the Framers' view. Aquinas attempts to base his theory on Aristotle's science in order to make Roman theology viable. Aquinas was Roman Catholic, which to the Framers did not stand upon a "*true bottom*" as Jefferson might say. The Framers evaded denominationalism by referring to their moral preference as the Christian philosophy. The Framers located natural law in the Judaeo Bible and the Christian New Testament in which the apostle John (1:1-18, with verse 10 testifying boldly) assigns Jesus as the originator of the world. Therefore, the Christian philosophy provides the source, foundation, and truth for their comprehension of natural law. While some Framers question the divinity of Jesus, their inquiry is no different from ours in terms of reasoning. Faith requires hope for what we believe to be fact we must support by the hope of its truth that leads to its fulfillment. Faith that the sun shall rise in the morning requires the hope that it will. Science requires faith in methodology and the hope that it uncovers reliable facts. All of these require a form of knowledge that supports its faith. One might refer to Alvin Plantinga's similar argument 1991: 15.[329]

Natural law relates to human nature and its purpose. While the tension between evolution and Christianity seems to be a matter of incompatible theories, it is actually physics and anthropology attempting to disprove or to curtail the influence of metaphysics. Yet, our drama sees how the latter serves our understanding in commerce. The good of capitalism does not justify its evil, nor does its evil justify those who desire to destroy its good. As God sees man's heart as evil, so he sees man's soul as worthy of redemption. What God does is to offer himself as the ransom for the evil in human nature. He is the only healer whose virtue is both necessary and sufficient for redemption. The Framers openly admit this as Washington laments the Framers likely overestimation of human nature's good. They looked forward to life after death. Thus, we must understand capitalism as a stage upon which our life drama reveals whether we choose to be virtuous or not. Fidel Castro's faith in communism fails to produce its promise. As Fidel Castro admits that his experiment with communism was a failure, which he now wishes he never had tried, so must capitalism admit its human faults, so we humans either admit or deny that our human nature vies for our choice between good and evil.

> "'Fidel Castro told a visiting American journalist that Cuba's communist economic model doesn't work, ...
>
> "Jeffrey Goldberg, a national correspondent for The Atlantic magazine, asked if Cuba's economic system was still worth exporting to other countries, and Castro replied: 'The Cuban model doesn't even work for us anymore' ...."[330]

Our question is, how does Fidel view his behavior in implementing his original faith in communism through violence now? Capitalism is theoretically and practically proper for an economic system. Our parallel between virtue and evil is the same as that between character and man, but man is not an absolute. Man is a finite creature of choice. When America, as a new government, converted to capitalism its motivational power for change drove the engine of conquest from east to west in a wave of ownership that disregarded our republican principles and especially virtue. It did inspire good men to labor industriously, but it enabled evil men to labor inhumanely for wealth. Our problem is that we accept the evil with the good as virtues of success when we praise capitalism as though pure in its motivations. While John Adams states in the Treaty of Tripoli that the United States government has no founding in Christianity, he does not mean that Christianity was not the faith of the majority of the colonies, as history would prove such a statement as nonfactual, but he means that our Republic is an empire of law and one of virtue. As a Christian, he understood the private nature of faith and its expression in principle. We accept all religions, but disallow their control over the minds of men, and, as Jefferson extols us, truth will win out.[331]

Today, some advocates of capitalism hail it as saintly and some antagonists curse it as devilish. History, when allowed to speak honestly, tells the story of man: some are good; some are bad. In all, tyrants and despots gained progress on the backs of slaves at the expense of lives and nature to harvest nature's resources. Slaves are made today by economic tyranny whose sword is money, whose whip is control, and whose chains are made of the links in the economic chain of necessity. We are neither free of slavery nor of serfdom.

We see this in the clamor for world integration that we label globalism. Third world countries are at the mercy of slave traders, especially in women and children.[332]

Our Framers knew that historically man exists more often as slave than as free. Therefore, their aspirations were to knit a government of principles whose fabric would hold a nation together for the longest possible time. Yet, they understood the nature of men, so their checks and balances offered reinforcement to the fabric of governmental structure.

We come to the scene when man again is poised to enslave humanity. Shall America rise to combat this evil? Our youth assemble for the battle. Our government seems to use them to support unrepublican ideologies. Truth shall triumph over evil. Our choices determine the character of our soul. Whose voice do you hear?

George Washington

> "Your Sentiment, that our affairs are drawing rapidly to a crisis, accord with my own. What the event will be is also beyond the reach of my foresight. We have errors to correct. We have probably had too good an opinion of human nature in forming our confederation. Experience has taught us, that men will not adopt & carry into execution, measures the best calculated for their own good without the intervention of a coercive power. I do not conceive we can exist long as a nation, without having lodged somewhere a power which will pervade the whole Union in as energetic a manner, as the authority of the different state governments extend over the several States ...
>
> "Would to God that wise measures may be taken in time to avert the consequences we have but too much reason to apprehend."[333]

Are we closer to or further from his fear? While the majority of states disfavored slavery in colonial America, one state held refuge in the threat to dissolve the union if the convention abolished slavery. The convention could not form a union without a bit more than two thirds of states ratifying our Constitution. Time proves certain decisions wise, although regrettable for the time.

While no rationalization justifies evil of the past, so the future will justify no hatred in the present. The same need exists to be a unified country for our own self-preservation. If we base our course on self-preservation, we shall come to the same conclusion as our Framers' did. A just government that rests on the majority finds its best fuel in the best principles of faith and governmental theory. They chose the Christian philosophy for their moral ground and republican principles knit from the experiences of ancient governments and their own contemporary experiences for our form of government. The principal of virtue bridges the gap modern secularists claim exists as separation between church and state.

When progress introduced machines to replace human labor, capitalist enterprise could proceed more rapidly and more efficiently. America observed the standard *to the conqueror goes the spoils* in justifying expansion. If we deny this, then we can neither free ourselves from such past calamities in the present or in our future nor unite ourselves by principles that agree with the virtue of humane beings. The human price in suffering continued as Blacks became free, our native Indians lost their lives for lands as capitalist speculators ravished the Midwest, which was government sponsored.[334] Later, the South suffered the same plunder from Northern capitalists known as carpetbaggers. We find this scenario in all societies whether black, white, yellow, or brown; there is no discrimination with greed. Does this recommend virtue as a pursuable principle?

Still, not all capitalists are as greedy as those who count human life as of little value when it stands in the way of profit. Nevertheless, profit is a prime mover in the greedy person's need to accumulate wealth. Do we still not see this in eminent domain claims from government intrusion today and the housing market? While the right argues for capitalism, it wears blinders and labels it the bankers, etc. when reality raises its head of capitalism's greed and man's evil in human nature. While the left argues for democracy, it wears cheerleader costume when societal divisions rise up. Neither left nor right alone or combined can provide national security or domestic tranquility based on their myopic vision. However, when factions violate our republican principles in order to subvert our Republic, then we are at war whether declared or undeclared or perceived or not. The Framers gave us the mint of ideas and the bank of trust that exists as our republican principles. Shall we adopt them?

Yet, we need capitalism as our economic theory, and it must play out in practice by men and women of all creeds and character. So, capitalism, like the hearts of men, is subject to virtue that each person chooses and that choice shapes his or her conscience. If we deny this human nature truth, then we cannot free ourselves from either governmental encroachment by policy or by law, which shreds our freedom, or personal decisions of injustice. The love of money motivates greed that pushes humanity aside. The love of God motivates love for humanity and balances work with a virtuous heart and character of soul. Thus, it is not a self-interested motivation in physical world terms, but a reconciliation of people in society and individuals in worship.

What humanity at large does not see is that the story of man is a descent from a Garden of Eden to the fields of bondage. As I view the story of Adam and Eve, I see the first cause of hardship with the election to know both good and evil. Can we not see the effects of this human wisdom? First, it alienated us from our creator, that is, direct spiritual knowing. Secondly, it alienated us form the Garden. Thirdly, it enslaved us to production and to the wiles of Pandora's Box. Man must gain sustenance by work, which is the first law of nature ushered in by that first choice. If Ockham's razor is sharp, then we must accept the simplest explanation of man's woes. If God exists, he can accomplish all things through nature as its creator, but his Word disciplines us to know his wisdom. We seek reconciliation and no better ground exists than our earliest thinkers' conclusion, namely that the Christian philosophy is the best moral system available to humanity. This is the one aspect absent in the United Nations campaign to govern humanity's standard of conduct. I submit it can only take from Christian values and deny it in order to persevere as *secular atheism*.

If we desire to save the earth, we must cease to exist for age deteriorates all things. God gives us the ground to exist. No form of government can retard, let alone annihilate, consumption of natural resources. However, capitalism must learn how to harvest with the least destruction. The earth provides the platform for man's struggle with both God's nature and his own nature. This fierce struggle is costly in its destructiveness. One may deny this scenario, but one cannot provide a concept that entails all aspects of life on earth that covers all man's actual activities as inclusive as God's word of truth that confirms man's existence and his natural right to life, liberty, and his pursuit of happiness. This is a fundamental republican principle.

If one is a seeker of *truth*, then absorb God's word, apply it to your life, and see if both your life and your government improve. God's moral way is what the scientific way mimics. Both man and government must obey it in order to be productive and nondestructive. We may deny this and continue our devolution into destruction that comes from hearts unredeemed. God informs us that he will restore nature and life ... in the end.

Appendix A: The Republican Principles[335]

We may use the republican principles to evaluate any issue past, present, and future. As virtue is one of the principles, it leads us to religion as it involves one's conscience. In religious parlance, conscience is a product of learned morals. While the Declaration of Independence focuses on the Old Testament's Yahweh (Hebrew) or Jehovah (Greek), the Framers ground the Constitution of the United States on the solid rock of the Christian philosophy as a moral teaching, but not all accept its soteriology. Law alone is stark, cold, and human. Natural law is vivid, warm, and celestial. We find that the meaning of secular in the eighteenth century, depending upon which definition one prefers, can mean *not bound by monastic rules*. This meaning clarifies our Framers' intent better than our modern interpretation.

Appendix B: Table of Government Powers[336]

*Ratification of Constitution and its +sources of constitutional authority and powers	National	Federal	Neither	Both
*Unanimous Consent		X		
+House of Representatives	X			
+Senate		X		
+Executive				X
+Federal Powers operate on Confederacy / Union of States	X			
+National Powers operate on individuals		X		
+Extent of powers	X (National Legislature)			
Mode of Amendment			X	

Appendix C. Glossary[337]

Activist

(See Cause Lawyering)

Alien

1. To make anything the property of another
2. To estrange; to turn the mind or affection; to make averse to; with from.

Alienable

That of which the property may be transferred.

> "Land is alienable, and treasure is transitory, and both must, at one time or other, pass from him, either by his own voluntary act, or by the violence and injustice of others, or at least by fate."
> Dennis Letters

Amoral

I researched this word and made an entry in my *Conceptionary* that is too long and complicated to add here. I will add my author's note taken from a paragraph of my conclusion from this research. Here it is:

> Mr. Brinton[338] discusses rationalism that spawns the doctrine that modern man can find all answers when he places faith in himself and in his intelligence using Popper's scientific method, but science focuses only on the physical while denying the metaphysical. "As *science* it provides neither a cosmology nor ontology, nor a full teleology. Science as science does not attempt to answer—does not even ask—the Big Questions of human destiny, of God's ways to man's, of Right and Wrong and Good and Bad. Some scientists as individuals come near not asking any of the Big Questions, come near guiding themselves in daily life by custom and authority, as do most of us most of the time." I

believe this forms the kernel of the 21st century's amoral stand as doctors, lawyers and evidently Wall Street brokers and bankers assume their work is subject to this same purist standard, but these latter are not after Truth, but money while the latter attempt to uncover Truth.

Angst

I use Kierkegaard's sense of anxiety by which he means "the dizziness of freedom," which embodies one's effort to achieve autonomy, which creates a tension between its allure and its disturbing influence.[339]

Atheism

The disbelief of a God.

Atheist

One that denies the existence of God.

Autocracy

Independent power; supremacy.

Barrier

1. A barricade; an entrenchment
2. A fortification, or strong place, as on the frontiers of a country.
3. A stop; an obstruction.
4. A bar to mark the limits of a place.
5. A boundary.

Belligerent

A country involved in a war or other armed international conflict. Cf. neutral (1).[340]

Burthen

A burden

Cause lawyering

"...one who advocates for social justice by combining the activities of litigation, community organizing, public education, and lobbying to advance a cause past its current legal limitations and boundaries."[341]

Citizen

A. 1. A freeman of a city; not a foreigner; not a slave.
   2. A townsman; a man of trade; not a gentleman.

3. An inhabitant; a dweller in any place.

B. A person who, by either birth or naturalization, is a member of a political community, owing allegiance to the community and being entitled to enjoy all its civil rights and protections; a member of the civil state, entitled to all its privileges.[342]

Civil

1. Relating to the community; political; relating to the city or government

2. Relating to any man as a member of a community

5. Not ecclesiastical

6. Not natural; as a person banished or outlawed is said to suffer civil, though not natural death.

Civil Rights

When we combine these terms, we conclude that our Civil Rights are a combination of our relation to community and to our creator, God, as the Framers' would comprehend this combination. As civil pertains to government and rights to God, then, we cannot separate church from state as the USSC adjudicated.

However, here is a court version:

"A 'civil right' is considered a right given and protected by law, and a person's enjoyment thereof is regulated entirely by the law that creates it." 82 CA 369, 373, 255, P 760, California Supreme Court

Should we accept this interpretation as representative of our natural rights from which all civil rights spring? The courts display a special and biased opinion toward man's law, which is destruction to unalienable rights.

Collective Choice

1. Social Choice attempts to derive these from individual choices, which are justified from collective action.
2. Collective Action attempts to describe and explain the ways in which groups conduct their affairs that emerge from actions of its members.[343]

Common

1. Belonging equally to more than one.
2. Having not possessor or owner
3. Vulgar; mean; not distinguished by any excellence; often seen; easy to be had; having little value; not rare; not scarce.
4. Public; general; serving the use of all.

5. Of no rank; mean; without birth or decent.

6. Frequent; usual; ordinary
(See Liberal)

Commonweal

1. A polity; an established form of civil life.
2. The public; the general body of the people.
3. A government in which the supreme power is lodged in the people; a republic

(Also known as *commonwealth* from *common* and *weal*, which see)

Compact
A contract; an accord; an agreement; a mutual and settled appointment between two or more, to do or to forbear something.

Complaisance
Civil; desirous to please.

Confederacy
A league; a contract by which several persons or bodies of men engage to support each other; union; engagement; federal compact. (See Consolidation; Federal; National; States; Union)

Consequentialism
An ethical theory that judges the rightness or wrongness of actions according to their consequences.
(See Aristotle's, *Ethics*; Utilitarianism; Virtue Ethics)

Constituent
n.f. 1. The person or thing which constitutes or settles any thing in its peculiar state.
2. That which is necessary to the subsistence of any thing
3. He that deputes another.
(See Depute)

Constitution

1. The act of constituting; enacting; deputing; establishing; producing.
2. State of being; particular texture of parts; natural qualities.
3. Corporeal frame.

4. Temper of body, with respect to health or disease.
5. Temper of mind.
6. Established form of government; system of laws and customs.
7. Particular law; established usage; establishment; institution.

Constitutional

1. Bred in the constitution; radical.
2. Consistent with the constitution; legal.

Consolidation

The act of uniting into a solid mass. (See Confederacy; Federal; National; States; Union)

"Each State, in ratifying the Constitution, is considered as a sovereign body, independent of all others, and only to be bound by its own voluntary act. In this relation, then, the new Constitution will, if established, be a FEDERAL, and not a NATIONAL constitution." Madison, Federalist #39

(See Confederacy; Federal; National; States; Union)

Contract

1. An act whereby two parties are brought together; a bargain; a compact.
2. An act whereby a man and woman are betrothed to one another.
3. A writing in which the terms of a bargain are included.

Corruption of Blood

"A defunct doctrine, now considered unconstitutional, under which a person loses the ability to inherit or pass property as a result of an attainder or of being declared civilly dead. Also termed *corruption of the blood....*" [344]

Czarism

autocratic rule[345]

Democracy

One of the three forms of government; that in which the sovereign power is neither lodged in one man, nor in the nobles, but in the collective body of the people.

"While many of the servants, by industry and virtue, arrive at riches and esteem, then the nature of the government inclines toward *democracy.*" Temple

"The majority having the whole power of the community, may employ all that power in making laws, and executing those laws; and there the form of the government is a perfect *democracy.*" Locke

Democratical

Pertaining to a popular government; popular.

"They are still within the line of vulgarity, and are democratical enemies of truth." Brown's Vulgar Errours, b.i.c.3.

Depersonalization

A person who suffers a severe emotional shock or prolonged stress withdraws from reality, but feels as though reality is withdrawing from him. He feels estranged from himself and from the world.[346]

Depute

(preceded by To) To send with a special commission; to impower one to transact instead of another.

Despotic

Unlimited in authority; arbitrary; unaccountable.

Despotism

Absolute power.

Disinterested

Without regard to personal advantage; not biased by particular views; impartial.

Dispassionate

Cool; calm; impartial; moderate; temperate.

Divine law

Law that emanates from a supernatural source, such as a deity. Cf. NATURAL LAW.[347]

Ectopic pregnancies

A pregnancy in an abnormal position, such as a cervical pregnancy. [348]

Embargo

A prohibition to pass; in commerce, a stop put to trade.

Equity

A. n.f. [equite, French; aequitas, Latin]

1. Justice; right; honesty.
2. Impartiality
3. [in law.] The rules of decision observed by the court of Chancery.

B. n. (14c) 1. Fairness; impartiality; evenhanded dealing <the company's policies require managers to use equity in dealing with subordinate employees>.

2. The body of principles constituting what is fair and right; natural law <the concept of "unalienable rights" reflects the influence of equity on the Declaration of Independence.>
3. The recourse to principles of justice to correct or supplement the law as applied to particular circumstances <the judge decided the case by equity because the statute did not fully address the issue>....
4. The system of law or body of principles originating in the English Court of Chancery and superseding the common and statute law (together called "law" in the narrower sense) when the two conflict <in appealing to the equity of the court, she was appealing to the 'king's conscience">; CHANCERY (2).
5. A right, interest, or remedy recognizable by a court of equity <there was no formal contract formation, so they sued for breach in equity>. [Cases: Equity key1.] [349]

(See Parity)

Establish

A. 1.To settle firmly; to fix unalterably.
2. To settle in any privilege or possession; to confirm.
3. To make firm; to ratify.
4. To fix or settle in an opinion.
5. To form or model.
6. To found; to build firmly; to fix immovably.
7. To make a settlement of any inheritance.

B. 1. To settle, make, or fix firm; to enact permanently
2. To make or form; to bring about or into existence.
3. To prove; to convince[350]

Establishment

A. 1. Settlement; fixed state
2. Confirmation of something already done; ratification.
3. Settle regulation; form; model of a government or family.
4. Foundation; fundamental principle; settled law.

B. 1. The act of establishing; the state or condition of being established.
2. An institution or place of business.
3. A group of people who are in power or who control or exercise great influence over something.[351]

Establishment Clause

(1959) The First Amendment [1791] provision that prohibits the federal and state governments from establishing an official religion, or from favoring or disfavoring an official religion over another.[352]

Amendment I [1791]

> "Congress shall make no law respecting an establishment of religion, or prohibiting the free exercise thereof;...."[353]

Executive Order

"(1862) An order issued by or on behalf of the President, usu. Intended to direct or instruct the actions of Executive agencies or government officials, or to set policies for the Executive branch to follow.—abbr. ex. Ord. [Cases: United States 28.]"[354]

Executive Powers

"(17c) Constitutional law. The power to see that the laws are duly executed and enforced. Under federal law, this power is vested in the President; in the states, it is vested in the governors. The President's enumerated powers are found in the U.S. Constitution, art. KKI, §2; governors' Executive powers are provided for in state constitutions. The other two great powers of government are the legislative power and the judicial power. [Cases: Constitutional Law 2620-2626.][355]

Falsification

Popper: "We say that a theory is falsified only if we have accepted basic statements which contradict it (cf. section 11, rule 2)...We shall take it as falsified only if we discover a *reproducible effect* which refutes the theory."[356]

Federal

A. 1. Form regards the Union as a CONFEDERACY of sovereign states.

> "the assent and ratification of the several States, derived from

the supreme authority in each State, the authority of the people themselves"

2. Relating to a league or contract
3. powers operate on the political bodies composing the Confederacy, in their political capacities

"Each State, in ratifying the Constitution, is considered as a sovereign body, independent of all others, and only to be bound by its own voluntary act. In this relation, then, the new Constitution will, if established, be a FEDERAL, and not a NATIONAL constitution."[357]

States "as political and coequal societies...."[358]

B. Of or relating to a system of associated governments with a vertical division of governments into national and regional components having different responsibilities; esp., of or relating to the national government of the United States.[359]

(See Confederacy; Consolidation; National; States; Union)

Federal Act

A statute enacted by the U.S. Congress.[360]

Federalism

Not in the Samuel Johnson, 1755 dictionary

A. 1. "A system of government, such as exists in the US, in which a central (or federal) government, both legislature an Executive, exists side by side with state or provincial government, again with both Executive and legislative powers. Both federal and state governments will derive what powers they have from the single federal constitution, but both are supreme in their particular fields, so that ...the state government cannot be construed as a delegation of federal power." [361]
2. Federalism in the European Union (EU) is a rule that a nation state must comply with the EU's rules of law over its own."[362] We should note that the EU uses a body of law referred to as *acquis communautaire*, which is some 100,000 pages.

B. (1787) The legal relationship and distribution of power between the national and regional governments within a federal system of government.[363]

Federal Law

(18c) The body of law consisting of the U.S. Constitution, federal statutes and regulations, U.S. treaties, and federal common law.[364]

Gentleman

1. A man of birth; a man of extraction, though not noble.
2. A man raised above the vulgar by his character or post.
3. A term of complaisance.
4. The servant that waits about the person of a man of rank.
5. It is used of any man however high.

God

1. The Supreme Being;
2. a false god; an idol;
3. Any person or thing deified or too much honored.

Good Faith

1. A state of mind consisting in:
(1) honesty in belief or purpose,
(2) faithfulness to one's duty or obligation,
(3) observance of reasonable commercial standards of fair dealing in a given trade or business, or
(4) absence of intent to defraud or to seek unconscionable advantage.
Also termed *bona fides*.[365]

Historicism

Argues that history determines both social and cultural outcomes, and these certain laws govern.[366]

Impartial

Equitable; free from regard to party; indifferent; disinterested; equal in distribution of justice; just. It is used as well of the actions as persons. (See Disinterested)

Inalienable

That cannot be alienated.

Integrity

1. Honesty; uncorrupt mind; purity of manners; uncorruptedness.
2. Purity; genuine unadulterated state.
3. Intireness; unbroken whole.

Intermixture

1. "A mass formed by mingling bodies.
2. Something additional mingled in a mass."[367]
3. Black's Dictionary conjoins intermixture with goods. It defines an intermixture of goods with the phrase confusion of goods, which means "the mixture of things of the same nature but belonging to different owners so that the identification of the things is no longer possible".

Jus sanguinis

[Latin "right of blood"] The rule that a child's citizenship is determined by the parents' citizenship. Most nations follow this rule.

jus soli

Latin "right of the soil"] The rule that a child's citizenship is determined by place of birth. This is the U.S. rule, as affirmed by the 14th amendment to the Constitution.

Justice

1. The virtue by which we give to every man what is his due.
2. Vindicative retribution; punishment.
3. Right; assertion of right

Kitsch

A German term that relates how art, music, literature, and popular culture lie about human conditions by using false heroes. Kitsch is the tactic the Nazi used. Watch for it in contemporary politics.[368]

Law

A. 1. A rule of action.
   2. A decree, edict, statute, or custom, publicly established as a rule of justice.
   3. Judicial process.
   4. Conformity to law; any thing lawful.
   5. An established and constant mode or process; a fixed correspondence of cause and effect.
B. 1. The regime that orders human activities and relations through systematic application of the force of politically organized society, or through social pressure, backed by force, in such a society; the legal system <respect and obey the law>.

2. The aggregate of legislation, judicial precedents, and accepted legal principles; the body of authoritative grounds of judicial and administrative action; esp., the body of rules, standards, and principles that the courts of a particular jurisdiction apply in deciding a controversies brought before them <the law of the land>.
3. The set of rules or principles dealing with a specific area of a legal system <copyright law>
4. The judicial and administrative process; legal action and proceedings<when settlement negotiations failed, they submitted their dispute to the law>.
5. A statue <Congress passed a law.—Abbr. L.>
6. COMMON LAW <law but not equity>.
7. The legal profession<she spent her entire career in law>.[369]

Legal

1. Done or conceived according to law
2. Lawful; not contrary to law

Legislature
The power that makes laws.

League
To unite; to confederate

Liberal

1. Not mean; not low in birth; not low in mind.
2. Becoming a gentleman.
3. Munificent; generous; bountiful; not parsimonious.[370]

(See Common; Vulgar)

Libertine
one who is unconfined; one who lives without the restraint of law; one without regard for the precepts of religion; as an adjective, a licentious or irreligious person.

Majority Will
The whole people of the United States, who form one nation of voters who win the electoral majority in each state that elects the person for a particular office, constitute the will of the majority, which would bind the minority.

Material

In context, *material* means *of such a nature that knowledge of the item would affect a person's decision-making.*[371]
(See Treason, Item 2.)

Moral

1. Relating to the practice of men towards each other as it may be virtuous or criminal; good or bad.
2. Reasoning or instructing with regard to vice and virtue.
3. Popular; such as is known or admitted in the general business of life.

Jefferson and Franklin to the reverend Stiles[372] summarized the virtues of the Christian philosophy. Jefferson condensed the New Testament to the words of Jesus in his Jefferson Bible.[373] Franklin provides a list of virtues at the end of which he advises the reader to imitate Jesus and Socrates.[374] Franklin shares with Reverend Stiles this comment about Jesus of Nazareth, which is,

> "As to Jesus of Nazareth, my Opinion of whom you particularly desire, I think the System of Morals and his Religion, as he left them to us, the best the World ever saw or is likely to see;...."

National

A. is a government that regards the Union as a consolidation of the States.

By intent, the national legislatures were the pools from which the federal legislature would come.

> "The idea of a national government involves in it, not only an authority over the individual citizens, but an indefinite supremacy over all persons and things, so far as they are objects of lawful government. Among a people consolidated into one nation, this supremacy is completely vested in the national legislature."[375]

We should distinguish in this quote whether the Federal has jurisdiction over the National as some interpret the Supremacy Clause.

(See Confederacy; Consolidation; Federal; States; Union)

B. 1. of or relating to a nation;
2. Nationwide in scope.[376]

National emergency

A national crisis or situation that requires immediate and extraordinary national response.[377]

(See Federal; National)

Natural Law

(15c) 1. A physical law of nature <gravitation is a natural law>.

2. A philosophical system of legal and moral principles purportedly deriving from a universalized conception of human nature or divine justice rather than from legislative or judicial action; moral law embodied in principles of right and wrong <many ethical teachings are based on natural law>.—Also termed law of nature; natural justice; lex aeterna; eternal law; lex naturae; lex naturalae; divine law; jus divinum; jus naturale; (in sense 2) normative jurisprudence; jure naturae. Cf. FUNDAMENTAL LAW; POSITIVE LAW; DIVINE LAW.

> "'Natural law, as it is revived today, seeks to organize the ideal element in law, to furnish a critique of old and received ideals and give a basis for formulating new ones, and to yield a reasoned canon of values and a technique of applying it. I should prefer to call it philosophical jurisprudence. But one can well sympathize with those who would salvage....' Roscoe Pound. *The Formative Era of American Law 29 (1938).*"[378]

Neutral

A person or country taking no side in a dispute; esp., a country that is at peace and is committed to aid neither of two or more belligerents. Cf. BELLIGERNT.[379]

Neutrality

1. The state or quality of being impartial or unbiased.
2. The condition of a nation that in time of war takes no part in the dispute but continues peaceful dealings with the belligerents.[380]

Ochlocracy

Government by the lowest classes; mob-rule[381]

Parity

A. Funk and Wagnalls
    1. Equality, as of condition, rank, value, etc.; also like a state or degree.

2. The equivalence in legal weight and quality of the legal tender of one class of money to another.
3. Par. (def. 3).
4. Equality between the currency or prices of commodities of two countries or cities.
5. Deals with farm prices, 7 and 8 do not deal with monetary values.[382]

B. *Black's Law Dictionary*, No entry
(See Equity)

Passion

A. Samuel Johnson
1. Any effect caused by an external agency.
2. Violent commotion of the mind.
3. Anger.
4. Zeal; ardour.
5. Love.
6. Eagerness.
7. Emphatically.

B. Neuroscientific studies address *intellectual passion* that drives both theology and science. It operates within and emerges out of a particular paradigm (Khun) or tradition (MacIntyre), which guides the criteria for what is reasonable.
...The way in which passion forms an inextricable element of rational inquiry has also been demonstrated by findings in the field of neuroscience.
... Neuroscientific studies have shown that human thinking cannot be so easily separated from human feeling and doing, because the formation of beliefs is mediated by emotional and psychological experiences that are mediated through neurobiological functioning (cf. Damaiso 1999). These developments do challenge the compartmentalization of thinking (reason) form willing (faith), but they also provide an opportunity to recover the more holistic anthropology of the Hebrew Bible and the New Testament (Shults 2003: 165-81)[383]

Perfidy

Treachery; want of faith; breach of faith.

Plenipotentiary

A negotiator invested with full power.

Popular

1. Vulgar; plebeian
2. Suitable to the common people
3. Beloved by the people; pleasing to the people
4. Studious of the favour of the people
5. Prevailing or raging among the populace: as, a popular distemper

(See Vulgar)

Popular Government

1. Cicero calls it a democracy
2. Adams says, popular government in the strictest sense, that is, pure democracy, where the people in themselves, and by themselves, perform all that belongs to government.... (See Chapter 1, Section 3: B.)

Postmodernism

Postmodernism takes on many shades of meaning. For instance, it may mean any or all of the following, which are:

1. "An actual state of affairs in society
2. The set of ideas which try to define or explain this state of affairs
3. An artistic style , or an approach to the making of things
4. A word used in many different contexts to cover may different aspects of all the above."[384]

Is a collection of ideas I will not discuss the elements of this view of the world, but it is necessary to emphasize that it plays a role in one's understanding of meaning in our current environment. The era of the ancients and Framers is uninfluenced by this model, but some today may be and that more or less. I leave it to the reader to investigate this broad encompassing field. One must start with Structuralism, Poststructuralism, and Deconstruction. Its antifoundational aspects influence moods and tempers that in turn affect those whose foundation is opposite these influences. I will include in the Bibliography some books pertinent to this subject.

(See Linguistics; Postmodernism; Semiotics)

Potentate

Monarch; prince; sovereign.

Radical

1. Primitive; original
2. Implanted by nature
3. Serving to origination

Reason

1. The power by which man deduces one proposition from another, or proceeds from premises to consequences; the rational faculty.
2. Cause; ground or principle.
3. Cause; efficient.
4. Final cause.
5. Argument; ground or persuasion; motive.
6. Ratiocination; discursive power.
7. Clearness of faculties.
8. Right; justice.
9. Reasonable claim; just practice.
10. Rationale; just account.
11. Moderation; moderate demands.

To Reason:

1. To argue rationally; to deduce consequences justly from premises.
2. To debate; to discourse; to talk; to take or give an account.
3. To raise disquisitions; to make enquiries.

Religion

A. 1.a. "A system of faith and worship usu. involving belief in a supreme being and usu. containing moral or ethical code; esp., such a system recognized and practiced by a particular church, sect, or denomination.

2. b. "In construing the protections under the Establishment Clause

and the Free Exercise Clause, courts have interpreted the term religion quite broadly to include a wide variety of theistic and nontheistic beliefs. [Cases: Religions Societies key1][385]

B. 1. Virtue, as founded upon reverence of God, and expectation of future rewards and punishments;
2. A system of divine faith and worship as opposite to others.[386]

Religious

Pious-disposed to the duties of religion

Religious Rights

When we combine the two terms, one understands his religious duties to be a just claim as a property or interest. This definition corresponds to both Adams' and Madison's tracts on property. I take the liberty to include the same correspondence with our civil rights. We ground our natural rights in both Religious and civil rights.

Republic

1. Commonwealth; state in which the power is lodged in more than one.
2. Republics-"…states accountable to their citizens."[387]

(See Chapter 5, Section 1: A-I)

Republican

Adj. Placing the government in the people.
n.s. [from republic] One who thinks a commonwealth without monarchy the best government.

Republicanism

"Usually used to denote a particular tradition in political thought, which defends government offices, representation of the people and the rule of law, as the pre-conditions of a free citizenry."[388]

Right

1. Justice; not wrong
2. Freedom from error
3. Just claim
4. That which justly belongs to one
5. Property; interest
6. Power; prerogative

Salutary

Wholesome; healthful; safe; advantageous; contributing to health or safety.

Secular

1. Something that is not spiritual; it relates to present world affairs; it is not holy, but worldly.

This, in every several man's actions of common life, appertaineth unto moral, in public and Politic secular affairs, unto civil wisdom. Hooker.

Even in this definition, Hooker's usage contains the juxtaposition that secular maintains in common parlance between public morals and politics that together generate wisdom.

2. Not bound by monastic rules

The Roman Catholic church always possessed its monastic laws and for a time they were codified and taught mainly through monastic schools, whereas the English laws were neither codified nor taught through institutions. Secular society had no academy for law, which permitted the monarchy to dictate the law. Eventually, this situation changed as the common law codified and universities established.

States

A national group of individual sovereign territories united as Confederacies. (See Confederacy; Consolidation; Federal; National; Union)

Subsidiarity

European Union (EU) term that, in this context, seems to mean that nation states are subsidiary (*subordinate; under another's control*) to the EU.

Subversion

Overthrow; ruin; destruction

Treason

1. An attempt to overthrow the government in one of two forms, which are:
   a. To make war against the state
   b. To materially support the state's enemies
2. The offense of attempting to overthrow the government of the state to which one owes allegiance, either by making war against the state or by materially supporting its enemies—also termed high treason; alta prodition. Cf. sedition.[389]

Madison quotes the constitutional article for the punishment of treason in his Notes regarding the powers conferred to the federal government.

a. About or

The use of *or* means one or the other condition exists, but both occurring at the same time is prohibited, which is the usual definition in logic. The text substantiates this interpretation as the next sentence addresses the need for two witnesses unless the accused gives a confession in open court.

b. Aid and comfort

What remains is to determine what *aid and comfort* means in the seventeenth century. Johnson says *aid* in general usage means *to succor, to support, to help.* In law, it means a subsidy. *Comfort* means *to support, assistance, or countenance.*

c. On subsidy

Johnson defines *subsidy* as *comfort,* as in money.[390]

I would link this with material support.

d. On *war*

1. Hostile action using armed forces
2. Hostile situation without armed forces[391]

Tribunal

1. The seat of a judge.
2. A court of justice.

(See Chapter 5, Section G: Extended Republic: Federal Government.)

Unalienable

Not to be transferred.

Hereditary right should be kept sacred, not from any unalienable right in a particular family, but to avoid the consequences that usually attend the ambition of competitors. Swift

Union

The act of joining two or more, so as to make them one. (See National; Consolidation) In civil and in law, union contains a religious sense.

> "Hence, it clearly appears, that the same advantage which a republic has over a democracy, in controlling the effects of faction, is enjoyed by a large over a small republic,--is enjoyed by the Union over the States composing it." Madison, Federalist #10

(See Confederacy; Consolidation; Federal; National; States)

Unmixed
Not mingled with any thing; pure; not corrupted by additions.

Urge

1. To incite; to push.
2. To provoke; to exasperate.
3. To follow close, so as to impel.
4. To labour vehemently.
5. To press; to enforce.
6. To press as an argument.
7. To importune; to solicit.
8. To press in opposition, by way of objection.

Vulgar
The common people.

Vulgarity

1. Meanness; state of the lowest people.
2. Particular instance or specimen of meanness.

Vulgarly
Commonly; in the ordinary manner; among the common people.

Virtue
1. Moral goodness
2. A particular moral excellence
5. Efficacy; power
6. Acting power
7. Secret agency; efficacy, without visible or material action.
10. One of the orders of the celestial hierarchy.

Virtue Ethics
An ethical theory that focuses on the character of the actor rather than on the nature of the act or its consequences.[392]
(See Aristotle's Ethics; Consequentialism)

Weal

1. Happiness; prosperity; flourishing state

2. Republic; state; public interest
(See Commonweal)
NOTE: *weal* does not mean *well* as the movie *Lean on Me* teaches.

Worship: 4. Adoration; religious act of reverence
To Worship: 1. To adore; to honour or venerate with religious rites.
Thou shalt worship no other God. Exod. Xxxiv.14

Author's Note:

Associating all the words, I find that some militants who use arms to advance their cause and are citizens of the United States fall within the Framers' definition of war. The courts will challenge this conclusion due to modern liberalism, but the people's general welfare and the nation's tranquility are both at risk. Should militants inspire a rebellion, then we must declare an overt case of war as our form of government is at risk, which meets the primary definition of armed forces, unless we restrict that to what we mean today by armed services. Our second definition (b) provides sufficient grounds for our premise. I place this in the context of our Constitution requiring an amendment by the states to change our form of republican government.

Appendix D: Table of Constitutional Convention's Principles of Government

Principles	Explanation	Means	Ends	Source
Limited government	Defines boundaries to "erect some barrier against the gradual innovations of an unlimited government."	Constitution	Provides definitions of government and its interaction of departments along specific functions.	Madison
Natural rights	God endowed.	Constitution	Makes rights sovereign and govt. guaranty of protector of natural rights.	Madison
Republic	Rule by law (constitutional), not by man (despotism, monarchianism, oligarchy, Judiciary, etc.).	Constitution	Makes law dependent upon the people through representation (America's modern contribution to government).	Madison
Federal republic (unmixed republican government)	It remained for the people of the U.S. by combining a federal with a republican organization to enlarge still more the sphere of representative Govt and by convenient partitions & distributions of power, to provide the better for internal justice & order, whilst it afforded the best protection agst. external dangers.			Madison, 1833, Majority Governments, Madison Manuscripts
No two or more departments must be controlled by the same hands.	Division of power of the branches, but with a negative.[393]	Executive appoints; legislature makes law.	Legislature confirms and Judiciary interprets application within the laws of the land.	Madison, *Federalist* #47
Each dept. a wall of its own				Madison, *Federalist* #47

Separation of powers	1. Apply checks and balances between. different departments. 2. using opposite and rival interests (He means "private" interests v. federal interests in the interest of public rights, p. 289.).	1. Members have as little agency in appointment of members of other depts. 2. a. ambition counteract ambition. b. personal motive to resist encroachment of the others."	"The great security against gradual concentration of the several powers in the same dept."	Madison, *Federalist* #51
Power or authority of the people-National Government	Voice or will of the people is primary control on the government.	Legislature is the people's direct link to representatives and to amendments.	Balance one dept. within constitutional limits.	Madison, *Federalist* #51
Legislative authority necessarily dominates.	Republican government.	Divide it into different branches to offset its dominance	Different modes of election; different principles of action to give them little connection in the nature of their functions and their common dependence on the society.	Madison, *Federalist* #51
Executive weaker than legislature needs to be fortified.	Legislative authority necessarily dominates.	Constitutional equilibrium: Balance by connection of Executive with weaker of legislature which is connected to its stronger half.	Balance of power between Executive and the legislature.	Madison, *Federalist* #51
Above principles from *Federalist* #51.	If not applied threatens liberty.	Applied is "the great security against gradual concentration of the several powers in the same dept."	Remedy is to provide the constitutional means and personal motives, to resist encroachments of the others.	Madison, *Federalist* #51
State codes facilitate federal legislation.	Local interests & circumstances drive federal legislation.	House of Reps drawn from state legislatures who bring knowledge to Congress.	Assemblage from all states unify state diversity into a federal code of a ratio of 1 to 30,0000.	Madison, *Federalist* #56
States balance federal.	House of Reps. Have common interest with their state.	Weaker than Senate, but relation with Executive balances power with Senate.	Strengthens will of the people and pits ambition in house against ambition with other departments.	Madison, *Federalist* #51
Representation either direct or indirect.	a. To make representatives dependent on the people b. rights of property same as personal rights.	a. Election every two (biennial) years b. establishment of a common standard for representative taxation	a. Short terms encourage common interest of representatives with the people b. balances difference in population of small and large states.	Madison, *Federalist* #52 a. #54: pg. 302–04 b. pg. 306–07

State legislators elect members of Congress; the two houses elect who returns. See note 1: Seventeenth Amendment.	To ensure that reps of merit and knowledge return to manage federal affairs.	Those in office know one another best and can discern upon close scrutiny who serves honorably.	Assists human virtue that is tested by advantage, but known to associates and less known to constituents.	Madison, *Federalist* #53
Apportionment of: 1. members of the several states determined by personal rights. 2. Property rights. Slaves counted as three-fifths of a person (for representation) and as property (for taxation). The constitution views slaves in their mix. "If law restored them their rights they would have an equal share in representation", p. 303. 1. Slaves as persons, i.e., as a moral person not part of irrational creation as are animals, which increases state representation. 2. Slaves as property generate taxes on "that proportion of wealth" of the states.	1. Personal Rights: House of Representatives from each state is based on number of state population, which creates a need for a census. 2. Personal property rights generates taxes.	Members of the House are elected by their peers in the House based on ability, etc.	Members scrutinize others and determine who contributes and returns those most capable.	Madison, *Federalist* #54; see Madison's letter to Robert Walsh, Montpellier, Nov. 27, 1819.
Human Nature	a. degree of depravity in all humans with b. a portion of esteem and confidence.	Human nature in republican government assumes this state more than does any other form of limited representation, which warrants caution in delegating authority and care of legislative trust.	Human nature is the reason for a balance of power crafted into the Constitution.	Madison, *Federalist* #55

Interests of constituents & circumstances	State interests in federal matters are known by state representatives from which state legislators elect House of Representatives members.	Human nature in republican government assumes this state more than does any other form of limited representation, which warrants caution in delegating authority and care of legislative trust.	Makes commerce, taxation, and the militia concerns of the federal government.	Madison, *Federalist* #56
Common Good of Society: "The aim of every political constitution is … to obtain for rulers men who possess most wisdom to discern, and most virtue to pursue, the common good of the society; and … to take the most effectual precautions for keeping them virtuous, whilst they continue to hold their public trust."	"The elective mode of obtaining rulers, is the characteristic policy of republican government.	"The means relied on in this form of government for preventing their degeneracy, are numerous and various. The most effectual one is such a limitation of the term of appointments, as will maintain a proper responsibility to the people." "They can make no law which will not have its full operation on themselves and their friends, as well as on the great mass of society. This has always been deemed one of the strongest bonds by which human policy can connect the rulers to the people together." *Note*: Obfuscated by the Congress to remove themselves from this connection in raises and in health care.	See Constitution #D.2.	Madison, *Federalist* #57

Census every ten years	1. to readjust apportionment of representatives in ratio of 1/30,000. 2. experience bears out this gradual increase. 3. a constitutional peculiarity, that on branch of the legislature is a representation of the citizens; the other of the states.	1. A scheduled census every ten years. 2. establishes roles and power barriers to balance each House.	1. Ensures representation based on state population. 2. balances the two houses of Congress to maintain equal power and in legislative subjects. 3. "and speaking the known and determined sense of a majority of the people. 4. the House of Representatives alone cannot only refuse, but they alone can propose the supplies requisite for the support of government.	Madison, *Federalist* #58
Senate: 1. qualifications 2. appointment by state legislatures. 3. equality of representation appointment .duration. 4. numbers. 5. powers invested in the Senate.	1. advanced age (thirty minimum) and a longer period of citizenship (nine years). 2. a. an *unnecessary* need for explanation for it is "the most congenial with the public opinion." b. Gives a "select appointment" and the states "an agency in the formation of the federal government, as must secure the authority of the former, and may form a convenient link between the two systems."	1. Senatorial trust; Stability of character. 2. Keeps the federal in touch with the states and a bond between the two systems. 3. Constitutional limit on legislation that conflicts with the Constitution. 4. See Republican Government #3.	3. See Constitution #D.1. 4. See Representation #6.	Madison, *Federalist* #62
Constitution of the Senate as it relates to duration of appointment.	A stable body to maintain a stable government and to quell the people stimulated to unwise action.	Builds a sense of national character to win respect of the people and other nations.	See Representation.	Madison, *Federalist* #63

Reason	"It would inevitably be connected with the spirit of preexisting parties, or of parties springing out of the question itself. It would be connected with persons of distinguished character and extensive influence in the community. It would be pronounced by the very men who had been agents in, or opponents of, the measures to which the decision would relate. The *passions*, therefore, not the *reason*, of the public would sit in judgment. But it is the reason, alone, of the public, that ought to control and regulate the government. The passions ought to be controlled and regulated by the government. "We found in the last paper, that mere declarations in the written constitution are not sufficient to restrain the several departments within their legal rights. It appears in this, that occasional appeals to the people would be neither a proper nor an effectual provision for that purpose. How far the provisions of a different nature contained in the plan above quoted might be adequate, I do not examine. Some of them are unquestionably founded on sound political principles, and all of them are framed with singular ingenuity and precision."			Madison, *Federalist* #49; p. 284, *The Federalist, Alexander Hamilton, James Madison, and John Jay, Introduction and Notes by Robert A. Fer*guson, 2006, George Stade, consulting editorial director

Virtue	A. 1. a. VI'RTUE. n.f. [virtus, Latin.] 1. Moral goodness: opposed to vice. Either I'm mistaken, or there is virtue in that Falstaff. Shakespeare. If there's a power above us, And that there is, all nature cries aloud Through all her works, he must delight in virtue, And that which he delights in must be happy. Addison. 1. b. 10. One of the orders of the celestial hierarchy. Thrones, dominations, princedoms, virtues, powers. Milton. A winged virtue through th' etherial sky, From orb to orb unwearied I does thou fly. Tickel.			*A Dictionary of the English Language, In Which The Words Are Deduced From Their Originals,* Volume 2, 1755, Samuel Johnson, First Edition
Justice	It remained for the people of the U.S., by combining a federal with a republican organization, to enlarge still more the sphere of representative Govt and by convenient partitions & distributions of power, to provide the better for internal justice & order, whilst it afforded the best protection agst. external dangers.			Madison, 1833, Majority Governments, Madison Manuscripts
Will of Society or Majority	Elections by state.	Majority in each. State wins electoral votes.	Elector casts vote.	Madison, *Spirit of Governments*

Appendix E: Bibliography

Adams, John. *Defense of the Constitutions of the United States*, volume 1, http://www.constitution.org/jadams/ja1_pre.htm.

Adams,_John. *Thoughts on Government*, Apr. 1776 Papers 4:86–93, http://www.constitution.org/jadams/thoughts.htm.

Allen, W. B. *George Washington: A Collection*, editor W. B. Allen.

Aitchison, Jean, *Linguistics*, 1999.

Appiah, Kwame Anthony and Gates, Henry Louis, Jr., Editors, *AFRICANA CIVIL RIGHTS, An A-Z Reference of the Movement That Changed America*, 2004.

Audi, Robert, General Editor, *The Cambridge Dictionary of Philosophy*, Second Edition, 1999.

Austin, Dacey, *The Secular Conscience, Why Belief Belongs in Public Life*, 2008.

Barnhart, Robert K. *The Barnhart Concise Dictionary of Etymology, The Origins of American English Words, ©1995, edited by Robert K. Barnhart.*

Barry, C. Michael. *Deism Examined*, http://www.truthandculture.com.

Barry, C. Michael. *Quote and Confusion,* a rebuttal to *Treaty of Tripoli*, article, February 1, 2009, Ed Buckner's speech to the Humanists of Georgia on June 22, 1997 and at Lake Hypatia, 1997, http://www.stephenjaygould.org/ctrl/buckner_tripoli.html.

Black's Law Dictionary, Ninth Edition, Bryan A. Garner, Editor in Chief, 2009, Thomas Reuters

Bradford, M.E. *Founding Fathers*, 1994, M.E. Bradford, foreword by Russell Kirk.

Brinton, Crane, *The Shaping of Modern Thought*, 1963.

Bryce, James. *The American Commonwealth, Volume II*, 1995.

Churchill, Winston S. *The Great Democracies, A History of the English-Speaking Peoples*,_volume IV, with an introduction by William Gallup.

Cicero, Marcus Tullius. *Cicero on the Commonwealth*, 1929, translated with notes and introduction by George Holland Sabine and Stanley Barney Smith.

Cicero, Marcus Tullius. *Fragments.*

Clayton, Philip, Editor. *The Oxford Handbook of Religion and Science*, 2008, paperback.

Cohler, Anne M., Basia C. Miller, and Harold S. Stone, editors. *Montesquieu, The Spirit of the Laws*, 1989.

Colapietro, Vincent M., *Glossary of Semiotics*, 1993.

Connolly,_Francis. *Man and His Measure*, 1964.

Conrad, Jessamyn. *What You Should Know about Politics, but Don't: A Nonpartisan Guide to the Issues*, 2008.

Dacey, Austin, *The Secular Conscience, Why Belief Belongs in Public Life*, 2008

Douglas, J. D. and Tenney, Merrill C., *The New International Dictionary of the Bible*, Pictorial Edition, 1967

Eagleton, Terry, *Reason, Faith, and Revolution, Reflections on the God Debate*, 2009.

Eco, Umberto, *A Theory of Semiotics*, 1976.

Federal Judicial Center, History of the Federal Judiciary, *Talking Points on Judicial*

Gutmann, Amy and Thompson, Dennis, *Democracy and disagreement*, 1996.

Herrick, James A., *The History of and Theory of Rhetoric, An Introduction, 2005.*

History, Section 4. Defining the Judiciary, Tenure, and Removal, http://www.fjc.gov/history/home.nsf/page/tu_sedition;

Fineman, Howard. *The Thirteen American Arguments, Enduring Debates That Define and Inspire* Our Country, 2009.

Foster, James C. and Susan M. Leeson, *Constitutional Law, Cases in Context,* Volume I Federal Governmental Powers and Federalism, 1992.

Gigot, Paul. *The Journal Editorial Report,* Fox News, October 9, 2010.

Goldenson, Robert. M., Ph. D, *The Encyclopedia of Human Behavior,* Volume 1, 1970.

Franklin, Benjamin, *Autobiography,* Editor, Gordon S. Haight, Ph.D., 1941

Heritage Guide to the Constitution, The, ©2005, Edwin Meese III.

Herrick, James A. *The History and Theory of Rhetoric, An Introduction,* 2005.

Iversen-Norman Associates, *The Zondervan Parallel New Testament in Greek and English,* 1975.

Jacoby, Susan, *The Age of American Unreason, Revised and Updated,* 2009.

Jefferson, Thomas. *First Inaugural Address,* March 4, 1801; *Jefferson, Writings,* 1999, Library of America.

Jefferson, Thomas. *Notes on the State of Virginia,* Query XVII; *Jefferson Writings,* 1984, The Library of America.

Jefferson, Thomas, *The Jefferson Bible, The Life and Morals of Jesus of Nazareth,* Beacon Press, 1998

Johnson, Samuel. *A Dictionary of the English Language,* first edition, 1755.

Kennedy, George A. *Aristotle on Rhetoric, A Theory of Civic Discourse,* Second Edition, 2007.

Ketcham, Ralph, *The Anti-Federalist Papers and the Constitutional Convention Debates,* 1986.

Koch, Adrienne. *Bicentennial Edition of Notes of Debates in the Federal Convention of 1787 Reported by James Madison with and Introduction by Adienne Koch*, 1966.

Lim, Timothy C. *Doing Comparative Politics, An Introduction to Approaches and Issues*, 2006.

Madison, James. *Madison Writings*, 1999, Library of America.

Madison, James. *Property*, March 27, 1792, http://www.TeachingAmericanHistory.org/library/index.asp?documentprint=600.

Madison, James. *Spirit of Governments*, February 18, 1792, National Gazette.

Madison, James. *The James Madison Papers*, volume 9, The Library of Congress, http://lcweb2.loc.gov/cgi-bin/query/r?ammem/mjmtext:@field(DOCID+@lit(jm090149)).

Madison, James. To-- --1 [1833] [Majority Governments] MAD. MSS., Madison, http://teachingamericanhistory.org/, add to end of URL: "library/index.asp?category=1",

Martinelli, Alberto. *The Political Democracies of the United States and the European Union*, Dipartimento di Studi e Politic Università degli Studi di Mano, Working Paper January, 2007.

Matthews, Peter, *The Concise Oxford Dictionary of Linguistics*, 1997.

Meacham, Jon. *Andrew Jackson in the White House, American Lion*, 2008.

Meese, Edwin, III, *The Heritage Guide to the Constitution*, 2005.

O'Grady, Dobrovolshy, and Aronoff, Contemporary Linguistics, Third Edition, 1997.

Oxford Handbook of Religion and Science, The, ©2006, Edited by Philip Clayton

Paul, Ron. *Sorry Mr. Franklin, We are All Democrats Now*, February 2, 2003, http://www.juntosociety.com/guest/rpaul/rp_Democracy020303.html.

Popper, Karl, *Popper Selections*, edited by David Miller, 1985.

Popper, Karl, *The Logic of Scientific Discovery*, 2002.

Posner, Richard A. *How Judges Think*, 2008.

Prothero, Stephen, *Religious Literacy, What Every American Needs to Know—and Doesn't*, 2007.

Quincy, Josiah. *Memoir of the Life of John Quincy Adams*, 1860.

Rakove, Jack N. *Original Meanings, Politics and Ideas in the Making of the Constitution,* 1996.

Rousseau, Jean-Jacques. *The Social Contract*, 1762.

Sandel, Michael J., *Democracy's Discontent, America in Search of a Public Philosophy*, 1996.

Saul, John Ralston. *Voltaire's Bastards, The Dictatorship of Reason in the West*, 1992.

Scruton, Roger. *Modern Philosophy: An Introduction and Survey, Third edition*, 2007.

Scruton, Roger. *Palgrave Macmillan Dictionary of Political Thought, Third edition*, 2007.

Schlesinger, Arthur M. and Fox, Dixon Ryan, editors. *A History of American Life*, XII Volumes.

Sowell, Thomas, *Intellectuals and Society*, 2009.

Stade, George. *The Federalist, Alexander Hamilton, James Madison, and John Jay,* with introduction and notes by Robert A. Ferguson, 2006.

Strauss, Leo, Natural Right and History, 1953.

Taleb, Nassim Nicholas, *The Black Swan: The Impact of the Highly Improbable*, 2007.

Taber's Cyclopedic Medical Dictionary, Edition 21, 2005.

Tocqueville, Alexis De, *Democracy in America,* renewed 1972.

http://www.state.gov/, United States, State Department, Bureau of Democracy, Human Rights, and Labor

Trask, R. L., *A Dictionary of Grammatical Terms in Linguistics*, 1993.

United States Constitution, The, article I, section 2 and section 3; article II, section 1; and article III, section 1; and amendment article XII ratified 1804.

Universal Declaration of Human Rights, December 10, 1948, General Assembly of the United Nations.

Valentine, Phil. *The Conservative's Handbook, Defining the Right Position on Issues from A to Z,* 2008.

Ward, Glenn, *Postmodernism,* 1997.

Westin, Drew, *The Political Brain, The Role of Emotion in Deciding the Fate of the Nation,* 2007.

Wilson, James. *Pennsylvania Ratifying Convention, November 20–December 15, 1787,* November 24, 1787.

Endnotes

1. *A History of American Life*, Arthur M. Schlesinger and Dixon Ryan Fox, editors, volume IV of XII, pg.314-315.
2. Ibid.
3. Ibid. p. 1888.
4. *The Spirit of the Laws,* book 3, pg. 21–30, 1989, Montesquieu, edited by Anne M. Cohler, et al.
5. Ibid. book 2, chapter 1, p. 10.
6. *The Barnhart Concise Dictionary of Etymology, The Origins of American English Words,* Robert K. Barnhart, 1995, p. 194.
7. *The Palgrave Macmillan Dictionary of Political Thought*, 3rd edition, pg. 593-94, roger Scruton, 2007. (no capitalization is used)
8. Madison, *Federalist* #10, p. 56, *The Federalist, Alexander Hamilton, James Madison, and John Jay,* 2006, George Stade, consulting editorial director, with introduction and notes by Robert A. Ferguson. Compare his thoughts with those of Montesquieu.
9. Ibid. Madison *Federalist* #10, p. 102.
10. Ibid. Madison *Federalist* #14, pg. 73–4.
11. *A Defense of the Constitutions of Government of the United States of America, Vol. 1,* Sidney, p. 147, § 18; http://www.constitution.org/jadams/ja1_pre.htm.
12. Ibid. Sidney, p. 160. § 19.
13. Ibid. Sidney, p. 161.
14. Ibid. Sidney, p. 165. § 21.
15. Ibid. Sidney, p. 258.

16. Ibid. Letter XXIII. Ancient Republics, and Opinions of Philosophers. Plato., pg. 106–07.

17. *Federalist Papers Authored by Alexander Hamilton, in The Federalist Alexander Hamilton, James Madison, and John Jay,* introduction and notes by Robert A. Ferguson, 2006; *Bicentennial Edition of Notes of Debates in the Federal Convention of 1787* Reported *by James Madison, with an Introduction by Adrienne Koch,* Bicentennial Edition, 1966.

18. *Bicentennial Edition of Notes of Debates in the Federal Convention of 1787 Reported by James Madison, with an Introduction by Adrienne Koch,* Bicentennial Edition, 1966, Mr. Gerry, Monday, May 31, 1787, p. 39.

19. *Montesquieu, The Spirit of the Laws,* Book 3, chapter 3, p. 23.

20. Ibid. pg. 22-24.

21. Ibid. p. 23.

22. Ibid. p. 27.

23. Ibid. book 4, chapters 4–5, pg. 35–36; book 5, chapters 1 and 2, p. 42.

24. Ibid. book 5, chapter 3, pg. 43–44.

25. Ibid. book 5, chapter 5, p. 45.

26. Ibid. book 5, chapter 5, pg. 46–47, and chapter 6, pg. 47–48.

27. Ibid. book 5, chapter 6, p. 48

28. Ibid. Mr. Madison, FN10, p. 110, July 2, 1787.

29. *Bicentennial Edition of Notes of Debates in the Federal Convention of 1787 Reported by James Madison, with an Introduction by Adrienne Koch,* Bicentennial Edition, 1966, Mr. Madison, p. 368.

30. *The Palgrave Macmillan Dictionary of Political Thought*, 3rd Edition, pg. 169-71. All references in this section are from this resource unless otherwise noted.

31. Ibid. pg. 107-08.

32. Ibid. pg. 640-41.

33. *Modern Philosophy: An Introduction and Survey,* Third Edition, p. 172.

34. *Doing Comparative Politics, An Introduction to Approaches and Issues,* p. 27, 2006, Timothy C. Lim.

35. *The Palgrave Macmillan Dictionary of Political Thought,* Third Edition, 2007, Roger Scruton, p. 172.

36. *Democracy and disagreements,* pg. 5, 32, 36-37.

37. *Montesquieu, The Spirit of the Laws,* Book 5, chapter 7, pg. 49–50.

38. *Jean-Jacques* Rousseau, *The Social Contract, 2004, Penguin Books.*

39. *The Anti-Federalist Papers and the Constitutional Convention Debates, The Clashes and The Compromises that gave Birth to Our Form of Government,* 1986, Ralph Ketcham, p. 276.

40. *Bicentennial Edition of Notes of Debates in the Federal Convention of 1787 Reported by James Madison with an Introduction by Adienne Koch,* p. vii, 1966.

41. Madison, *Federalist* paper #10, *The Federalist, Alexander Hamilton, James Madison, and John Jay,* George Stade, consulting editorial director, with introduction and notes by Robert A. Ferguson.

42. *American Lion,* John Meacham, 2008, p. 164.

43. Ibid. p. 414.

44. *The Heritage Guide to the Constitution*, Edwin Meese, III, 2005, p. 413.

45. *Bicentennial Edition of Notes of Debates in the Federal Convention of 1787 Reported by James Madison, with an Introduction by Adrienne Koch,* Bicentennial Edition, 1966, p. 140.

46. Adrienne Koch 1913-1971, received her doctorate from Columbia in history. She taught at Tulane, Berkley, and the University of Michigan, then went to the University of Maryland as professor of history. Her acclaim is a specialist in 18th century American history.

47. *Bicentennial Edition of Notes of Debates in the Federal Convention of 1787 Reported by James Madison with an Introduction by Adrienne Koch,* pg. xix–xx, 1966.

48. *A History of American Life,* Arthur M. Schlesinger and Dixon Ryan Fox, editors, Volume IV of XII, p. 313; Ibid. p. 311.

49. *The Anti-Federalist Papers and the Constitutional Convention Debates,* Ralph Ketcham, 1986, p. 6.

50. *Black's Law Dictionary,* Ninth Edition, p.1875, "Toute exception non surveillée tend à prendre la place du princpe".

51. *The Anti-Federalist Papers and the Constitutional Convention Debates,* Ralph Ketcham, 1986, p. 5.

52. *The Federalist, Alexander Hamilton, James Madison, and John Jay,* introduction and notes by Robert A. Ferguson, Federalist #14, p. 74, 2006.

53. *The Anti-Federalist Papers and the Constitutional Convention Debates,* Ralph Ketcham, 1986, p. 6.

54. *Spirit of Governments,* James Madison, February 18, 1792, National Gazette.

55. Natural Right and History, p. 12.

56. Ibid.

57. *The Great Democracies, A History of the English-Speaking Peoples, Volume IV,* p. 121, Winston S. Churchill with an Introduction by William Gallup.

58. Andrew *Jackson in the White House, American Lion*, John Meacham, 2008, pg. 48.

59. Ibid.

60. Madison *Federalist* #39, p. 242, *The Federalist, Alexander Hamilton, James Madison, and John Jay,* introduction and notes by Robert A. Ferguson.

61. *The Dictionary of Etymology, The Origins of American English Words,* Robert K. Barnhart, 1995, p. 773, means ample or abundant, having substance or reality.

62. Ibid. p. 308, Meacham is speaking of Jackson.

63. Ibid. pg. 48–49, 143, and 309 respectively.

64. *The American Commonwealth, Volume II,* pg. 923–4, 1995, James Bryce.

65. Ibid.

66. *The Federalist, Alexander Hamilton, James Madison, and John Jay,* introduction and notes by Robert A. Ferguson Madison, *Federalist* #48, p. 276.

67. Ibid. Madison, *Federalist* #14, pg. 74–5.

68. *Fragments,* Cicero

69. *Cicero on the Commonwealth,* p. 57, 1929, Marcus Tullius Cicero. Translated with notes and introduction by George Holland Sabine and Stanley Barney Smith; this is repeated by Montesquieu, book 2, chapter 2, p. 10.

70. *Ibid.* p. 133

71. Ibid., p. 139

72. *A Defense of the Constitutions of Government of the United States of America, Vol. 1,* Preface, p. 5, http://www.constitution.org/jadams/ja1_pre.htm.

73. Ibid. p. 7.

74. Ibid. pg. 9–10.

75. Ibid.

76. Ibid. pg. 16–17, Letter II.

77. Ibid. pg. 17–18, Letter III. St. Marino.

78. Ibid. Preface, p. 20, Letter III. St. Marino.

79. Madison, *Federalist* #14.

80. *A Defense of the Constitutions of Government of the United States of America, Vol. 1,* Preface, p. 20, Letter III. St. Marino.

81. Ibid., p. 22, Letter IV. Biscay; merindades: municipalities of Burgos, which is a province of northern Spain.

82. Ibid.

83. Ibid.

84. Ibid. p. 23, Letter IV. Biscay.

85. Ibid. p.25, Letter V., Switzerland, Democratical Cantons, Appenzel.

86. Ibid. Preface, p. 28, Letter VII. Glaris.

87. Ibid. Preface, p. 31, Letter XI. Aristocratical Republics. The Canton Of Berne.

88. Ibid. Preface, p. 51, Letter XXVII. Mixed Governments. Machiavelli's Discourses Upon The First Decade Of Livy. Book I. C. 2.

89. Ibid. Preface, Sidney, p. 138. § 16. p. 84, Letter XXVII. Mixed or Composed Governments. Sidney, Page 22, § 10.

90. *Notes on the Debates in the Federal Convention of 1787.*, p. 39, Mr. Mason, May 31, 1787.

91. *Pennsylvania Ratifying Convention, November 20–December 15, 1787,* by James Wilson, November 24, 1787.

92. From the Madison copy of the constitution, http://avalon.law ; from the ratified constitution: Article III, Section 3. Treason.

93. *Bicentennial Edition of Notes of Debates in the Federal Convention of 1787 Reported by James Madison, with an Introduction by Adrienne Koch,* Bicentennial Edition, 1966.

94. Ibid.

95. Ibid.

96. Ibid.

97. Ibid. Mr. Hamilton, June 18, 1787.

98. Ibid. Mr. Governor Morris, July 2, 1787.

99. Ibid. p. 233.

100. 1Corinthians1:10-25

101. Ibid. Mr. Madison, FN8, July 2, 1787.

102. Ibid. Mr. Madison, FN8, July 2, 1787.

103. *Political Brain,* pg. 140-41.

104. Ibid. p. 417.

105. Ibid.

106. Ibid. p. 419.

107. Ibid. book 2, chapter 2, p. 10; book 3, chapter 2, p. 21; book 4, chapter 1, p. 31, book 5, chapter 6, p. 48.

108. *The Palgrave Macmillan Dictionary of Political Thought,* Third Edition, p. 593, 2007, Roger Scruton.

109. Ibid.

110. Madison, *Federalist* #10, p. 56, *The Federalist, Alexander Hamilton, James Madison, and John Jay,* introduction and notes by Robert A. Ferguson.

111. Ibid.

112. Madison, *Federalist* #39, p. 210, *The Federalist, Alexander Hamilton, James Madison, and John Jay,* introduction and notes by Robert A. Ferguson.

113. Ibid, p. 212.

114. Ibid. p. 26.

115. Ibid. p. 27.

116. Ibid.

117. Ibid. p. 26.

118. Ibid. p. 27.

119. Ibid.

120. Ibid.

121. Ibid.

122. Ibid, pg. 26-27.

123. Speech in Congress on "Self-Created Societies" as quoted in *Madison Writings*, Library of America, p. 551.

124. Ibid. p. 552.

125. Madison, *Federalist* #39, p. 25.

126. Ibid.

127. Ibid. p. 26.

128. Ibid.

129. *Thoughts on Government,* John Adams, Apr. 1776 Papers 4:86–93, http://www.constitution.org/jadams/thoughts.htm.

130. *A Dictionary of the English Language, First Edition, in Which the Words Are Deduced from Their Originals, and Illustrated in Their Different Significations by Examples from the Best Writers to Which Are Prefixed, A History of the Language, and An English Grammar.* By Samuel Johnson, A.M. In Two Volumes, 1755, Volume I.

131. *Black's Law Dictionary,* Ninth Edition, p. 602.

132. Ibid. book 5, chapters 1–7, pg. 42–51.

133. *The Spirit of the Laws,* book 5, chapter 6, p. 48, 1989, Montesquieu, edited by Anne M. Cohler, et al.

134. Montesquieu, *The Spirit of the Laws*, Book 20, pg. 337-397. Part 4, Chapter 21, p. 390 new worlds.

135. *Barnhart Concise Dictionary of Etymology, The Origins of American English Words*, p. 735.

136. *The Zondervan Parallel New Testament in Greek and English,* 1Timothy 6:10, p. 620.

137. John Adams, Defense of the Constitutions of Government of the United States, 1787, chapter 16, document 15, University of Chicago Press.

138. *Property*, James Madison, March 27, 1792

139. *Property*, James Madison March 27, 1792, http://www.TeachingAmericanHistory.org/library/index.asp?documentprint=600.

140. *Black's Law Dictionary*, p. 601.

141. *The United States Constitution*, V Amendment [1791].

142. Madison, June 6, 1787, pg. 76–77, *Bicentennial Edition of Notes of Debates in the Federal Convention of 1787 Reported by James Madison*, with an introduction by Adrienne Koch, June 26, 1787.

143. *Bicentennial Edition of Notes of Debates in the Federal Convention of 1787 Reported by James Madison, with an introduction by Adrienne Koch,* June 26, 1787.

144. http://teachingamericanhistory.org/convention/delegates/ for a biography of all the delegates

145. *Bicentennial Edition of Notes of Debates in the Federal Convention of 1787 Reported by James Madison, with an Introduction by Adrienne Koch,* Bicentennial Edition, 1966, Mr. Madison, May 31, 1787, p. 39.

146. Ibid. Mr. Washington, September 17, 1787, p. 655.

147. Ibid. Mr. Wilson, May 31, 1787, p. 40.

148. Ibid. Mr. Wilson, May 31, 1787, p. 40

149. Ibid. Mr. Madison, May 31, 1787.

150. Ibid. Mr. Madison, May 31, 1787.

151. Ibid. Mr. Gerry, May 31, 1787, p. 41.

152. Ibid. p. 41, Vote results: Massts. ay. Connect. divd. N. York ay. N. Jersey no. Pena. ay. Delawe. divd. Va. ay. N.C. ay. S. C. no. Georgia. ay.

153. Ibid. Mr. Spaight, Monday May 31, 1787.

154. Ibid. Mr. Rand, May 31, 1787, p. 42.

155. Ibid. Mr. Madison, Wednesday June 6, 1787, p. 75.

156. Ibid. Col. Mason, June 4, 1787, p. 64.

157. Madison, *Federalist* #63, p. 351; *The Federalist, Alexander Hamilton, James Madison, and John Jay,* introduction and notes by Robert A. Ferguson, 2006.

158. Ibid. Madison, *Federalist* #63, p. 352.

159. Ibid. Madison, *Federalist* #63, p. 348.

160. Ibid.

161. Ibid. Madison, *Federalist* #62, p. 343.

162. Date of capture is September 22, 2010.

163. *Black's Law Dictionary*, p. 1670, (Uniform Law Commissioners).

164. *Majority Government*, 1833, Madison

165. Madison, *Federalist* #62, p. 343.

166. Ibid.

167. Ibid.

168. *The Palgrave Macmillan Dictionary of Political Thought*, pg. 204-05.

169. Madison, *Federalist* #62, p. 343.

170. *Cicero On the Commonwealth*, . pg. 58, 133, fn74

171. *Majority Government*, 1833, Madison

172. Ibid.

173. Ibid.

174. Ibid., See also *The James Madison Papers,* vol. 9, The Library of Congress; *The Writings of James Madison,* edited by Gaillard Hunt, James Madison. Majority Government, 1834. http://lcweb2.loc.gov/cgi-bin/query/r?ammem/mjmtext:@field(DOCID+@lit(jm090149))

175. See *The Heritage Guide to the Constitution*, Edwin Meese, III, p. 3.

176. *A Defense of the Constitutions of the United States*, John Adams, Volume 1, p. 104, LETTER XXVIII, MIXED GOVERNMENTS; http://www.constitution.org/jadams/ja1_00.htm; MONTESQUIEU, SPIRIT OF LAWS, B. II. C. VI. OF THE CONSTITUTION OF ENGLAND

177. http://www.constitution.org/jm/jm.htm; Madison: *Speech in the Virginia Ratifying Convention on Direct Taxation June 11 1788*

178. Ibid. Last sentence in the quote: "I conceive they will be more likely to produce disputes, in rendering it convenient for the people, than run into interfering regulations."

179. Ibid.

180. Letter to *John Wayles Epps*, Monticello, June 24, 1813, Library of America, p. 1282.

181. *The Writings of James Madison,* Speeches in the Virginia Convention, June 11—Power to Lay Taxes, http://xtf.lib.virginia.edu/xtf/view?docId=2003_Q3/uvaBook/tei/b001615579.xml;chunk.id=d51;toc.depth=1;toc.id=d51;brand=default.

182. Ibid.

183. *The Writings of James Madison,* Speeches in the Virginia Convention, June 11—Power to Lay Taxes.

184. *Bicentennial Edition of Notes of Debates in the Federal Convention of 1787 Reported by James Madison, with an Introduction by Adrienne Koch,* Bicentennial Edition, 1966, Mr. Gerry, Mr. Madison, FN8, p. 110, July 2, 1787.

185. Madison, *Federalist* #48, p. 276; *The Federalist, Alexander Hamilton, James Madison, and John Jay,* introduction and notes by Robert A. Ferguson, 2006.

186. Ibid. Madison, *Federalist* #51, p. 290.

187. *The Zondervan Parallel New Testament in Greek and English*, Matthew 12:25, p. 36.

188. Ibid. Madison, *Federalist* #51. p. 290, *The Federalist, Alexander Hamilton, James Madison, and John Jay,* introduction and notes by Robert A. Ferguson, 2006.

189. Ibid. Madison, *Federalist* #51.

190. Ibid. Madison, *Federalist* #10, p. 56.

191. and conquer.

192. *Madison Writings, Federalist* #27, p. 149.

193. Constitutional Law, Cases in Context, Volume I Federal Governmental Powers and Federalism, 1992, Foster, James C. and Susan M. Leeson, p. 652.

194. *The Heritage Guide to the Constitution, Edwin Meese III, 2005,* p. 5.

195. Madison, *Federalist* #14, pg. 75–76.

196. *Black's Law Dictionary*, Ninth Edition, p. 1874.

197. Ibid. p. 76.

198. Madison, *Federalist* #51, p. 290, , *The Federalist, Alexander Hamilton, James Madison, and John Jay,* introduction and notes by Robert A. Ferguson, George Stade, consulting editorial director.

199. Ibid. *Federalist* #62, pg. 342–43, The rest of that section follows:

> "But it is superfluous to try, by the standard of theory, a part of the Constitution which is allowed on all hands to be the result, not of theory, but "of a spirit of amity, and that mutual deference and concession which the peculiarity of our political situation rendered indispensable." A common government, with powers equal to its objects, is called for by the voice, and still more loudly by the political situation, of America. A government founded on principles more consonant to the wishes of the larger states, is not likely to be obtained from the smaller states. The only option, then, for the former, lies between the proposed government and a government still more objectionable. Under this alternative, the advice of prudence must be to embrace the lesser evil; and, instead of indulging a fruitless anticipation of the possible mischiefs which may ensue, to contemplate rather the advantageous consequences which may qualify the sacrifice."

200. *The Conservative's Handbook, Defining the Right Position on Issues from A to Z,* p. 36, 2008, Phil Valentine.

201. Madison, *Federalist* #51, pg. 290–91, *The Federalist, Alexander Hamilton, James Madison, and John Jay,* 2006, introduction and notes by Robert A. Ferguson, George Stade, consulting editorial director.

202. *A Dictionary of the English Language, First Edition, In Which the Words Are Deduced from Their Originals, and Illustrated in Their Different Significations by Examples from the Best Writers to Which Are Prefixed, A History of the Language, and An English Grammar.* By Samuel Johnson, A.M. In Two Volumes, 1755.

203. Madison, *Federalist* #51, pg. 290–91, *The Federalist, Alexander Hamilton, James Madison, and John Jay,* 2006, introduction and notes by Robert A. Ferguson, George Stade, consulting editorial director.

204. *AFRICANA CIVIL RIGHTS, An A-Z Reference of the Movement That Changed Am*erica, pg. 114-115.

205. *Bicentennial Edition of Notes of Debates in the Federal Convention of 1787 Reported by James Madison, with an Introduction by Adrienne Koch,* Bicentennial Edition, 1966, Mr. Gerry, Monday, May 31, 1787.

206. *Madison, Writings,* p. 152, 1999, Library of America, "Letter to Thomas Jefferson Octr. 24. 1787."

207. *How Judges Think,* Introduction, 2008, Richard A. Posner.

208. *Jefferson Writings*, Letter To Justice William Johnson, June 12, 1823, p. 1472, The Library of America.

209. Ibid.

210. Votility is one answer to both knowing and expressing one's opinion and giving feedback to representatives, www.votility.com.

211. *Defense of the Constitutions of the United States, Volume I, Preface, Grosvenor Square, January* 1, 1787, by John Adams, http://www.constitution.org/jadams/ja1_pre.htm.

212. Alexander Hamilton, *Federalist #9 The Union as a Safeguard Against Domestic Faction and Insurrection; For the Independent Journal.* http://www.foundingfathers.info/federalistpapers/hamilton.htm.

213. Madison, *Federalist* #63, p. 350, *The Federalist, Alexander Hamilton, James Madison, and John Jay,* 2006, introduction and notes by Robert A. Ferguson, George Stade, consulting editorial director.

214. Ibid. Madison, *Federalist* #63, p. 349. (See Chapter 6, Section 4)

215. Ibid. Hamilton, *Federalist* #9, pg. 47–48.

216. Ibid. Madison, *Federalist* #39, pg. 209–215.

217. *Thomas Jefferson, Writings,* pg. 1470–71, a letter to Justice William Johnson, "The Supreme Court and the Constitution," Monticello, June 12, 1823, 1999, Library of America.

218. *Thomas Jefferson, Writings,* pg. 1470–71, a letter to Justice William Johnson, "The Supreme Court and the Constitution," Monticello, June 12, 1823, 1999, Library of America.

219. *Original Meanings, Politics and Ideas in the Making of the Constitution,* Jack N. Rakove, pg. 366–68. The quote is as follows: "Democracy has no forefathers, it looks to no posterity, it is swallowed up in the present and thinks of nothing but itself." I find it astounding that this quote is not from the *Memoir of the Life of John Quincy Adams.* Even the *Los Angeles Times* quotes it in its May 14, 1995, article "The Democracy Dilemma," which bases it on Rakove's *James Madison and the Creation of the American Republic.*

220. Notes on the State of Virginia, Query XVII, *Jefferson Writings,* p. 287, 1984, The Library of America.

221. James 2:8, King James Version, *The Zondervan Parallel New Testament in Greek and English.*

222. I found an article by Representative Ron Paul, dated February 2, 2003, and entitled "Sorry, Mr. Franklin, We Are All Democrats Now" that is posted at http://www.juntosociety.com/guest/rpaul/rp_democracy020303.html.

223. *The Political Democracies of the United States and the European Union*, Alberto Martinelli, Dipartimento di Studi e Politic Università degli Studi di Mano, Working Paper 1/07, p. 8.

224. *The Palgrave Macmillan Dictionary of Political Thought, Third Edition,* 2007, Roger Scruton, pg. 245–46

225. *Black's Law Dictionary,* Ninth Edition, p. 1565, 2009, Bryan A. Garner, editor in chief

226. *Thomas Jefferson, Writings,* pg. 494–95, "First Inaugural Address, March 4, 1801, 1999, Library of America. See Conduct; Culture; Democracy; Determinism; Federal; Free will; Government; Metaphysics; Power; Secularism.

227. *The Palgrave Macmillan Dictionary of Political Thought,* Third Edition, 2007, Roger Scruton, p. 593.

228. *Jefferson Writings*, p. 663.

229. Madison, *Federalist* #39, *The Federalist, Alexander Hamilton, James Madison, and John Jay,* p. 210, 2006, introduction and notes by Robert A. Ferguson, George Stade, consulting editorial director; *good behavior*: History of the Federal Judiciary, Talking Points on Judicial History, Federal Judicial Center, Section 4. Defining the Judiciary, Tenure and removal, p. 2, http://fjc.gov/history/home.nsf/page/talking_co_tp.html.

230. Jefferson Writings, The ANAS. 1791-1806. SELECTIONS, Explanations of the 3. Volumes bound in marbled paper, February 4, 1818, p. 661-673.

231. *The Sedition Act Trials*, Bruce A. Ragsdale, Federal Judicial Center, 2005, p. 40.

232. Reply: (Mis)Understanding Good-Behavior Tenure, The Yale Law Journal, Saikrishna Prakash and Steven D. Smith, from *How To Remove a Federal Judge*, 116 Yale L.J. 72 (2006).

233. Madison, *Federalist* #10, pg. 210–11, *The Federalist, Alexander Hamilton, James Madison, and John Jay,* introduction and notes by Robert A. Ferguson.

234. Ibid. Madison, *Federalist* #39; *Black's Law Dictionary,* Ninth Edition, pg. 1886–87, Appendix C, 2009, Bryan A. Garner, editor in chief, p. 211.

235. Jefferson to William Johnson, Monticello, June 112, 1823, *Jefferson Writings*, Library of America, p. 1469.

236. Madison, *Federalist* #43, p. 243, *The Federalist, Alexander Hamilton, James Madison, and John Jay,* introduction and notes by Robert A. Ferguson.

237. Ibid. Madison Federalist #39

238. *Black's Law Dictionary,* Ninth Edition, p. 764, Bryan A. Garner, editor in chief.

239. *Madison Writings,* p. 864, 1999, Library of America; Notes on the State of Virginia, Query XVII, *Jefferson Writings,* p. 287, 1984, The Library of America.

240. Madison, *Federalist* #49, p. 280, *The Federalist, Alexander Hamilton, James Madison, and John Jay,* introduction and notes by Robert A. Ferguson, 2006.

241. Ibid.

242. Ibid. Madison, *Federalist* #62, pg. 343–44.

243. Ibid. Madison, *Federalist* #62, pg. 344–45.

244. Democracy, the Worst Form of Government Ever Tried, by Bevin Chu, http://www.LewRockwell.com

245. *A Defense of the Constitutions of Government of the United States of America*, LETTER XXX. Ancient Republics, and Opinions of Philosophers, p. 94, John Adams; author's note: Item number 6 is the best definition of the American extended Republic that I have seen, apart from the whole body of Madison's *Federalist* articles and his Convention Debate Notes. What this item does is to set apart the idea that America is some form of democracy. *A Defense of the Constitutions of Government of the United States of America,* John Adams, LL.D., Apr. 1776.

246. Ibid. Letter XXXI. Ancient Republics, and Opinions of Philosophers, p. 95

247. Madison, To-- --1 [1833] [Majority Governments] MAD. MSS., pg. 19–20, http://teachingamericanhistory.org/library/index.asp?category=1 (See Desideratum).

248. Madison, *Federalist* #39, p. 215, *The Federalist, Alexander Hamilton, James Madison, and John Jay,* introduction and notes by Robert A. Ferguson, 2006, George Stade, consulting editorial director.

249. Ibid. Madison; *Federalist* #48, p. 276.

250. Ibid. Madison, *Federalist* #51, p. 288.

251. Author's note: I adapted his notes to this table. (See file: F:\Attache\That Confounded Man\Articles\Republican Principles\Republican Colonial v Modern Left_Liberal\Juxtapostion of Principles.docx) *The Federalist, Alexander Hamilton, James Madison, and John Jay,* p. 215, 2006, introduction and notes by Robert A. Ferguson; *Federalist* articles 10, 39, and 63 by James Madison

252. Madison, *Federalist* #10, *The Federalist Alexander Hamilton, James Madison, John Jay, George Stade,* consulting editorial director, with introduction and notes by Robert A. Ferguson, pg. 51–59, 2006 (See Democracy; Disinterested; Federalism; Negative Law; Positive Law; Republic; Republican Principles; State; Tribunal).

253. See my note p. 325, *The Federalist Alexander Hamilton, James Madison, John Jay, George Stade,* consulting editorial director, with introduction and notes by Robert A. Ferguson, 2006.

254. *A Defense of the Constitutions of Government of the United States of America,* John Adams, LL.D., Apr. 1776.

255. Jefferson to William Johnson, Monticello, June 12, 1823

256. *Aristotle on Rhetoric, A Theory of Civic Discourse*, Second Edition, p. 73.

257. *The History of and Theory of Rhetoric, An Introduction*, p. 278.

258. There are eight occurrences in 371 pages.

259. *Madison Writings*, 1999, Library of America, p. 864

260. Madison *Federalist* #39, *The Federalist, Alexander Hamilton, James Madison, and John Jay,* introduction and notes by Robert A. Ferguson, p. 242.

261. *Madison Writings,* p. 864, 1999, Library of America.

262. Intermixture does not appear in the *Barnhart Dictionary of Etymology, The Origin of American English Words.* It does occur in the *Shorter Oxford English Dictionary* as intermingle: "mix or mingle together."

263. The Pacificus-Helvidius Debates of 1793–1794: Toward the Completion of the American Founding (1793), Pacificus Number 1, pg. 8–17 and Helvidius Number 2, June 22, 1793, pg. 855–64, Alexander Hamilton & James Madison, 1793, http://teachingamericanhistory.org/library/index.asp?category=1.

264. *A Dictionary of the English Language, in Which the Words Are Deduced from Their Originals, and Illustrated in Their Different Significations by Examples from the Best Writers to Which Are Prefixed, A History of the Language, and An English Grammar.* By Samuel Johnson, A.M. In Two Volumes, 1755.

265. *Speech on Amendments to the Constitution*, James Madison, June 8, 1789.

266. Ibid.

267. Ibid.

268. Helvidius 1, p. 64, http://teachingamericanhistory.org/library/index.asp?category=1.

269. *Black's Law Dictionary*, Ninth Edition, p. 1874.

270. The Constitution of the United States, Article. I. Section. 1. "All legislative Powers herein granted shall be vested in a Congress of the United States, which shall consist of a Senate and House of Representatives."

271. *Black's Law Dictionary*, p. 117.

272. Helvidius 1, p. 59, The Pacificus-Helvidius Debates of 1793–1794: Toward the Completion of the American Founding (1793).

273. Ibid. Helvidius 1, p. 59.

274. *Jefferson Writings, Thomas Jefferson letter to William Johnson, 12 June 1823, p. 1476*

275. The Supreme Court and the Constitution *To Justice William Johnson, Monticello, June 12, 1823, Jefferson Writings,* p. 1469, 1984, Library of America.

276. *Black's Law Dictionary*, p. 983, under *legislative power* (17c) Constitutional law [Cases: Separation of Powers key 2340-2446.].

277. See Bartolome De Las Casas (1484-1566); Franciscus de Victoria (1480-1546); Johann Gottlieb Heineccius (1681-1741); Sir James Mackintosh, M.P.-member of Parliament; John Taylor (1753-1824)-American

278. Plato has a sophisticated system of the art of rhetoric that involves the human soul and *logoi*, the logical study of arguments. *The History and Theory of "Rhetoric, An Introduction,* p. 68, James A Herrick.

279. http//:www.truthandculture.com, *Deism Examined*

280. *In Unfurl the Flag*, by C. Michael Barry, subtitled *How Inalienable are America's Rights,* 2000, unpublished, I made this point to the USSC. (I did use the incorrect word)

281. Popper, Karl, p. 53, *Popper Selections*, edited by David Miller, 1985.

282. Ibid. p. 57.

283. Popper, Karl, p. 66, *The Logic of Scientific Discovery*, 2002.

284. Taleb, Nassim Nicholas, p. 44, *The Black Swan: The Impact of the Highly Improbable*, 2007.

285. *George Washington, A Collection,* p. 522, "Farewell Address, 1796," editor W. B. Allen.

286. Ibid. p. 533, "To the General Assembly of Presbyterian Churches, May 1789." See Endnote # l xxxv.

287. James Wilson, *Of the Natural Rights of Individuals*, 1790–91, Speech at the Pennsylvania Ratifying Convention, December 3, 1787 (slavery and representation, importation of slaves).

288. *The Encyclopedia of Human Behavior*, p. 305.

289. Republic, 1604, meant to the colonialists, a nation that is governed by elected representatives. Republican, 1712, was one who favored such a system.

290. *Original Meanings*, Rakove, Jack N., p. 42.

291. *The Barnhart Concise Dictionary of Etymology, The Origins of American English Words*, p. 242.

292. *Palgrave MacMillan Dictionary of Political Thought*, pg. 530-31.

293. *Jefferson Writings*, p. 673.

294. Ibid. p. 1466, *Calvin and Cosmology*, to John Adams, 1823.

295. *Reason, Faith, and Revolution, Reflections on the God Debate*, Terry Eagleton, p. 76, 2009.

296. Christopher Dawkins, *God is Not Great.*

297. Universal Declaration of Human Rights, December 10, 1948, General Assembly of the United Nations.

298. United States, State Department, Bureau of Democracy, Human Rights, and Labor, http://www.state on December 24, 2010.

299. General Report on the Activities of the European Union, 2009, chapter 3, p. 63, European Commission.

300. Bureau of Democracy, Human Rights, and Labor, Washington, DC, December 10, 2010, Remarks at the Eleanor Roosevelt Human Rights Award Ceremony, http://www.state.gov/g/drl/

301. *Black's Law Dictionary*, p. 596.

302. Richard A. Posner, *How Judges Think*, p.5.

303. *The Thirteen American Arguments, Enduring Debates That Define and Inspire Our Country,* 2009, Howard Fineman.

304. *What You Should Know About Politics, But Don't, A Nonpartisan Guide to the Issues,* 2008, Jessamyn Conrad.

305. Jefferson: Thomas Jefferson to Joseph C. Cabell, Feb. 2, 1816, *Writings 14:421–23.*

306. "Deism Examined," http://www.truthandculture.com.

307. *The Works of the Honorable James Wilson*, L. L. D., Volume 1, p. 182, 1804.

308. Hebrews 7:25-28, *The King James Version*, p. 652.

309. Chapter 3, Section 2.

310. Intellectuals and Society

311. *Voltaire's Bastards, The Dictatorship of Reason in the West*, p. 235

312. Ibid. pg. 248–9

313. *A History of American Life*, The Revolutionary Generation, 1763-1790, p. 314.

314. Ibid. p. 25

315. http://www.whalingmuseum.org/library/amwhale/am_index.html

316. *The Journal Editorial Report,* Paul Gigot, Fox News, October 9, 2010; President Obama; President George W. Bush, Sarah Palin among others, including the History Channel that also declares America to be a democracy. Our nonplussation is serious, but it is changeable through education. They seem to assume the part is the whole as did Andrew Jackson.

317. *Federalist Papers,* Madison, #10, *The Federalist*, pg.51-59.

318. *Heritage Guide to the Constitution*, p. 3.

319. *A Dictionary of the English Language, In Which the Words Are Deduced from Their Originals, and Illustrated in Their Different Significations by Examples from the best Writers to Which Are Prefixed, A History of the Language, and An English Grammar.* By Samuel Johnson, A.M. In Two Volumes, 1755. Johnson places the source name at the end of the last line of the quote.

320. *George Washington, A Collection,* pg. 306, 335, 565, 593–4, 597–98, 1988, edited by W. B. Allen.

321. Madison, *Federalist* paper #14, *The Federalist, Alexander Hamilton, James Madison, and John Jay,* George Stade, consulting editorial director, with introduction and notes by Robert A. Ferguson.

322. History of the Federal Judiciary, Talking Points on Judicial History, Defining the Judiciary, Tenure and Removal. http://www.fjc.gov/history/home.nsf/page/talking_co_tp.html.

323. *A Dictionary of the English Language, In Which the Words Are Deduced from Their Originals, and Illustrated in Their Different Significations by Examples from the best Writers to Which Are Prefixed, A History of the Language, and An English Grammar.* By Samuel Johnson, A.M. In Two Volumes, 1755.

324. See the treatment of democracy in Roger Scruton's *The Palgrave Macmillan Dictionary of Political Thought*, pg. 169–71, 2007.

325. Constitution as recorded in Madison's Notes, September 12, 1787 Article 1, Section 6

326. *Federalist* #43, p. 241, *The Federalist, Alexander Hamilton, James Madison, and John Jay,* introduction and notes by Robert A. Ferguson, 2006.

327. I use the meaning of *a summary of the action* as found in *Man and His Measure,* p. 1355, 1964, Francis Connolly.

328. Roscoe Pound, *An Introduction to the Philosophy of Law*, 1982 renewed, p. 10.

329. *The Oxford Handbook of Religion and Science*, p. 190.

330. Right Wing News, Van Helsing, article not dated; http://rightwingnews.com/marxism/fidel-castro-gives-up-on-communism/

331. See my Treaty of Tripoli, Quote and Confusion article, February 1, 2009, a rebuttal to Ed Buckner's speech to the humanists of Georgia on June 22, 1997 and 1997 at Lake Hypatia, http://www.stephenjaygould.org/ctrl/buckner_tripoli.html.

332. Children for Sale, The Stockholm Congress Against the Commercial Exploitation of Children, Ellen Lukas, Insight, Family Research Council; US Department of State, Trafficking in Persons Report (TIP) 2009; Slavery Now 2004 Report, Department of Defense.

333. *To John Jay, Mount Vernon, August 15, 1786, George Washington, A Collection,* pg. 333, 334; 1988, edited by W. B. Allen, pg. 333, 334.

334. http://www.allshookdown.com/newhistory/download.html.

335. See Appendix: Table of Constitutional Convention's Principles of Government.

336. *The Federalist, Alexander Hamilton, James Madison, and John Jay,* George Stade, consulting editorial director, with introduction and notes by Robert A. Ferguson, Madison, *Federalist* #39, pg. 209-215.

337. All definitions are from the following source, unless otherwise noted: *A Dictionary of the English Language, in Which the Words Are Deduced from Their Originals, and Illustrated in Their Different Significations by Examples from the Best Writers to Which Are Prefixed, A History of the Language, and An English Grammar.* By Samuel Johnson, A.M. In Two Volumes, 1755.

338. Brinton, Crane, *The Shaping of Modern Thought*, chapter 3: Rationalism, pg. 82-107.

339. *The Cambridge Dictionary of Philosophy*, Second Edition, 1999, Robert Audi, General Editor, Pg. 29-30.

340. *Black's Law Dictionary, p. 175*

341. *Ibid.* p. 251.

342. Ibid. p. 278.

343. *The Palgrave Macmillan Dictionary of Political Thought,* p. 107.

344. Ibid. p. 397.

345. http://www.merriam-webster.com/dictionary/czarism

346. *The Encyclopedia of Human Behavior*, Robert. M. Goldenson, Ph. D., p. 313.

347. *Black's Law Dictionary*, p. 549.

348. *Taber's Cyclopedic Medical Dictionary*, Edition 21, 2005, pg. 722; 1876.

349. *Black's Law Dictionary*, p. 619.

350. *Black's Law Dictionary*, p. 626.

351. Ibid.

352. Ibid.

353. Ibid. p. 1888.

354. Ibid. p. 651.

355. Ibid. p. 626.

356. Popper, See Section: 5: On Our Destiny.

357. *Federalist*, James Madison, #39, *The Federalist, Alexander Hamilton, James Madison, and John Jay,* George Stade, consulting editorial director, with introduction and notes by Robert A. Ferguson, p. 213.

358. Ibid.

359. *Black's Law Dictionary*, p. 685.

360. Ibid.

361. *The Palgrave Macmillan Dictionary of Political Thought, Third Edition,* p. 369, 2007.

362. Ibid. pg. 245–46.

363. *Black's Law Dictionary*, p. 687.

364. Ibid.

365. *Black's Law Dictionary*, p. 762.

366. *Shorter Oxford English Dictionary,* Sixth Edition, electronic version.

367. *A Dictionary of the English Language, in Which the Words Are Deduced from Their Originals, and Illustrated in Their Different Significations by Examples from the Best Writers to Which Are Prefixed, A History of the Language, and An English Grammar.* By Samuel Johnson, A.M. In Two Volumes, 1755.

368. *The Palgrave Macmillan Dictionary of Political Thought,* p. 245-46, 2007, Roger Scruton.

369. *Blacks's Law Dictionary*, p. 962.

370. In this case, parcimonious is misspelled in Johnson's 1755 facsimile, but I corrected it. It is probably an optical scanning error.

371. Ibid. p. 1066, See *Material in the Glossary.*

372. Letter to Ezra Stiles, 1790, "As to Jesus of Nazareth".

373. *The Jefferson Bible, The Life and Morals of Jesus of Nazareth,* Jefferson, Thomas, Beacon Press, 1998.

374. *Autobiography,* Benjamin Franklin, editor, Gordon S. Haight, Ph.D., 1941, pg. 130-131.

375. *Federalist* paper #39, James Madison, *The Federalist, Alexander Hamilton, James Madison, and John Jay,* George Stade, consulting editorial director, with introduction and notes by Robert A. Ferguson, p. 214.

376. *Black's Law Dictionary,* p. 1121

377. Ibid. p. 1122.

378. Ibid. p. 1127.

379. Ibid. p. 1140.

380. Ibid.

381. Ibid., p. 1185; *Cicero On The Commonwealth,* p. 58

382. *The Reader's Digest, Great Encyclopedic Dictionary,* p. 980.

383. *The Oxford Handbook of Religion and Science,* p. 494.

384. *Postmodernism,* p. 5.

385. *Black's Law Dictionary,* p. 1405.

386. The two definitions conflict with the former a modern version to suit the court's view and the traditional that altogether refutes the modern interpretation, which is contra to translation. *A Dictionary of the English Language, In Which the Words Are Deduced from Their Originals, and Illustrated in Their Different Significations by Examples from the Best Writers to Which Are Prefixed, A History of the Language, and An English Grammar.* By Samuel Johnson, A.M. In Two Volumes, 1755.

387. *The Palgrave Macmillan Dictionary of Political Thought,* p. 594, 2007, Roger Scruton

388. Ibid.

389. *Black's Law Dictionary,* p. 1639.

390. *A Dictionary of the English Language, In Which the Words Are Deduced from Their Originals, and Illustrated in Their Different Significations by Examples from the Best Writers to Which Are Prefixed, A History of the Language, and An English Grammar.* By Samuel Johnson, A.M. In Two Volumes, 1755.

391. *Black's Law Dictionary*, p. 1720.

392. Ibid. p. 1706.

393. The Pacificus-Helvidius Debates of 1793–1794: Toward the Completion of the American Founding (1793). See *intermixture*.

Index

Symbols

A

B

C

D

E

F

G

H

I

M

P

Q

R

S

T

U

V

W

X

Z